Precarious Lives and Marginal Bodies in North Africa

After the Empire: The Francophone World and Postcolonial France

Series Editor: Valérie K. Orlando, University of Maryland

Advisory Board
Robert Bernasconi, Memphis University; Claire H. Griffiths, University of Chester, UK; Alec Hargreaves, Florida State University; Chima Korieh, Rowan University; Mildred Mortimer, University of Colorado, Boulder; Obioma Nnaemeka, Indiana University; Alison Rice, University of Notre Dame; Kamal Salhi, University of Leeds; Tracy D. Sharpley-Whiting, Vanderbilt University; Nwachukwu Frank Ukadike, Tulane University

Recent Titles
Precarious Lives and Marginal Bodies in North Africa: Homo Expendibilis, by Hervé Anderson Tchumkam
Global Revolutionary Aesthetics and Politics after Paris '68, by Martin Munro, William Cloonan, Barry Falk, and Christian Weber
Francophone African Narratives and the Anglo-American Book Market: Ferment on the Fringes, by Vivan I. Steemers
Ethnic Minority Women's Writing in France: Publishing Practices and Identity Formation (1998-2005), by Claire Mouflard
Theory, Aesthetics, and Politics in the Francophone World: Filiations Past and Future, by Rajeshwari S. Vallury
Refiguring Les Années Noires: Literary Representations of the Nazi Occupation, by Kathy Comfort
Paris and the Marginalized Author: Treachery, Alienation, Queerness, and Exile, by Valérie K. Orlando and Pamela A. Pears
French Orientalist Literature in Algeria, 1845–1882: Colonial Hauntings, by Sage Goellner
Corporeal Archipelagos: Writing the Body in Francophone Oceanian Women's Literature, by Julia Frengs
Spaces of Creation: Transculturality and Feminine Expression in Francophone Literature, by Allison Connolly
Women Writers of Gabon: Literature and Herstory, by Cheryl Toman
Backwoodsmen as Ecocritical Motif in French Canadian Literature: Connecting Worlds in the Wilds, by Anne Rehill
Intertextual Weaving in the Work of Linda Lê: Imagining the Ideal Reader, by Alexandra Kurmann
Front Cover Iconography and Algerian Women's Writing: Heuristic Implications of the Recto-Verso Effect, by Pamela A. Pears
The Algerian War in French-Language Comics: Postcolonial Memory, History, and Subjectivity, by Jennifer Howell

Precarious Lives and Marginal Bodies in North Africa

Homo Expendibilis

Hervé Anderson Tchumkam

LEXINGTON BOOKS
Lanham • Boulder • New York • London

Published by Lexington Books
An imprint of The Rowman & Littlefield Publishing Group, Inc.
4501 Forbes Boulevard, Suite 200, Lanham, Maryland 20706
www.rowman.com

6 Tinworth Street, London SE11 5AL, United Kingdom

Copyright © 2021 The Rowman & Littlefield Publishing Group, Inc.

All rights reserved. No part of this book may be reproduced in any form or by any electronic or mechanical means, including information storage and retrieval systems, without written permission from the publisher, except by a reviewer who may quote passages in a review.

British Library Cataloguing in Publication Information Available

Library of Congress Cataloging-in-Publication Data

Names: Tchumkam, Hervé, author.
Title: Precarious lives and marginal bodies in North Africa : homo expendibilis / Hervé Anderson Tchumkam.
Description: Lanham : Lexington Books, [2021] | Series: After the empire: the Francophone world and postcolonial France | Includes bibliographical references and index. | Summary: "Precarious Lives and Marginal Bodies in North Africa sheds light on marginal bodies and the (post)colonial State, revealing the deep interconnectedness of the past with the recent situation of North Africa. Insecurity is not the consequence of a society perceived as uncivilized, but rather the result of an indecent society"— Provided by publisher.
Identifiers: LCCN 2020056041 (print) | LCCN 2020056042 (ebook) | ISBN 9781793640758 (cloth) | ISBN | 9781793640772 (paper) | ISBN 9781793640765 (epub)
Subjects: LCSH: Marginality, Social—Africa, North. | Precarious employment—Africa, North. | Africa, North—Economic conditions. | Africa, North—Social conditions.
Classification: LCC HN781.Z9 M2683 2921 (print) | LCC HN781.Z9 (ebook) | DDC 305.5/680961—dc23
LC record available at https://lccn.loc.gov/2020056041
LC ebook record available at https://lccn.loc.gov/2020056042

Contents

Introduction: *Homo Expendibilis* in North Africa   vii

1   *Memento Mori*: The Living Dead of Colonial Algeria   1
2   The Immigrant Body as Body of Exception   35
3   Women Body, Pathological Body   71
4   Precarious Lives: Slum Dwellers and Social Outcasts   105

Conclusion: Decentering the Center, Recentering the Periphery   135

Bibliography   149

Index   159

About the Author   169

Introduction
Homo Expendibilis *in North Africa*

In October 1988, thousands of youths invaded the streets of Algeria and literally took control of the streets in response to the austerity measures declared by the State at a time when the unemployment rate was very high among young people.[1] When the state of siege was declared in reaction to the youth riots, the monster that had been nurtured by the State escaped from its control, and the country plunged into darkness. Elite military forces were assigned to reestablish order, and the violent repression of civilians ensued, creating a fertile ground for religious leaders to emerge as the only ones capable of both uniting the people and offering them a better future. The 1988 Algerian riots would lead to the black decades of the 1990s, opening the door to two decades of extreme violence in the form of Islamic terrorism, which should be analyzed not only in terms of security but also as the result of a sociopolitical context in which the State itself creates insecurity (Tchumkam 2018). In May 2003, in Algeria's neighboring country Morocco, Casablanca was shaken by a series of terrorist attacks; the suicide bombers were young people from Sidi Moumen, a shantytown in the poor suburbs of Casablanca. Seven years later in Tunisia, a street vendor named Mohamed Bouazizi set himself on fire in response to the humiliation he experienced at the hands of members of the police force. One year later, in 2011, outraged by Bouazizi's self-immolation and fed up with the rampant social injustices that were proliferating under a dictatorial leadership, citizens chose the path of violent protest in the form of a civil disobedience that would later be known as the Jasmine Revolution, or the Tunisian Revolution.

While the three important political moments that I have just highlighted might seem unrelated, and while it is true that each upheaval was nurtured in a particular social and historical context, I submit that they are in fact all related. The link between the riots in Algeria, mass protests in Tunisia, and suicide bombing in Morocco is, I argue, that feeling of being fed up that was expressed by entire segments of populations that had been neglected, forgotten, or quite simply sacrificed. Using the powerful expression coined by Martin Evans and John Phillips (2007) who applied it to the specific case of Algeria, I would say that what was witnessed in those three North African countries was nothing more or less than the "anger of the dispossessed." As a matter of fact, the above-mentioned three events can also be seen as sharing the same commonality with the Hirak movement, the peaceful protests that led to the resignation of Algeria former President Abdelaziz Bouteflika whose reign lasted twenty years. Notwithstanding the respective national specificities and the difference in the manner that State power was confronted, one can argue that the citizens were affirming their unhappiness with the lack of civil and social protections that they are faced with or better, exposed to. I argue that what John Phillips and Martin Evans (2007, 297) characterize as the anger at the authoritarian nature of the regimes and the anger at generalized economic disaffection in the case of Algeria can also be observed in the Jasmine Revolution in Tunisia. The same anger could also very well be the result of the feeling of having been excluded from social protection, a marginality that in my opinion resulted in the Sidi Moumen youths' radicalization. Revolt is therefore central to the understanding of marginal bodies in that it takes many forms, from rioting as a political action to resistance and insurrection, as the only media of speech and visibility for those who have been reduced to inaudibility and invisibility. While I am focusing on North African countries formerly colonized by France, I must note that similar situations are prevalent in the rest of the continent where socially disqualified people face a life that has morphed into survival.

As a matter of fact, the current social and political experience in Africa in general and in Francophone North Africa in particular could lead us to wonder whether the entire continent is struggling to emerge from "out of the dark night" to borrow a phrase from Achille Mbembe (2019). While the representation of a "nightmarish Africa" remains "dear to certain know-all Western intellectuals" (Ramonet 1997), support for this very problematic stereotype is out of the question. Instead, it is important to produce a realistic and objective examination of the facts, which demonstrate that even as Africa evolves, tangible signs of liberation from its long "nightmare" are slow in coming. Wars and conflicts continue to hinder development. Unemployment in its various forms remains ever present, as does underemployment. On the political front, democratic change and consolidation are blocked because countless forms of authoritarianism continue to harden and seek desperately to survive.

Within such a context, addressing issues of precarious lives and marginal bodies requires a cautious approach and conceptualization as well as special consideration. The least that can be said is that the African continent remains trapped in what was once considered the landmark for its autonomy and therefore its emergence: independence. Challenges abound in both matters of civil defense and social welfare, which respectively guarantee fundamental freedoms and ensure the security of individuals and property within the framework of the rule of law and protect against risks likely to cause decline in an individual's situation. We could ask: Who are these dispossessed and what are the mechanisms that create an iniquitous division of space, labor, and visibility possible in Africa in general, and more specifically in North Africa? To answer this question, we must explore the metamorphoses of the human condition in North Africa as it is represented in the fiction, from the colonial period to the present. For what is at stake here is the meaning (or lack thereof) that certain lives acquire from the moment they are excluded from society, stripped of their basic human rights, and reduced to poverty, hopelessness, and ultimately a symbolic or even physical death. Moreover, once we understand that entire segments of the population have been cast aside, it becomes even more interesting to raise the question of why the lives of these people do not matter. In short, what becomes of these people who have been cast into oblivion and depoliticized by the very State structure whose mission it is to guarantee their civil and social liberties?

We must first of all recognize that the marginal lives of North Africa have been excluded from networks of capital production and social recognition. With that awareness, our initial interpretation of marginality in North Africa will be based on a sociological approach related to labor and social protection. We should note, however, that marginality deriving from lack of social welfare is not just a matter of being excluded, as the notion of exclusion presents certain limitations that have been outlined by Robert Castel. In his article "Les pièges de l'exclusion" (The pitfalls of exclusion), the French sociologist warns about the uses of the term *exclusion*. The first reason, he states, is that the notion of exclusion "nomme une foule de situations différentes en gommant la spécificité de chacune. Autrement dit l'exclusion n'est pas une notion analytique. Elle ne permet pas de conduire des investigations précises des contenus qu'elle prétend recouvrir" "names a host of different situations by erasing the uniqueness of each. In other words, exclusion is not an analytical concept. It does not allow us to do precise research on the contents it claims to cover" (1995, 13). According to Castel, in using the notion of exclusion, there is a risk of applying a purely negative conception to a situation without explaining its origins or its manifestations. Secondly, he continues, "parler d'exclusion conduit à autonomiser des situations limites qui ne prennent sens que si on les replace dans un processus. L'exclusion se donne en effet pour l'état de ceux qui se trouvent places en dehors des circuits vivants des échanges sociaux" "speaking of exclusion leads to autonomizing the limiting situations that only have meaning if they can be placed in a process. Exclusion in effect can be seen as the state of those who find their place outside the living circuits of social exchanges" (1995, 14).

This warning deserves to be taken seriously, because, as a matter of fact, as he argues, most of the time the notion of exclusion refers to situations that convey a deterioration, exemplified by the fact that people who were once socially integrated through labor can become vulnerable due to the precarization of their working conditions. In response to the fact that the notion of exclusion appears problematic in terms of understanding how a category of people experiences disenfranchisement, Castel proposes the notion of "désaffiliation sociale" "social disaffiliation," which seems particularly relevant for one of the ways in which I perceive the marginal bodies and precarious lives of North Africa as mediated through fiction. In point of fact, according to Castel, affiliation is possible under two conditions: the first is labor, which makes it possible for a person to be inserted into society, and the second is sociability (*sociabilité*), which relies on social relations and inserts the individual into social bonds (*liens sociaux*) (see Claude 2011).

In this sense, disaffiliation entails lack of participation in collective forms of protections, and particularly the protection that stems from labor. Unlike exclusion, which signifies a fixed negative situation, disaffiliation results from the processes of marginalization and the shattering of social bonds. Danièle Debordeaux explains Castel's notion of disaffiliation in the following terms:

> La désaffiliation caractérise un processus de rupture du lien social que vivent un certain nombre de personnes particulièrement démunies. Cette notion se différencie donc de la paupérisation car elle ne se réduit pas à la dimension économique de leur situation mais concerne également le tissu relationnel dans lequel elles s'insèrent (ou plutôt ne s'insèrent pas). Elle désigne non pas un état mais un processus fait de ruptures d'appartenances qui peuvent se lire sur deux axes—un axe d'intégration-non intégration par le travail qui va de l'emploi stable à l'absence complète de travail en passant par toutes les formes d'emplois précaires—un axe d'insertion-non insertion dans une sociabilité socio-familiale qui va de l'inscription dans les réseaux solides de sociabilité (familiale ou extra-familiale) à l'isolement social total.

> Disaffiliation characterizes a process of rupturing the social tie experienced by a certain number of people who are particularly deprived. This notion is thus differentiated from pauperization because it is not reduced to the economic dimension of their situation, but also concerns the relational fabric in which they are inserted (or rather, not inserted). It designates not a state, but a process made up of breaks in belonging that can be read on two axes: an axis of integration/nonintegration through work that ranges from stable employment to the complete absence of work as well as all forms of precarious jobs—an axis of

insertion/noninsertion in a sociofamilial sociability that ranges from inscription in the solid networks of sociability (familial or extra-familial) to total social isolation. (1994, 94)

From the above definition of the notion of disaffiliation (a combination of both joblessness and social isolation) coined by Castel, it appears that the concept indeed has much in common with the term *social disqualification* that Serge Paugam, another French sociologist, has employed to understand the rise of new forms of precarity. As the author of *La disqualification sociale* puts it in no uncertain terms:

Étudier la disqualification sociale ou, en d'autres termes, le discrédit de ceux dont on peut dire, en première approximation, qu'ils ne participent pas pleinement à la vie économique et sociale, c'est étudier la diversité des statuts qui les définissent, les identités personnelles, c'est-à-dire les sentiments subjectifs de leur propre situation qu'ils éprouvent au cours des diverses expériences sociales, et enfin, les rapports sociaux qu'ils entretiennent entre eux et avec autrui. Ce n'est pas l'analyse en elle-même des conduites en situation de pauvreté qui constitue l'axe essentiel de la recherche, mais plutôt le rapport au statut des populations qui occupent les derniers échelons de la hiérarchie sociale, c'est-à-dire l'identification partielle ou totale à un ensemble de comportements plus ou moins systématisé et relativement fixe, correspondant à des rôles sociaux reconnus comme légitime par elles et par la société.

Studying social disqualification, or in other terms, the discredit of those who we might say, as a first attempt, that they do not fully participate in the economic and social life, means to study the diversity of the statuses that define them, personal identities, that is, the subjective feelings of their own situation that the experience through various social experiences, and finally the social ties that they maintain with themselves and with others. It is not analysis in itself of the conduct in situations of poverty that constitutes that essential axis of the research, but rather the link to the status of the populations that occupy the lowest echelons of the social hierarchy, that is, the partial or total identification of a group of behaviors that are more or less systematized and relatively fixed, corresponding to those social roles that are recognized as legitimate by them and by society. (2011, 17)

Having discussed the sociological tools necessary to my conception of the precarious lives of North Africa and that have to do with social protections, I must now point out the second hermeneutic tool of precariousness in North Africa, which has to do with civil protections and more specifically the ways in which politics in North Africa has become both biopolitics and thanatopolitics, or what Achille Mbembe has named "necropolitics." All three notions have in common the centrality of the body as a site of expression of sovereign power, whether in its reduction to a pure biological object or in its subjection to suffering, abuse, pain, hunger, and ultimately death. If we look at colonialism, which viewed colonized bodies both as "corps de chair et de sang de l'individu singulier" "bodies of flesh and blood of the singular individual" and as a "corps social, comme population qui produit des richesses et se reproduit" "social body, like a population that produces riches and reproduces," to use Vincent Grégoire's (2007, 61) classification, which includes the use of female bodies in the colonial empire as carefully studied in the collection edited by Martine Spensky (2015), it is striking that human life has entered the realm of politics, in this case with the classification of populations divided into social groups (colonized, colonizers) or sexual groups (men, women). The place of sexuality in the process of expenditure that Martine Spensky (2015), Christelle Taraud (2012), and Catherine Brun and Todd Shepard (2016), for instance, have carefully scrutinized as yet another characteristic of sovereignty is not surprising, especially if one considers Achille Mbembe's interpretation of Georges Bataille. Mbembe writes: "Sexuality is inextricably linked to violence and to the dissolution of the boundaries of the body and self by way of orgiastic and excremental impulses" (2004, 15).

On another level, the value of the human body as a commodity that is paradoxically subject to expendability features in all past and current debates on the migration of bodies between North Africa and Europe, with particular attention given not just to the condition of the immigrant once in Europe but also to the abuses, battles, and hardships faced by African migrants in search of Europe, tribulations that Robert Press has summarized as "dangerous crossings" (2017). The expendability of bodies is even more glaring when we consider the treatment of slaves, as well as the social disqualification that affects the impoverished masses trying to survive in the Casbah of Algeria or the slums of Morocco, to name but a few examples. Both during colonial times when race or racism, in Foucault's words, was "the condition for the acceptability of putting to death" (2003, 256) and in the postcolonial era where we see the construction of a necropolitics understood by Achille Mbembe as "contemporary forms of subjugation of life to the power of death" with the rise of "new and unique forms of social existence in which vast populations are subjected to conditions of life conferring upon them the status of living dead" (2003, 39–40), the citizen of North African countries has simply been reduced to a body over which sovereign authority has the power of life and death. Indeed, from the colonial era to the present, when immigration has become a hot topic, what is at stake here is control over people's bodies.

In *Homo Sacer: Sovereign Power and Bare Life* (1998), Giorgio Agamben extends the reflections of Michel Foucault on biopower, understood as specific power techniques enforced over individual bodies and populations. That control over bodies corresponds to political mechanisms unleashed by the sovereign power. Quite specifically, sovereign power, in the sense understood by the Italian philosopher, is today organized around control over the bodies of citizens. Inspired by ancient Greece, Agamben begins with a fundamental distinction between the terms *bios* and *zoè*, "two terms that, although traceable to a common etymological root, are semantically and morphologically dinstict: *zoè*, which expressed the simple fact of living common to all living beings (animals, men or gods) and *bios*, which indicated the form or way of living proper to an individual or group" (1998, 1). What is interesting in this distinction, as Agamben suggests and is in agreement with Foucault, is that the individual becomes a pawn in political strategies. Agamben thus offers evidence of the importance of biological life that becomes a stake in the management of human beings:

> What defines the status of the *homo sacer* is therefore not the original ambivalence of sacredness that is assumed to belong to him, but rather both the particular character of the double exclusion into which he is taken and the violence to which he finds himself exposed. This violence—the unsanctionable killing that, in his case, anyone may commit—is classifiable neither as sacrifice nor as homicide, neither as the execution of a condemnation to death nor as sacrilege. (1998, 82)

It becomes clear that the goal of sovereignty, according to Agamben, is not life as it is characterized for the citizen, one who is able to speak and make use of his or her rights, but rather bare (or naked) life, one that is reduced to the silence of refugees, the deported, and the banished: that of the *homo sacer,* relentlessly subject to the discipline, imprisonment, or death of the body. My use of the concept of biopolitics to analyze the relation between sovereignty and citizens' lives in North Africa rests at the juncture between the figure of the *homo sacer* as treated by Agamben and the notion of the government of bodies inspired by Michel Foucault. In both cases, we are dealing with a politics that becomes a form of expendability: the offspring of those who yesterday were subjected to forced labor, rape, and heavy taxation, or reduced to cannon fodder in the colony, are today reduced to bodies at the disposal of postcolonial States. Agamben himself had already signaled that necropolitics can become thanatopolitics:

> Along with the emergence of biopolitics, we can observe a displacement and gradual expansion beyond the limits of the decision on bare life, in the state of

exception, in which sovereignty consisted. If there is a line in every modern state marking the point at which the decision on life becomes a decision on death, and biopolitics can turn into thanatopolitics, this line no longer appears today as a stable border dividing two clearly distinct zones. (1998, 122)

It is therefore at this crossroads of biopolitics, necropolitics, and thanatopolitics that I position myself to propose the figure of the *homo expendibilis*, the expendable person, the expendable (wo)man. Combining the figure of the *homo sacer*, the one who can be put to death in a manner that is classified neither as sacrifice nor as homicide, as Agamben explains, and the victims of necropolitics that are faced with a sovereign power that deploys "new technologies of destruction [that] are less concerned with inscribing bodies within disciplinary apparatuses [than] inscribing them, when the time comes, within the maximal economy now represented by the 'massacre,'" as Mbembe writes (2004, 34), I am proposing the figure of the *homo expendibilis* as a new means of interpreting the marginal bodies and precarious lives in former French colonies in North Africa.

The *homo expendibilis* is therefore that person who is not only exposed and subjected to biopolitics, necropolitics, and thanatopolitics, but additionally, who is also kept at the periphery of social life. The main difference that I see between the *homo sacer*, characterized by unsanctionable death in Agamben's studies, and the *homo expendibilis* is that the *homo expendibilis* is not only subjected to the power of death; s/he can be left alive and still be turned through political and social systems into the living dead, thereby embodying what Mbembe called a "form of death-in-life" (2003, 21). In other words, the *homo expendibilis*, unlike the *homo sacer* or the subject whose life is subjugated to the power of death, is a type of zombie whose existence is both necessary and expendable. If the colonized, the casualties of wars, and prisoners are victims of biopolitical or necropolitical political apparatuses, they do differ from the poor, the disabled, and the disenfranchised who are not literally subjected to biological death, but who are nonetheless exposed to symbolic death. What makes the homo expendibilis peculiar in my opinion is that before or beyond mere death, they are characterized by dehumanization and relegation at the margins of the polis, a marginality that they will oppose by resorting to various mechanisms of resistance. Thus, the *homo expendibilis* in my understanding differs slightly from the *homo sacer* and the victims of necropolitics or thanatopolitics in the sense that *homo expendibilis* is also, beyond the issue of the right to live, a victim of what Paugam called social disqualification, and in that sense, this person experiences Castel's "social disaffiliation" in that they are not being protected. I argue that the *homo expendibilis* is that person who is not only exposed to irredeemable death but who can also be alive and yet dead in the symbolic sense, because of the lack of access to social welfare, and can consequently be trapped in social disintegration/degradation. The *homo expendibilis* in North Africa, in my analysis, clearly exceeds the categories discussed by Agamben and Mbembe, and cover the expendable lives that are the racialized, colonized subject, the exile or immigrant who is an eternal "stranger," the woman who suffers male domination, the poor, the disabled, the slave, and the many other invisibles who inhabit the slums of major North African cities, as well as the common person who becomes engulfed in the violence of terrorist attacks. The *homo expendibilis* is the vulnerable subject whose life is reduced to survival, who is faced with death but also has no social protection; in short, the subaltern who has been made both invisible and inaudible but who will nevertheless strive to assert his or her right to exist, or what Muhammad Ali Nasir has called the "right to life" (2017) in the context of biopolitical or, we could even add, necropolitical governmentality.

Furthermore, and of greater interest for me, the *homo expendibilis* who is subjected to all we have seen above in terms of biopolitics, necropolitics, or thanatopolitics will refuse to remain a mere victim and will reinvent ways to resist his circumstances, including sometimes resorting to a violence that is first and foremost a liberating violence in Frantz Fanon's sense, although at times self-destructive. In an article entitled "Thanatopolitics or Biopolitics? Diagnosing the Racial and Sexual Politics of the European Fra-Right," Jemina Repo observed that "the interest in race in political/IR theory is more disposed to analyze the thanatopolitical metaphysics of exclusion instituted by sovereign power . . . is reflected in the popularity of certain post-Foucauldian frameworks like Agamben's (1998) concept of bare life and Esposito's (2008) immunization (rather than postcolonial or critical race theory, which is rarely cited or employed)" (2016, 112). My study will address that particular blind spot by specifically proposing a postcolonial-grounded approach to the ability of the sovereign to let live or let die, through an understanding of mechanisms of production and the agency of the *homo expendibilis* in North African contexts, going beyond Foucault's biopolitics as well as Agamben's bare life and Esposito's immunization, to inscribe the expendable people in the context of (formerly) colonized African societies that govern the living dead, to borrow the words of Andrew Norris (2000). For it is undeniable that in North Africa, from the colonial era to the present, one can observe a series of mechanisms that cause the human species to enter into the sphere of politics defined by Foucault as "biopower" (2004). And it is literature that appears to offer interesting representations or mediations of this state of affairs.

PRECARIOUS LIVES AND MARGINAL BODIES IN NORTH AFRICAN FICTION

The study of African literatures is generally underpinned by two core methodological claims. The first sees States as boundaries of knowledge and thereby turns the political into epistemological boundaries. In this regard, there is an inclination to limit the study of African societies based solely on the country's colonial past. The second methodological claim is that the study of these societies depends heavily on an analysis that emphasizes antagonistic human groups. For instance, studies often scrutinize the encounter between colonized and colonizers. While this approach has its benefits, it seems to me important to take a closer look at individuals—or rather, groups of individuals—that are not merely general categories like "natives" or "colonizers," but instead social, sexual, or symbolic categories (poor and disenfranchised, street children, peasants, slaves, disabled, forces exiles, abused women). When it comes specifically to the literature produced in North Africa or by North African writers, Marc Gontard earlier signaled a divide between critics who focus on content analysis and those who regard "écriture" as a fundamental element of the text. He noted that literary criticism on North African literary productions followed two main groups: on the one hand, those for whom "the Maghrebian text is Maghrebian before it is a text [and who are] primarily interested in the text as a historical or sociological document, as a political or ideological message, assuming that it is no more than a simple 'reflection' of the real" (1992, 36), and on the other hand, a second group of critics for whom "a text, even a Maghrebian text, is first of all a literary text that must be read like any other text, regardless of the culture to which it belongs," adding that this approach has the distinct advantage of "respecting the aesthetic purpose of the North African texts, its 'literariness,' and of distinguishing the text from the 'real' that serves as its referent by emphasizing the formal mediation of meaning and the process of symbolization, thereby avoiding the pitfalls of naïve sociologism" (1992, 36–37). It is, however, important to note that critical studies have evolved since Gontard's powerful warning about the necessity not to overvalue North African literature by the nature of its reception, and the study of francophone North African literature has since followed different and yet important trajectories.

More recently than Marc Gontard, Jane Hiddleston, in her article entitled "État Présent: Francophone North African Literature," has provided an insightful overview of the evolution of criticism and stresses the recent "renewed attention to the memory and representation of colonialism and its demise in North Africa" as well as the fact that "given the persistence of widespread anxiety about the colonial past in France alongside the emergence of new tensions in North Africa, the very meaning of 'postcolonialism' in

North Africa, fifty years or more after independence, is again under scrutiny" (2015, 82). Indeed, North African literature has become the mirror of a society in crisis, beginning with colonial exploitation and continuing into current social and political turmoil throughout the various French-speaking countries that make up North Africa. In this sense, postcolonialism goes beyond a return to the past and also attempts to comprehend the lingering effects of colonial legacy. While this work does not follow Hiddleston's suggestion of observing the interaction between francophone and arabophone cultures as a means to achieve a wider grasp of the transnational connection in North Africa, it does take up her recommendation that "if postcolonial theory created the foundation for a better understanding of North African literature as it evolved before and after independence, criticism now needs both to understand the preoccupation of francophone writers from the Maghreb and to establish conceptual frameworks for reading that would be appropriate to the concerns of our time" (2015, 90). Hiddleston ultimately calls for a form of interdisciplinary research that provides a deeper understanding of literature, which should be considered as rooted in a wider context of political transition and cultural reinvention. I would submit that returning to the colonial period and following major themes and marginal figures in North African literature, with a special emphasis on the use of bodies both by colonial and postcolonial powers as a means to understand the metamorphoses of the *homo expendibilis* (the expendable person), could constitute the basis for a renewed approach to francophone North African fiction and society. For in fact, a central concern to this study is the effect of biopower on the North African body, from the colonial to postcolonial perspectives. How are marginal bodies inscribed in the novels from Francophone North Africa, and what does this representation tells us about the relation between sovereignty or colonial forces and the citizens? This book bridges francophone studies and postcolonial studies, two fields that "have often been seen as rival if not antagonistic academic fields," in Alec Hargreaves and Jean-Marc Moura's words, who add that "where work in the second has been led by Anglophone scholars for whom the politics of culture has been of primordial importance, the first has generally been preferred by scholars in France who have seen in 'postcolonialism' an oversimplified and unduly politicized 'Anglo-Saxon' approach to the culture of the formerly colonized people" (2007, 307).

In that regard, this project aims to study North Africa at the junction of literary analysis, political philosophy, and social sciences such as history and sociology, by means of an analysis of social categories related both to civil protections (those that guarantee fundamental liberties and guarantee the security of people) and to social protections (those that protect from illnesses, poverty, etc.) and that can lead to social degradation. I have chosen to read both male and female authors from Algeria, Tunisia, and Morocco.

While I could have limited my study to a corpus of works from a specific country, I am framing my analysis within the context of former French colonies. And because each of these has a specific historical and social context, I am not arguing that they are homogeneous. Rather, I hope to show that beyond differences, with regard to social order in the wake of independences, there seems to be a kind of social uniformization whereby one can find a common ground between the three countries, which is the social disqualification of the dispossessed and the rise of insecurity that derives from the resistance to marginalization, humiliation and ultimately, dehumanization. Given that literature is firmly grounded into its political context, my readings of the selected novels discussed here will aim at scrutinizing the societal dimension represented by texts. My reading of novels as sociological accounts focuses on the narrative in so far as it offers an illuminating glimpse into the North African political and social drama since colonization. In clear, I am interested in novels whose narratives describe unequal social arrangements, but furthermore, offer paths to reflect on how fiction authors through their imagination disrupt and challenge systems of inequality in which the homo expendibilis is inscribed. In doing so, my objective will be to reassess violence insofar as it crystallizes the disjunction between the socially disqualified and the holders of power—colonial, political, and religious. Taking my cue from Achille Mbembe's notion of "necropolitics," I will investigate the ways in which literary productions from North Africa, to the extent that they inscribe in a central way the interrogation of the value of human lives, record the expression of sovereignty in the power to decide who lives and who dies. Of particular interest for my analysis in Mbembe's "necropolitics" is subjectivization that Mbembe grounds in a discussion of Hegel's understanding of the relation between death and "becoming a subject." Mbembe writes:

> Within the Hegelian paradigm, human death is essentially voluntary. It is the result of risks consciously assumed by the subject. According to Hegel, in these risks the "animal" that constitutes the human subject's natural being is defeated. In other words, the human being truly *becomes a subject*—that is, separated from the animal—in the struggle and the work through which he or she confronts death (understood as the violence of negativity). It is through this confrontation with death that he or she is cast into the incessant movement of history. Becoming subject therefore supposes upholding the work of death. To uphold the work of death is precisely how Hegel defines the life of the Spirit. The life of the Spirit, he says, is not that life which is frightened of death, and spares itself destruction, but that life which assumes death and lives with it. Spirit attains its truth only by finding itself in absolute dismemberment. (2003, 14)

In the light of the definition of the process of becoming a subject in Hegel that Mbembe circumscribes, the literary production of North Africa studied in this book mediates marginal figures who, through resistance to invisibility and inaudibility by means of solitary or collective revolt (oppressed peasants and women), terrorism (slum children), hunger strikes (exile and immigrants), uphold the work of death. Indeed, by staging a resistance to the colonial or postcolonial oppressive order, these characters in the novels risk their lives in the confrontation with death. Additionally, the marginal bodies that I analyze in this book differ from the victims of necropolitics that Mbembe identifies in the context of war as a means of achieving sovereignty. In this specific case, my paradigm is that of social categories that are disqualified from civil and social protections. What stands out from this shift of paradigm, from camps and wars to social categories, is that the excluded resist to their condition, and affirm their right to exist. The emphasis on social categories is important because neither Agamben's *homo sacer* nor Mbembe's wounded or slain bodies are based on social categories, and much less on precarity. In clear, the homo expendibilis is the person pushed away from a livable life, dehumanized, faced with insecurity and deprived of agency but who, in response, stages a resistance to their marginal condition. The focus on revolt, insurrection and resistance in the novels discussed will offer an interpretation of the link between marginal bodies in their significance and political power in the society represented by the novels, Francophone North Africa. The result, I argue, is the proliferation of insecurity. My reading of the novels studied in this essay will therefore emphasize the causality link that exists between precarity and insecurity, for in an attempt to emerge from the margins and claim their place in what Jacques Rancière calls the "distribution of the sensible," precarious lives erect their marginal bodies and take the form of a dangerous class that will challenge the social and political order upheld by authority figures, either at personal or collective levels.

Furthermore, this book will contend that if one fails to understand precarization in African contexts, and most specifically in North Africa, from colonial times to this era, then one can understand neither the politics nor the rise of insecurity of the present. Thus, the representation and the uses of marginal bodies will be central to this study, since corporeal representations do not merely reflect natural reality; they also reveal cultural productions that convey the metamorphosis of the real and consequently expose the arena of oppression and resistance. Recent studies have charted new critical perspectives on Maghrebi literature. Charles Bonn's *Lectures nouvelles du roman algérien* (2016) and Valerie Orlando's *The New Algerian Novel* (2017) offer contemporary theoretical perspectives on the Algerian novel, emphasizing what can be called a Franco-Algerian comparatism that emphasizes cosmopolitan and global perspectives with regard to a binary relation between the North and the South. In *Aspects du roman marocain* (2006), Moroccan scholar Abdallah Mdarhri Alaoui offer a synthesis of Moroccan fiction by identifying five important moments, ranging between 1950 and 2000. This chapter underlines salient trends and themes at work in the Moroccan novel in French, but also in a few cases analyzed, in Arab. In *Le roman tunisien de langue francaise* (2004), Jean Fontaine provides readers with a thematic and historical reading of the Tunisian novel in French, shedding light on topics and themes in three types of novels that he classifies as ethnographic novels, historical novels, and autobiographical novels. My book, while acknowledging the outstanding contribution by the authors of the above-mentioned essays, goes beyond national boundaries and literary traditions to identify an emerging figure, at least at it appears in fiction, that effectively links the three Francophone countries/literatures in North Africa. The historical and political reasons for my choice are inspired by Fanny Colonna and Zakya Daoud's book, *Être Marginal au Maghreb* (1993), an edited volume that brings together anthropologists, historians and sociologist who reflect on social order in North Africa, including Egypt. Fanny Colonna suggests "une *uniformisation progressive* des sociétés et des cultures du Nord de l'Afrique (uniformisation qui est aussi à l'œuvre semble-t-il au Sud du Sahara) versus celle d'une diversification profonde, endogène et irrépressible" (3–4). This standardization (*uniformisation* in French) in the essay seems to rest on the existence of marginal social groups that are excluded by the independent State. I extend the reflection on marginal citizens in my work by adding to Colonna's independent States, the colonial administration, the dominant male, and the slave master. I also shift the analysis from Anthropology, Law and History to novels that I read in their societal dimension.

Therefore, the present work begins with the postulate that the precarious lives in North Africa have become true bodies of exceptions, that is, bodies that are dangerous and unworthy of being regarded as valuable as citizens with full rights, despite being members of their nations. Basing my approach on the notion of "bare life" theorized by Giorgio Agamben in *Homo Sacer: Sovereign Power and Bare Life* and that of "precarious lives" developed by Judith Butler in *Precarious Life: The Powers of Mourning and Violence*, I propose that we can observe in colonial and postcolonial North Africa a mutation whereby the socially disqualified human categories literally become expendable even while necessary for the exercise of sovereign power. For if Agamben's *homo sacer* could be put to death without his death being considered homicide, in the case of the social categories that I am studying in this book, being put to death is doubled by the person's construction as a precarious life not even deserving to be mourned. Thus, by combining Agamben and Butler, that is, by adding the unsanctionable murder that anyone may commit with them to the conditions of humans that do not count as humans, whose lives are not mournable, I will explore the hypothesis that the *homo expendibilis*, the expendable person, constitutes the figure of the periphery whereby the center is challenged, remapped, and ultimately redefined. One major reason for analyzing and understanding the ambiguity of the socially disenfranchised people has been emphasized by French philosopher Guillaume le Blanc, who writes:

> Signaler que des vies sont jetables, c'est d'emblée indiquer le caractère ambivalent de l'exclusion qui, d'un côté, arrache des vies de la communauté, les extirpe de la cité des humains, mais pour les maintenir, de l'autre côté, dans une marge de la cité où il sera toujours possible de puiser, et aussi à l'intérieur de la cité, en les poussant, malgré tout, à la consommation.
>
> To signal that lives can be thrown away indicates right away the ambivalent nature of exclusion, which on the one hand snatches lives from the community, uproots them from city of human beings, but to keep them, on the other hand, at the margin of the city where it will always be possible to tap them, and also inside the city, by pushing them, despite everything towards consumption. (2011, 40–41)

I argue that those lives that can be "thrown away," to use le Blanc's terminology, occupy a central place in the remapping of North African contemporary societies insofar as they signal the threshold between the center and the periphery, and contribute to a redefinition of power and agency. Hence, I ask the following questions: What is the value of human lives when these very humans are reduced to their pure biological expression? What is the relationship between death and politics in North Africa? How does one understand the central paradox of necessity and expendability that the socially disqualified are trapped into? What political and social mechanisms are put in place by sovereign power to turn human lives into lives that can be put to death without homicide, and that furthermore do not even deserve to be mourned? In short, what does the intersection of precarization and stigma tell us about the prevalence of insecurity in North Africa and beyond? To answer these questions, *Homo Expendibilis* will investigate the polemic distribution of space, visibility, and speech in North Africa in four chapters. The following chapters are a collection of more or less successful, analysis of the fictional representation and significance of various social categories whose bodies enter the sphere of politics. Such categories that are subjected to death but also simultaneously socially disqualified is what I call *homo expendibilis*, the expendable person.

Chapter 1, "*Memento Mori*: The Living Dead of Colonial Algeria," will go beyond the classic distinction between colonized and colonizers to reflect on peasantry as a primordial category of expenditure, needed but exploited, and victims of exclusive inclusion in the social order of colonial Algeria. Analyzing the oppressed and peasants in revolt in Mohammed Dib's *L'incendie* and Azzédine Bounemeur's *Les bandits de l'Atlas*, I will show that the daily life of colonized people, and to a further extent of peasants in rural Algeria, was a constant meditation on the knowledge that they could be made subject to death. In response, the peasant resistance and the place that it held in the efforts of decolonization will be analyzed, with a special emphasis on the ways in which the peasantry played a central role in the efforts of decolonization only to be cast out by the new ruling elite on the eve of independence, in the sense that Frantz Fanon wrote about in his seminal essay, The *Wretched of the Earth*.

Chapter 2, "The Immigrant Body as Body of Exception," offers a reflection on the paradox of immigration, by underlining two determining paradoxes of transhumance from North Africa to France: the paradox of invitation and rejection, and the contradiction between the denial of asylum rights and the surge in humanitarian effort. Building on Albert Bensoussan's *Mirages à 3*, Mehdi Charef's *Le thé au harem d'Archi Ahmed*, and Fawzia Zouari's *Ce pays dont je meurs*, I will contend that the current debate on immigration from Africa to Europe puts forward humanitarianism only as a means to refuse to take the necessary measures to protect basic human rights. Extending Sidi Mohammed Barkat's *Le corps d'exception* from the colonial context to immigration, I will suggest that the immigrant body is a body characterized as dangerous, unworthy of hospitality, and yet included in France through its very exclusion.

Winifred Woodhull (1993), Valerie Orlando (1999), Anne Donadey (2001), Allison Rice (2012) and Mildred Mortimer (2018),[2] to name only a few, have offered insightful readings of the feminine figure, both as characters in novels and as authors in the Maghreb. Building on their works, chapter 3, "Women Body, Pathological Body," rests on the intersection between human(women) biology and politics to offer a reading of *Le châtiment des hypocrites* and *La jeune fille et la mère*, two novels by Leïla Marouane, through the lens of the insertion of the female body into the realm of biopolitics, that is, a politics of the body wherein women are reduced to their corporeal otherness. Using Pierre Bourdieu's *Masculine Domination* along with Giorgio Agamben's *The Use of Bodies*, I will suggest that women's bodies in Algeria have gradually become slave bodies[3] and that although these women struggle for rights over their own bodies, those very bodies are not quite their own. As a consequence, in response to rape and other forms of bodily torture, women resort to violence as a means to move out of precarity. And in so doing, by joining the fight against colonial and postcolonial injustices and resisting humiliation, women take an active part in the erection of a "decent society," that is a society whose institutions do not humiliate the people under their authority, and whose citizens do not humiliate one another, in the words of Avishai Margalit (1998).

Chapter 4, "Precarious Lives: Slum Dwellers and Social Outcasts," analyzes the central figures of slum children as social pariahs or better, outcasts in Mahi Binebine's *Les étoiles de Sidi Moumen* as well as the female black slave in *Le sommeil de l'esclave*. By interpreting precarious lives as ones that have been cast out and hidden from public sight, in this chapter I will follow the cue of French philosopher Guillaume le Blanc to submit that while the precarious beings are not out-of-society per se, their living conditions exclude them from relations of power and deprive them of all the elements necessary for an effective pursuit of happiness. I will submit as well that while the act of speech in the precarious is hindered by their social invisibility, it nevertheless constitutes an element that democracy needs to be attentive to at the very least, and better, to protect. Resistance to relegation through terrorism by slum children and through reclaiming one's body usage in the case of the female slave will be paramount to our understanding of how street children, social outcasts, and the black female slave reclaim the periphery and affirm their right to exist.

My work here will be to analyze vulnerability, to scrutinize the ways in which some social categories are shunted outside the realm of society because of sickness, gender, social class, poverty, unemployment, and physical handicap. Moreover, it will be my contention that the construction of precarious lives in fact reveals the common vulnerability of both those who take part in the distribution of the sensible and those who are outcasts. Ultimately, I will propose that the marginal bodies of North Africa, by affirming their right to exist and their civil competence, offer a perception of the society that marginalized them, and thus, as inaudible and invisible peripheral people, they challenge the idea of the center, thereby forcing a reconceptualization of democracy and citizenship. Such is the important contribution that I believe this book will bring to the broader discussion on Africa, democracy, and human rights.

NOTES

1. For further reading on political violence in Algeria from colonial times to the recent present, see for instance Malika Rahal's article "Fuse Together, Torn Apart. Stories and Violence in Contemporary Algeria." *History & Memory,* Vol. 24, No. 1 (Spring/Summer 2012): 118–51.

2. Winnifred Woodhull, *Transfigurations of the Maghreb: Feminism, Decolonization, and Literatures.* Minneapolis, University of Minnesota Press, 1993. Valerie Orlando, *Nomadic Voices of Exile: Feminine Identity in Francophone*

Literature of the Maghreb. Athens, Ohio University Press, 1999. Anne Donadey, *Recasting Postcolonialism: Women Writing Between the Worlds*. Portsmouth, Heineman, 2001. Allison Rice, *Polygaphies: Francophone Women Writing Algeria*. Charlottesville &London, University of Virginia Press, 2012. *Mildred Mortimer, Women Fight, Women Write: Texts on the Algerian War*. Charlottesville &London, University of Virginia Press, 2018.

3. I use the notion of slavery in this context in the sense defined by Giorgio Agamben in *The Use of Bodies* (2015). For the philosopher who uses Aristotle's discussion of slavery, the slave's activity is use of the body, not for economic production, but for the necessary tasks that reproduce bodily life (zoe), so that the master can pursue bios.

Chapter 1

Memento Mori
The Living Dead of Colonial Algeria

THE EXPENDABLE LIVES OF FELLAHS IN MOHAMMED DIB'S *L'INCENDIE*

"N'oubliez pas que cette terre est la vôtre. Elle vous a vu naitre et grandir. Aujourd'hui, on nous en chasse. Que Dieu les punisse" "Do not forget that this land is your land. It has seen your birth and growth. Today, we're being chased out. May God punish them." These words, a call to remember as well as a malediction, are pronounced by the father of the three main characters in Rachid Bouchareb's film *Hors la loi* (2010).[1] This film revisits the troubled history of Algeria from the beginning of the 1900s until the independence of that country, which, as we all know, experienced a bloody war in which numerous military and civil victims, on one side (Algeria) as well as the other (France), seem to be in the grips of either an economy of memorial excess or collective amnesia. What interests me about the opening of Bouchareb's film is the father's bitterness at the arrival on his property of an Algerian caïd, accompanied by two French gendarmes; the caïd informs him that he must vacate his property, a verdict that is at the very least arbitrary and against which he argues that the land has been in his family's possession from time immemorial up to own parents, who left it to him. The conversation between the Algerian peasant and the caïd turns on an intractable judgment that leaves the peasant powerless: he has three days to leave his land because it is "the law." Chased from his property with wife and children, this is the start of a life without guideposts for the Algerian peasant. We should note that because *Hors la loi* came out only five years after the Law of February 23, 2005, whose main goal was to celebrate France's colonial grandeur through all the benefits of its civilizing mission, the film was a remarkable effort to highlight a return to a history without which the histories of France and

Algeria would be completely different today. Furthermore, Bouchareb's film, like his *Indigènes/Days of Glory* (2006), which preceded it, is an invitation to return to the colonization of Algeria to understand its subtleties and especially to attempt an approach to the meanings of the lives of the colonized so that that they might be understood in ways other than through the prism of the binary relationship of colonizer-colonized.

In other words, the presence of the caïd who brings with him the two French gendarmes onto the site of expropriation is highly suggestive in that it summons us to scrutinize more closely the categories of subalterns created by colonization. In essence, if the colonized is in general a victim of oppression, that category itself remains fragmented, with subcategories, leading to the observation that in the grand scheme of the colonized, there are categories that are doubly debilitating. It is specifically the figure of the fellah, the peasant indigene, who interests me in this part of my study, where I will begin with a reading of the novel *L'incendie* by Mohammed Dib (1954). In *Lecture présente de Mohammed Dib* (1988), Charles Bonn had emphasized the ways in which *L'incendie* had brought to light the political consciousness of peasants that was unprecedented. Adejir Tar for his part had already underlined how from silence in Dib's *La grande maison* (1952), peasants have become articulate in *L'incendie*, voicing their indignation with regards to confiscated land, to France, to the colonists and, last but not least, to the colonial legal system (1992). Building on Bonn's idea of the emergence of peasant's speech ("émergence de la parole paysanne"), I would like to reflect on the ways in which the peasants as marginal figures contribute to recasting the idea of resistance. What are the processes of social disqualification at work in the novel? What is the value of the lives of Algeria's peasants, trapped as they are between inclusion and exclusion in the sociopolitical sphere? How can we characterize their work? And finally, what lessons about the precarious lives of peasants during colonization can be drawn about the *sans-part*, that is those excluded from visibility, audibility, and speech (those excluded from what French philosopher Jacques Rancière has called the "distribution of the sensible")[2] and the invisible in colonial society in Algeria, and more generally in Africa? Those are the questions that will guide my analyses, which aim to highlight the juridical and political frameworks that make the life of the colonized expendable, and even more, that of the peasant who is doubly marginalized—first because he is among the colonized and then because as a fellah, he is reduced to his pure biological expression.

Mohammed Dib's *L'incendie* recounts the story of peasants in Bni Boublen, a tiny village perched among the mountains, a village where a tragedy is played out that reveals almost point by point the link between poverty and the domination of a colonized people. In the novel's prologue, Mohammed Dib introduces the reader to a land beyond space and time in which a particular kind of life is played out, an existence built around agriculture and breeding that takes place among the colonists. We are furthermore dealing with a place that is even more remote because in the novel, that place is on a continent that is literally forgotten. Dib employs a commonplace from colonial-era African literature when in a particularly meaningful allusion to spatial distribution, he emphasizes that the fellahs—that is, the peasants—occupy lower Bni Bublen. If the mention of lower Bni Boublen's geographical location supposes an upper Bni Boublen inhabited by French colonists, even more compelling is the novelist's summary, in the prologue, of the life of the fellahs: "Ces hommes vivent à la lisière des bas fonds cultivables, fixés sur la montagne, déjà relégués du monde. Pourtant, trois kilomètres seulement les séparent de Tlemcen. Leur existence se passe en journées agricoles et pastorales chez les colons. Elle est si archaïque, et les gens se montrent si simples, qu'on les croirait issus d'un continent oublié" "These men live at the edge of the lowest cultivable areas, set against the mountain, already set removed from the world. Yet, only three kilometers separates them from Tlemcen. Their existence is spent in days of farming and herding among the colonists. Their life is so archaic, and the people seem so simple, that you'd think they came from a forgotten continent" (7–8).

That passage about space is followed by a description of the children who incarnate and personify poverty, so to speak, downtrodden as they are like their parents by hunger. In the preceding citation, we saw the emergence of the condition of the colonized, whose body becomes the quintessential site of colonial domination, just as Dib's mention of a forgotten continent recalls most opportunely for the reader Frantz Fanon's excellent study, *The Wretched of the Earth*, a work in which Fanon explores the mechanisms of dehumanization of the colonized and analyzes that trauma within the framework of the colonial system. In fact, and rightly so, the description with which *L'incendie* opens fits perfectly with the carving of space that Fanon had already observed in his work and which, we should point out, was published amid the fullness of colonial violence in Algeria.

The characterization of lower Bni Boublen in terms of the space occupied by the colonists corresponds in several ways to Fanon's thinking on the polemical distribution of space, and thus existence in the context of colonization in Africa:

> The colonized's sector, or at least the "native" quarters, the shanty town, the Medina, the reservation, is a disreputable place inhabited by disreputable people. You are born anywhere, anyhow. You die anywhere, from anything. It's a world with no space, people are piled one on top of the other, the shacks squeezed tightly together. The colonized's sector is a famished sector, hungry for bread, meat, shoes, coal, and light. The colonized's sector is a sector that

crouches and cowers, a sector on its knees, a sector that is prostrate. It's a sector of niggers, a sector of towelheads. (2004, 4–5)

In this world torn in two, lower Bni Boublen is essentially the supreme space for the deterioration and crisis of fundamental human rights. If occupation of that space allows a view of spatial disequilibrium, it is first and foremost because it is not only in the colonial context that we are dealing with a clash through which colonization maintains and exerts its power but also because that spatial division follows the criteria of exclusion and marginalization that operate through a distinction between the center and the periphery. In considering the movement of the fellahs and the spaces assigned to them, we understand that space in this novel goes beyond aesthetic considerations to serve as the ultimate time or place for the exercise of power.

The space for whites is closed off from fellahs, except those given permission, and their movement is conditioned by a space for "laisser passer" "coming and going," whereas the space allotted to or endured by the peasants is open, and the colonizer has absolute freedom of movement within it. Colonization organizes space in such a way that power closes in on itself, and thus controls the conditions of economic and political existence. This hypothesis from the reading is indeed confirmed by the omnipresence of the motif of travel in this novel, from the famine- and poverty-racked village to the city, which is the temple of village curiosity, the site of all hope and the storehouse of resources that are left to rot out in the open. Through his tale, Mohamed Dib appears to transform the colonized into the mythical character Tantalus. The resources produced by the colonized are within their reach, yet at the same time paradoxically removed from their control. They cultivate the lands but have no right to their harvests, which are stolen through the colonizer's ruse. We might even speak of a disproportionate occupation of space that leads to the nonexistence of the colonized, as do Abraham Moles and Elizabeth Rohmer, who say that "si l'espace n'existe que par ce qui le remplit, l'être n'existe que parce qu'il remplit l'espace" "if space only exists by what fills it, the human being only exists if he fills that space" (Moles & Rohmer 1978, 129).

Beyond space, the body of the colonized, as described in *L'incendie,* itself also becomes the site where power is expressed in the bleakest of manners. The novel abounds in descriptions of bodies in a way similar to its description of space. The colonists are depicted as well-heeled, for the most part, whereas the colonized bodies, those of the peasants and their families, are starved bodies, thin, reduced to surviving on the city's garbage (164). These colonized bodies, described in this way, truly attest to how, through the exploitation that followed the expropriation of the peasants, the colonists reap the fruits of the colonial system, while the colonized literally become living beings who are already dead, sometimes even before birth, because their subaltern status seems to precede their entry into the world. This death before birth, suggested by Mohammed Dib's writing on colonial pillaging might, as already indicated, be the most powerful description of the body of the colonized. While these bodies appear in fiction and do seem to be a unique illustration of the descriptive function of novelistic representations, yet, according to Georges Balandier, "la métaphore corporelle est d'abord un moyen de la formation des théories politiques, absolutistes (voire totalitaires) ou libérales. Elle peut devenir l'institution imaginaire du pouvoir, et le révélateur de l'imaginaire qui fonde le pouvoir et permet de le soustraire à la loi du temps qui le dégrade, le frappe de précarité" "the metaphor of the body is first a means of formation of political theories, absolutist (indeed totalitarian) or liberal. It can become the imaginary institution of power, and the revealer of the imaginary which is the basis for power and allows it to be taken out of the law of time which degrades it, strikes it with precarity" (Balandier 1985, 27). We can indeed see that if the metaphor of the body is able to speak of power, it has all the means to signify, or at least to give shape to, what we call "nonpower," that is, the absence of power.

This nonpower in colonial Algeria, as shown in the reading of Mohammed Dib is basically articulated around a causal chain whose importance is that it is the summation of the avatars of colonization. In following Balandier, we could say that while the metaphorical body, the colonized body, is subject to illness, suffering, and death, the sovereign (the colonist in this context) on the other hand enjoys a "double existence": natural, through the physical, mortal body, and "mystique par sa propriété d'être corps politique non assujetti à la maladie et à la mort, établi dans la plénitude et la durée" "mystical through his/her ownership of a political body not subjected to disease and death, established in fullness and duration" (2005, 27). In this political fracas, as Balandier would say, the colonizer progressively takes on the form of the sovereign king, while the colonized cease being citizens and become subjects, with the fictional space of *L'incendie* completely assuming the look of a monarchy, where in place of a sovereign king, the colonial system has organized a multiplication of little kings, each and every one of them a duplication of the king, who in this case is the depository of the French political power installed in Algeria through its occupation in 1830.

To understand the imbalance in the encounter between French colonists and Algerians as it is fictionalized by Mohammed Dib, we must go back in Algeria's history to identify and understand the processes of social disqualification implemented by the French colonial authorities. The historian Todd Shepard provides several analytical keys to the matter in his remarkable study, *The Invention of Decolonization*. Shepard tells us that the paradox characterizing Muslim French citizens of Algeria between 1830 and 1960 could be found in the fact that while Algeria was an integral part of France, the natives of this colony were subjects of the nation, but not full citizens. Despite the gains of the revolution of 1848, which saw the declaration of the abolition of slavery and the Second Republic's declaration that the French territories in North Africa were in effect an extension of France, the matter of acquisition of French nationality by indigenes of Algeria continued to be deferred. If, in this view, everything indicated that Algerians were "French citizens" in their duties but were without citizenship rights, it was, Shepard says, because Algeria was administered according to models that defined its relationship—and thus that of its people—to France: the assimilationalist system articulated around the profound and radical transformation of Algerian social structures and traditions, and the system of coexistence that truly drew lines of demarcation between the different groups living in Algeria and that emphasized the difference in the individual relationships of these groups to the French State.

Thus, writes Shepard, if in the assimilationist model, "the state and its local agents would tear down what they described as local traditions and structures that promoted superstition and ignorance, conditions that prevented men from acting as individuals and joining the corps of citizens" (2006, 22), whereas in the case of coexistence it was a matter of governing the groups of Algerians by means of their separation, it nevertheless remains true that "until the end of War World II, while forms of domination based on coexistence predominated, most officials in Algeria and politicians in the metropole insisted that their goal was assimilation" (2006, 24). We can see that in the two cases evoked by the historian, the common denominator in this marginalization of Algeria is really the notorious civilizing mission, its real pretext for imperial domination.

It is effectively this imperialist position disguised under the veil of the civilizing mission that is at play in the tale of colonial plunder written by Mohammed Dib, and we can read on page 8 in the prologue, that "la civilisation n'a jamais existé; ce qu'on prend pour la civilisation n'est qu'un leurre. Sur ces sommets, le destin du monde se réduit à la misère" "civilization never existed; what we take for civilization is just a trap. From atop these heights, the fate of the world is reduced to misery." By denouncing the great lie and deceptions of the masterminds of the civilizing mission, Mohammed Dib, through his novel, seems to be on the same page as Aimé Césaire who was already saying in the 1950s—during the colonial period itself—that not only did colonization not put the colonizer in contact with the colonized but especially and also that "between colonization and civilization there is an infinite distance; that out of all the colonial expeditions that have been undertaken, out of all the colonial statutes that have been drawn up, out of all the memoranda that have been displayed by all the ministries, there could not come a single human value" (2000, 34). *L'incendie* by Mohammed Dib does succeed—through the gaze of Omar, a child who slowly comes to the realization that the plan spreads the injustices imposed on the peasants, who are even more disadvantaged than other categories of the colonized—in drawing the reader's eye to the maneuverings and subterfuges of colonial authority, which, beyond governing through assimilation and coexistence, promotes the law of divide and conquer among the colonized, as can be seen in the schism between the peasants living in desperate conditions and what we can call the "evolved colonized" who are won over to the cause of the colonial master and very proud of their petty privileges—which still do not make them free men.

Why insist on the category of fellahs as "sacrificial victims" and how otherwise can we understand their banishment from Algerian society in *L'incendie*, if not by digressing to analyze these fellahs as members of the most particularly precarious category? If in *L'incendie* the appropriation of property, that is, expropriation of the indigenes and confiscation of their lands, seems to be the first enterprise in colonization, it is because some lives are absolutely not worth being mourned. Clearly, these are lives that are subject to control and domination, with their humanity turned to self-invalidation in the process of submission, so that their deaths warrant no form of mourning. Winifred Woodhull (2000) has pointed out the ways and explained the reasons that, in her opinion, Mohammed Dib has adopted the realist aesthetic of anticolonial literature to highlight the life of the ordinary Algerian in his trilogy devoted to the French presence in Algeria. According to Woodhull:

> If Dib opts for realism at a specific historical juncture, he does so in order to respond to the expectations of the publishers most likely to make his work available in France, and to get the attention of a certain sector of the French reading public. But as an Algerian, Dib certainly does not consider realism to be intrinsically better suited to conveying, responding to, or transforming social reality than other discourses. (2000, 75)

Woodhull's reflection thus considers Mohammed Dib's trilogy of novels not just from the viewpoint of his esthetic choices, but also of his reception in France. Guy Dugas, for his part and in fact several years before Woodhull, presented a remarkable analysis of theme of the gaze in Dib's *L'incendie*, stating that he classifies this theme according to three criteria, namely, "who looks?" "who looks at whom (or what)?" and "who looks how?" (1984, 2). Beginning with the sequence of elements in the responses to these three questions, Dugas proceeds to distinguish social and ethnic categories and thus reveals that from that perspective, women, children, and fellahs belong to the same universe, whereas the colonizer in all variants has a very particular gaze. The critic ends up isolating three kinds of gazes: "the gaze of witness," the "complicit gaze," and the "inquisitor's gaze." Dugas concludes his thoughts by emphasizing "l'importance et la variété de la thématique du regard dans *L'incendie*—de sujets, d'objets et de manifestation multiples" "the importance and the variety of the thematic of the gaze in *L'incendie*—of multiple subjects, objects, and manifestations," before adding that this interpretation "lui a permis de mettre en évidence les soubassements psychologiques des personnes en présence et, tout à la fois, 'la configuration sociale' nouvelle produite par le face à face colonial" "allowed him to show the psychological substructures of the people and at the same time, the new 'social configuration' produced by the colonial encounter" (1983, 7).

While Woodhull approaches Dib's work from the perspective of avoidance that allows French readership to sidestep the "French question," I would like to extend Guy Dugas's thoughts on the social configuration resulting from the colonial encounter and propose that what is new in *L'incendie* is found in the interplay the author creates among his characters and his readers, namely, in the empty space that he leaves open to interpretation and that turns on the precarious lives that neither Woodhull nor Dugas mentioned, despite the accuracy and finesse of their analyses of Dib's novelistic production. To do this, I would like to begin by presenting a long reply from Comandar, the old man with mystical traits who is in charge of training, or indeed initiating, the young Omar and sensitizing him to the precarious condition of the peasantry. Comandar presents his ideas in these terms:

> Les fellahs ne quittent jamais Bni Boublen; s'ils le quittent, ils ne sont plus bons à rien. Leurs voix sont admirablement nostalgiques, leur salut plein de chaleur. Mais la colonisation blesse: ses yeux ont désespérément peur et les yeux des hommes sont désespérément durs. Le colon considère le travail du fellah comme totalement sien. Il veut, de plus, que les gens lui appartiennent. Malgré cette appartenance en titre, le fellah est pourtant maître de la terre fertile. Bétail et récoltes, partout la vie est sa génération. La terre est femme, et le même mystère de fécondité s'épanouit dans les sillons et dans le ventre maternel. La puissance qui fait jaillir d'elle des fruits et des épis est entre les mains du fellah. Puissant et redoutable, il doit être; il lui faudrait un jour protéger par les armes son foyer et ses champs.

> The fellahs never left Bni Boublen; if they leave it, they are never good for anything again. Their voices are admirably nostalgic, their greeting full of warmth. But colonization wounds: its eyes are full of desperate fear and the eyes of the men are desperately hard. The colonist considers the work of the fellah as totally his own. Furthermore, he wants the people to belong to him. Despite this virtual affiliation, the fellah is nevertheless the master of the fertile land. Cattle and harvest, everywhere life is of his creation. The earth is female, and the same

mystery of fertility unfolds in the furrows and the mother's womb. The power that causes the fruits and spikes to push forth from her is in the hands of the fellah. Powerful and formidable, it must be; one day he will have to protect his hearth and his fields with arms. (27)

Through Comandar's words, including the preceding quote, we are effectively in the presence of what Vincent Jouve calls "l'effet personnel" "the personal effect," inasmuch as the character functions as a token for the author and also shows a "volonté esthétique" "esthetic will" and "instance réflexive" "reflective instance" to offer a dual plane: that of the "lectant jouant" "lecturer at play" et du "lectant interprétant" "interpreting lecturer." A propos to the lecturer at play and the one who interprets, Jouve writes: "le premier saisit le personnage comme un pion narratif dont il s'agit de prévoir les mouvements sur l'échiquier du texte. Le second l'appréhende comme l'indice d'un projet sémantique" "the first takes the character as a narrative pawn in order to foresee the movement on the chessboard of the text. The second apprehends him as the indicator of a semantic project" (Jouve 1992, 92). Making use of the poetics of the text is capital here inasmuch as that type of character identification allows the reader to better understand and interpret the writer's aesthetic choices. Clearly, the choice of the enigmatic character Comandar, a former soldier for France who also ended up expropriated and relegated, as the one who announces the urgent need for resistance, the Algerian writer urges us to go beyond the question of the simple act of dissidence, and more precisely to the nature and stakes of the sacrificial act as a profanatory act in a postcolonial context hinging on the absurd.

With regard to the gaze of the characters, this interpretation seems all the more pertinent because, as Philippe Hamon puts it:

Le regard des personnages, la relation que le personnage a avec les objets et les spectacles du monde; ce regard pourra (comme, éventuellement, les autres sens du personnage) dans la mesure où il est prédéterminé par toute une série de canons et de grilles culturelles, et notamment de catégories esthétiques (le beau et le laid, le sublime et le médiocre, le réaliste et le romantique, etc.) qui découpent le réel en "scènes," "tableaux," "spectacles," etc., se trouver accompagné d'un commentaire évaluatif sur sa "compétence" à regarder, sur son *savoir-voir*, commentaire pris en charge soit par le personnage lui-même, soit par un autre personnage délégué à l'évaluation, soit par le narrateur; le regard n'a donc pas seulement, ici, une fonction purement utilitaire de ventilation d'une fiche documentaire prenant la forme d'une description "optique" (comme c'est le cas dans de très nombreux textes réalistes), mais devient le lieu d'une intrusion normative, devient carrefour normatif, l'évaluation frappant aussi bien la compétence du regardeur, que son regard, que l'objet regardé, ou que le "profit" retiré par le regardeur du spectacle regardé. Une "passion" est alors, souvent, la manifestation symptomatique, dans le texte, de l'affleurement de ce normatif (plaisir ou déplaisir, répulsion ou dégoût, chagrin ou ennui, colère ou satisfaction, etc.).

The gaze of the characters, the relationship between the character and the objects and spectacles of the world; this gaze can (as with, eventually, the other meaning of character) inasmuch as it is predetermined by an entire series of cultural canons and framework, and especially the esthetic categories (the beauty and the ugly, the sublime and the mediocre, the realistic and the romantic, etc.) that carve up what is real into "scenes," "tableaux," "spectacles," etc., to find itself accompanied by an evaluatory commentary on its ability to look, on its *savoir-voir* [knowing how to see], a commentary controlled either by the character itself, or by another person who has been selected to evaluate, or by the narrator; the gaze, then, does not have a purely literary function here as an "optic" (as is the case in very many realist texts), but becomes the locus for a normative intrusion, becomes the normative crossroads, with the evaluation hitting upon the authority of the gazer as well as his gaze, the gazed-upon object, or the "benefit" obtained by the gazer from the spectacle that is gazed upon. A "passion" is then, often, the symptomatic manifestation, in the text, of the outgrowth of this normative (pleasure or displeasure, repulsion or distaste, chagrin or ennui, anger or satisfaction, etc.). (Hamon 1984, 105–6)

To be precise, the narrator's commentary evaluating the urgency for struggling for the right to exist seems to be neutral, whereas Comandar's and certain other characters' commentary betrays a normative position torn between anger and disappointment. Presenting the perspective of Comandar and revealing his gaze consequently invites us to consider the sacrificial act in the text, or at least to highlight its tensions and its aporias. As Guy Dugas demonstrated so well in his article on the theme of the gaze in *L'incendie*, the instances where the colonist or the colonial administrator is presented as the subject who gazes reveal a specific position. Whereas the colonized peasant's gaze is an inquisitive gaze, seeing the colonist and rejecting Kara Ali, the Algerian who collaborates with the colonizer, the gaze of the colonial administration's auxiliaries (gendarmes or police) is a gaze that is empty, for truly it sees nothing, either because of a refusal to look or because the gaze betrays no expression at all. This construction of invisibility for the visible minorities—that is, the peasants of Bni Boublen—functions as a major element in the colonial plan, which essentially manages lives without content, since these lives have been so emptied of their political significance and reduced to one specific use, that it consequently imprisons them in a state of absolute precarity.

On this matter, Guillaume Le Blanc reflected on precarious lives in his work entitled *Vies ordinaires, vies précaires* (Ordinary Lives, Precarious Lives). In his chapter devoted to invisible lives, the philosopher questions how life in its very indeterminacy is threatened by suffering, and proposes not to limit himself to the definition of suffering, but to look further, to understand the reasons for suffering. It is therefore important, Le Blanc indicates, to understand how the ordinary person functions, and what the modalities of his or her existence are, but above all, what the consequences are for that person. Le Blanc writes, "Ce qui est alors révélé dans la souffrance, c'est non seulement la vulnérabilité d'une vie, qui régresse aux limites de l'humain, le malmenant, défaisant ce qui a été péniblement esquissé—l'ébauche d'une vie, son nouage dans un ensemble de normes—mais c'est de manière plus dramatique encore, l'engendrement d'une forme d'invisibilité sociale qui confère à la déshumanisation sa puissance dramatique propre" "What is then revealed in suffering is not only the vulnerability of a life, which regresses to the limits of what is human, abusing it, undoing what has been painfully given shape—the sketch of a life, its being woven into a set of norms—but even more dramatically, the engendering of a form of social invisibility that confers upon dehumanization its own dramatic power" (2007, 163).

Withered bodies of women and children, permanent hunger, and the repeated mention of how the villagers under domination struggle to survive, all these attest to the extreme vulnerability of the life of peasants in Bni Boublen. Furthermore, the evocation of the "jours sauvages de la liberté" "wild days of freedom" (29) referring to the years preceding the arrival of the French is a fully clear indication that France's intrusion into Algeria totally dismantled a way of life that was organized and had its own norms.

If the fellahs become the truly voiceless, including in decisions affecting their fates and sometimes their lives, we should add that in *L'incendie*, this absence of voice is doubled by an absence of visibility, and we can then agree with Le Blanc, who says that "il existe une déshumanisation de la vulnerabilité engendrée par la souffrance sociale, laquelle n'est pas simplement privation de voix mais, tout aussi bien, privation de visage, rendu invisible, privation d'une vie qui confine à la perte irrémédiable, à l'octroi d'un blanc comme seul espace d'indétermination, et, pire, de résignation" "there is a dehumanization of vulnerability born from social suffering, which is not simply the deprivation of voices, but also a deprivation of face, rendered invisible, a deprivation of life that verges on irremediable loss, that leaves a blank as the only space of indetermination, and worse, of resignation" (2007, 163). In this space occupied by peasants, Dib refers to children who are reduced to poverty and whose vulnerability had been so dehumanized that in that space, "le destin du monde se reduit à la misère" (8). We should make it quite clear that if Le Blanc refers to the contours of these invisible lives, it is by training his analyses most often on the absence of work. Now in *L'incendie*, it is not just the matter of unemployment (for the peasants whose lands have been taken from them), but also of the production of a labor whose products are taken away from those whose work produced them. The reduction of the fellahs to their bodies as it appears in Mohammed Dib acquires a new signification when one recalls Gilbert Meynier's statements that discrimination against the peasants was so well organized that until 1918, it was the peasants who financed their own dispossession, since the tax they unjustly paid was used to finance colonial administration (1962, 1).

Consequently, the body of the fellah can be said to be that zone of indeterminacy between slave (an individual deprived of freedom and who becomes the property of the French colonist, exploitable as a material good) and the *homo sacer*, whose condition is defined by Giorgio Agamben as follows:

> What defines the status *of homo sacer* is therefore not the originary ambivalence of the sacredness that is assumed to belong to him, but rather both the particular character of the double exclusion into which he is taken and the violence to which he finds himself exposed. This violence—the unsanctionable killing that, in his case, anyone may commit—is classifiable neither as sacrifice nor as homicide, neither as the execution of a condemnation to death nor as sacrilege. (1998, 82)

With respect to the domination that creates the form of slavery in Mohammed Dib's novel, it suffices to point out that the fellahs are transformed into an alterity through a process of desocialization, that while they are ostensibly free, they are possessed by the colonists, as can be seen in the hardening response of the colonists when the peasants attempt to initiate a strike. Furthermore, and to return to the matter of precarity that stamps them, the humanity of the fellahs is simply deferred, and they are left to oscillate between life and death, existence and inexistence, in short, between freedom and prisons. The proof can be found in the many illustrations of peasant imprisonment and arrests in the novel, without the peasants really understanding why. Furthermore, in Dib's tale, everything seems to point to the fact that ultimately the peasants are in an even deeper situation of exception since the suspension of their rights is not an exceptional, temporary measure, but has a permanent character. Thus, they are imprisoned without due process, they have their goods taken from them without legal cause, and they are turned into exiles in their own native land, upon which "la véritable richesse était rassemblée entre les mains des colons" "the true riches were taken up by the hands of the colonists" (31), whose fraud and arrogance knew no bounds. Moreover, as one character in the novel recalls, "le colon considère le travail du fellah comme totalement sien. Il veut, de plus, que les gens lui appartiennent" "the colonist considers the work of the fellah as totally his own. And even more, he wants the people to belong to him" (27).

As on a plantation, Algerians who refuse to work or those who instigate dissidence are arrested and tortured, like Hamid Saraj who was denounced by another one of the colonized who was a collaborator, Kara Ali. Additionally, simple supposition is enough to cause massive arrests of peasants by gendarmes, after which "les demandes d'explication de la part des autorités avaient lieu dans une chambre secrète. Les fellahs en gardaient longtemps les traces [en raison de quoi] les femmes et les enfants plus morts que vifs passaient dans l'angoisse ces journées" "calls for explanation by the authorities took place in a secret chamber. The fellahs long bore the traces of these, with the women and children spending these days more dead than alive in their anguish" (177–78). It could not be any clearer that these shared conditions of the novel's fellahs validate their identification with slaves, whether through their forced labor that assured the master (the colonist) his capital, through their "possession" by that same colonist, or through their dehumanization, which reduced them to the status of things. In any case, the colonized literally became a thing, a slave, given that as Aimé Césaire confirmed, "between colonizer and colonized there is room only for forced labor, intimidation, pressure, the police, taxation, theft, rape, compulsory crops, contempt, mistrust, arrogance, self-complacency, swinishness, brainless elites, degraded masses" (2004, 42).

To identify the fellah as *homo sacer*, I will begin by recalling that in Agamben's thinking, the *homo sacer* is an enigmatic figure from archaic Roman law who could not be sacrificed but was paradoxically allowed to be killed. In associating this philosophical precondition with Algeria's colonization, the contradiction associated with citizenship that Shepard wrote about and that I mentioned earlier is a framework for the production, or rather the transformation, of the colonized Algerian into a *homo sacer*. If not, how else can we understand that for a native of a territory that is recognized as an extension of France, and thus, we can say, France, access to total citizenship by Algerians was always challenge? Emmanuelle Saada has remarkably pointed out, with regards to legal structures in colonial Algeria, that "The process of colonization was continually traversed by law and legal structures. Far from being a pure exercise of force, colonization involved diverse levels of codification, and at the same time, was necessarily responsive to diverse juridical contingencies" (2002, 105). Clearly, the distinction between citizen and subject was central in separating and differentiating the Europeans from the "indigènes" in colonial times.[3] Better yet, how can we understand that in the aftermath of the war with Algeria, France advanced a kind of ethnicity that was based on race, and created a legal framework in which, as Shepard explains:

> The idea that those people French law defined as Muslim French citizens were part of an ethnoracial group different from that of other French citizens left the sphere of common sense to shape the legal categories established by the French government in July 1962. "Racialized ethnicity" explained why some people with French nationality ("Muslims") were Algerian, while other people from Algeria (pieds noirs) could remain French. (2006, 230)

Indeed, this change in legal categories occurred, as the historian says, in the aftermath of the war with Algeria, and not in the period in which the novel of Mohammed Dib is set, that is, during the war of national liberation.

Nevertheless, from the inequitable treatment reserved for the citizens of Algeria, and with its basis on race, ethnicity, and religion, it becomes very clear that the hesitation to permit any Algerian to benefit from full French citizenship after occupation was already in itself a measure of disqualification, as shown by the works of Emmanuelle Saada, Olivier Le Cour Grandmaison and with regards to the contested citizenship of Algerian women in particular, the work of Marc André.[4] It was an attempt to create an exception in which the Algerian, even though on French territory, did not have the same rights as other French, notably the colonists and Europeans of Algeria. In a way, the sacrality of the Muslim Algerian occupying a territory that had been declared French had already found its perfect contradiction in the fact that his life still remained subject to a death that could not be considered homicide, and even less as an execution of the condemned. A clear illustration of this position of the subject who is included in but at the same time excluded from the legal framework is seen in *L'incendie* in the scene where a worker's death is quickly recharacterized by M. Marcous, the colonist who owns the farm where the latter worked, as an "accident dû à l'imprudence de l'indigène" "accident due to the indigene's negligence" (77). Right after affirming that other workers should not speak to the gendarmes and declaring that the worker's death is a consequence of its own negligence, M. Marcous orders his workers to return to work as if nothing ever happened, otherwise their salary would be reduced for missing hours of work. Altogether, the condition of the peasant workers in Dib who are subjected to forced labor, taxation, and death corresponds to the colonized who was characterized by Albert Memmi as someone who "enjoys none of the attributes of citizenship; neither his own, which is independent, contested and smothered, nor that of the colonizer. [. . .] As a result of colonization, the colonized almost never experiences nationality and citizenship, except privately. Nationally and civically he is only what the colonizer is not" (1965, 96).

Next and an even more serious example, when confronted with the crowd of other Arab[5] workers at the scene of the so-called accident, the white farmer intimidates them into quickly returning to their work, by threatening them that lost hours would be deducted from their pay, their source for a decent living. The explicit commentary from Comandar bears witness to the fact that the death of a fellah does not even deserve an inquest, much less any sentiment: "Qu'est-ce que la mort d'un fellah? Un déchirement brutal et rapide. Et c'est tout. Après, il n'y a plus rien; et tout est comme avant" "What's the death of a fellah? A brutal and rapid agony. And that's all. After that, nothing; and everything is like before" (79). On this point, the poetics of Mohammed Dib, a poet, attests to the lack of value of the fellah's life. The tempo in the above quotation "un"/ "tout"/ "rien" and the short sentences chosen by the writer definitely mimics the brutality of the killing. In consequence, language becomes the only place left to bear witness to the abuse endured by the workers whose lives are made insignificant and valueless. The link between Agamben's *homo sacer* and the precarious lives described by Judith Butler is clear, inasmuch as the scene that I have just recalled raises the questions that Butler already had posed, namely, "Who counts as human? Whose lives count as lives? And, finally, What *makes for a grievable life?*" (2006, 20) Without responding to these questions, I will nevertheless simply point out that they brilliantly sum up the existence as well as the living conditions of the fellahs shown to us in Mohammed Dib's novel. In the final analysis, the fellahs no longer own their bodies, by rarely if ever being able to decide how they are used, to the point that their torture, their expendability, in short, their symbolic or physical death does not even deserve to be mourned. The sacrificable death of the fellahs is thus exposed as licit murder, not worthy of weeping.

On the whole here, I have attempted to show that *L'incendie* by Mohammed Dib is a novel of the denunciation of precarized marginality (fellahs) and that the awareness of an unjust situation is inscribed in an esthetic of revelation. Through this analysis, I intended to present a reading of the simple categorization of Dib's work as a novel of denunciation, to underscore the link between aesthetics and politics in the presentation of precarious lives. This incursion in Dib's novel leads me to formulate two observations. First, a sociohistorical observation: *L'incendie* exposes the colonized subaltern, but goes beyond in asking us to reflect upon a subcategory of the colonized subaltern, namely, the fellah, the peasant. In doing so, Dib succeeds in drawing the reader's and critic's attention to the fact that even in the colonial situation, it is important to remain attentive to the diverse degrees of subalternity, by observing the border that separates an ordinary life from a precarious life, and by questioning the mechanisms, stakes, and modalities of this reduction of the individual to a purely biological dimension. Albert Memmi was therefore right to observe that "the most serious blow suffered by the colonized is being removed from history and from community" (1967, 91). For in reality, if the colonized is generally a subaltern, it could be that social condition and class are overladen by a racial condition that creates a category that needs to be emphasized, and is related to the problem of the very existence of the colonized who is not of the same race as the colonizer. Such is perhaps what one of Dib's characters suggests when speaking about laws: "Elles sont faites de telle sorte que par notre seule existence nous sommes coupables" "They are made in such a way that by our very existence we are guilty" (156). The novel thus certainly seems to explore the question of the right of the colonized to exist, but after the matter of colonization, it becomes the question of the socially disqualified, the poor or indigent proletarian. My second observation is a philosophical one and has to do with the fact that the precarization we see in the novel's colonial context indicates a radical rethinking not only of the place of the fellah but more generally of the colonized, in what Jacques Rancière has called the distribution of the sensible, namely, "un découpage des temps et des espaces, du visible et de l'invisible, de la parole et du bruit qui définit à la fois le lieu et l'enjeu de la politique comme forme d'expérience" "a carving out of time and spaces, of the visible and the invisible, of the speech and noise that defines both the place and the stakes of politics as a form of experience" (2000, 14). Clearly, beyond the simplistic binary division used to think about colonialism in North Africa, we must recognize the complexity of the invisible, as well as the nuanced combination between race, class, and gender.

If we consider Gayatri Spivak's (1995) reflection on the subaltern as one who cannot speak, we must note that in the case of Algeria and in *L'incendie* in particular, the question needs to be shifted from the ability to speak to the ability to be heard. In other words, as can be seen in Dib's novels, the subaltern speaks but are they heard, given that they are constructed by colonial power as invisible? And if it is true that politics bears not only upon what is visible and speakable but also upon who has the power to see and to speak, it then becomes indisputable that "être invisible, c'est avoir déjà perdu sa voix, c'est aussi ne plus avoir de visage . . . si le visible sous-tend l'audible, seul l'audible rend cependant visible [car] c'est finir par ne plus être vu et ne plus être vu, c'est ne plus pouvoir être entendu" "to be invisible means that the voice has already been lost, and also no longer having a face . . . if the visible underlies the audible, only the audible, however, creates the visible [for] it means ending up being no longer seen, and no longer being seen, means no longer being able to be heard," according to Le Blanc (2007, 165). We can then understand how it is up to the precarious in the colony to respond to their invisibility by a form of visibility that transcends the ability to be seen and heard. Even though *L'incendie* does not depict a violent confrontation, we should still point out that there is a raising of national consciousness that is witnessed in several passages, of which I will cite only one: "Si vous abandonnez votre terre . . . vos enfants, vos petits enfants et arrière-petits-enfants . . . jusqu'à la dernière génération, vous demanderont des comptes. Vous n'aurez point mérité d'eux, de votre pays, de l'avenir" "If you abandon your lands, your children, your grandchildren, your great-grandchildren, all the way to the last generation will ask you to account for yourselves. You will not have deserved them, your land, your future" (45). From this perspective, and given that in the silence of each fellah there is a volcano just waiting to explode, Mohammed Dib can therefore be seen as the author who has best shown that the peasantry, and not the colonized intellectual elite, is the soul of the Algerian people. In doing so, Dib moves the precarious from the periphery and recenters them as artisans of a coming resistance. For in reality, given that the fellahs likely represent the extreme figure of precarity in colonial Algeria, they become central for being the best placed to unleash and effect what Albert Memmi calls absolute revolt, namely, "celle qui, n'ayant plus rien à sauvegarder, n'est plus arrêtée par rien. Ni par la peur de mourir ni, peut-être plus gravement encore, par les valeurs communes avec l'oppresseur. La révolte absolue, c'est la guerre, la découverte de la violence et de la crainte qu'elle inspire" "the result of a situation where those who revolt, having no longer anything to protect, are no longer restrained in any way. Neither by fear of death, nor, which is perhaps more serious still, by the respect of values they share with the oppressor. Total revolt means war, the discovery of violence and of the terror it inspires" (1968, 24). In the following section, I will now turn to the analysis of Azzédine Bounemeur's *Les bandits de l'Atlas* as a fictional representation of the resistance of the homo expendibilis, the expendable man who decides to break the colonial condition.

RESILIENCY FROM THE MARGINS: AZZÉDINE BOUNEMEUR'S *LES BANDITS DE L'ATLAS*

In an article entitled "Au temps de la France: Identités collectives et situation coloniale en Algérie" (In the time of France: Collective Identities and the Colonial Situation in Algeria 2013), Raphaëlle Branche offers an original reading of the colonial situation that begins with an analytical framework of the regimes of historicity. Her particularly inspired reflection shows that every colonial or imperialist breakthrough is not only motivated by but also based upon the substitution of one spatio-temporal order (that of the colonized) for another (that of the colonizer). If it is indeed undeniable that French colonization in Algeria suspended "Algerian time" (so to speak) to the benefit of what Branche calls "France's time," it remains, she emphasizes, that despite its grand cultural, political, and even military deployments, colonial time was never truly able to obliterate the temporalities that preceded it. For Branche, the separation between colonizers and colonized that is based on biology or space is not sufficient for an understanding of the colonial fracture, as that division fails to account for "la complexité des groupes qui continuent le plus souvent à être organisés selon des principes préexistants à la colonisation" "the complexity of the groups who most often continue to be organized according to principles that preexist colonization" (2013, 200). With respect to that very subject of the complexity of groups who oppose the temporal order imposed by colonization, it is worth noting that it is quite common in the criticism of francophone artistic production to analyze the problematics of violence through an emphasis on the group as, for example, an analysis that generally sets colonizers against colonized. Without of course denying the relevance of such an approach, we can begin with some remarks formulated by Branche and follow with my own proposal to extend the exploration of marginal figures from the colonial period in North Africa by reflecting not so much on the two antagonistic macro-groups, the "indigenes" and the "colonizers," but rather on two specific social categories, namely, peasants and bandits, who, as we shall see, often come from the peasantry. From this perspective, this study proposes a reading of *Les bandits de l'Atlas* (1983) by Azzédine Bounemeur, who places special emphasis upon the modalities and conditions under which peasant violence erupts as a mode of resistance. In so doing, we will not only question violence as a matter of evil but inscribe that violence into a logic of de-linkage between the powerholders (whether political, social, religious, colonial, etc.) and the *sans-parts*—the stakeless— truly marginal figures who are seen in peasants whose entire life is a series of decisions based upon the awareness of what I call, using the Latin expression, *memento mori*, in other words, an enduring meditation upon the imminence of death, which consequently determines the choices and actions of individuals who are reduced to their pure biological expression.

I began this chapter with an allusion to Rachid Bouchareb's film *Hors la loi*, and specifically to the first scene where we see a family being chased from its lands by a colonial administrator, brought to life in the film by the figure of the gendarme. Likewise, land is at stake in *Les bandits de l'Atlas*, or at any rate it is the control of land that structures the story by the Algerian writer. At the very beginning of the novel we read: "Sur les contreforts, remparts aux fortes pentes, se dresse cette terre, couverte de forêts jusqu'au jour où les hommes chassés par les envahisseurs qui se succédèrent vinrent s'y installer. Ils y mirent le feu et la défrichèrent. Seul le maquis subsista sur les pentes abruptes" "On the foothills, ramparts with steep slopes, this land rose up, covered in forests until the day when the men, chased by the invaders who succeeded them, established themselves there" (7). This short description immediately plunges the reader into the novel that tells, in epic form, the history of Hassan, a young Algerian who is to learn through a difficult apprenticeship about life and its injustices, and who ends up a "bandit," truly outside the law, and even more singular because his crime aims to reestablish a temporal, spatial, and cultural order broken by French colonization. In reality, and this is why I was already making reference to it in my introduction with my reflection based on the work of Raphaëlle Branche, the objective of the French colonizers in Algeria was to impose a temporal order that was their own, with the intervening time perceived here not only as a given in the present but likewise as the normative principle erasing the past, redefining the present, and consequently conditioning the future. Thus, to speak of the time of France also means observing and analyzing the ways in which the management of space follows the criteria of excluding the colonized. To that end, it is important to underscore that Bounemeur's novel suggests a division of space that simultaneously implies a division of visibility and speech: "Coupé du monde, dans l'arrière pays, chaque territoire porte le nom ancestral du clan: les Beni . . . les Beni . . . Sur chaque groupement règne un caïd. Il est le seul lien entre le colonisateur et ce monde où il règne en seigneur" "Cut off from the world, in the back country, each territory bears the name of its ancestral clan: the Beni . . . the Beni . . . Over each group there is a leader. He is the sole link between the colonizer and this world over which he rules as lord" (10). Two observations on this passage can be made a priori.

First, from the viewpoint of space, we find ourselves in the presence of an unbalanced and arbitrary management of the land's surface, making the lands occupied by the peasants into a space that is cut off from the world, a kind of location that is outside of place and time. Consider the following: "Les autorités coloniales nommaient au caïdat des hommes issus de familles nombreuses, généralement les plus puissantes. Dans chaque village il n'y avait que trois ou quatre maisons de tuiles, murs de terres, plats de terre. Le reste c'étaient des gourbis jusqu'à l'infini. La maison du caïd était grande, ceinte de murs" "The colonial authorities appointed men who came from large families, generally the most powerful, as the leaders. In each village there were only three or four tiled houses, earthen walls, earthen ovens. The rest were just a succession of foxholes. The *caïd*'s house was large, surrounded by walls" (20). The mention of the caïd's house, which so strongly contrasts with the unsanitary and dilapidated housing of the peasants, places house and living quarters at the very heart of the problematic of space. Now in Gaston Bachelard's *La poétique de l'espace*, he suggests that every lived-in space carries within it the essence of the concept of home. In analyzing space as a metaphor for the home, Bachelard writes that we must "go beyond the problems of description—whether this description be objective or subjective, that is whether it gives facts or impressions—in order to attain to the primary virtues, those that reveal an attachment that is native in some way to the primary function of inhabiting" (1969, 4). Following this theoretical orientation of establishing a bond with the primary function of habitation, we can duly declare that if the space occupied by the peasants is a world-beyond/world-outside, it is because it is a space *within* the world, the one occupied by the colonizers and their local representatives. Consequently, the novel suggests that the division of space itself is already justification for the contrasts found in the text, to wit, world/world-beyond, existence/nonexistence, living/surviving, and finally, life/death. We find ourselves within a dark tableau, a terrible struggle between the colonized and the colonizers, with the latter controlling "les grandes plaines, les plateaux riches" "the large plains, the rich plateaux," whereas the former, by the millions, "refoulés sur ces territoires inaccessibles, travaillaient la moindre parcelle, défrichaient le maquis, labouraient ce qui était labourable" "pushed back into the inaccessible lands, worked at the smallest plots, cleared the maquis, ploughing anything that could be plowed" (32).

Next, a second observation: That citation highlights a figure who acts as a bridge between the colonizer and the colonized, the figure of the caïd who is described as having the power of life and death over the indigenes. The caïd is a paradoxical figure, both central and marginal, and one we must stop and observe so that we might better understand the radicalization of the peasants who choose to revolt. In reality:

Non seulement la puissance coloniale se donnait les moyens de posséder la terre, mais elle réordonnait aussi les relations des hommes à leur territoire, en incitant à faire table rase des liens passés pour qu'émergent des individus là où la société indigène lui opposait des logiques collectives. La fabrication coloniale était là: elle imaginait des individus nouveaux, nés avec la France, qui leur proposait un présent et un avenir pour le prix de leur passé. Ainsi se retrouvaient-ils à égalité sur la terre algérienne et l'antécédence des indigènes était effacé.

Not only did the colonial authority give itself the means to possess the land, but it also reordered the relationships between men and their land, by inciting an erasure of the past links so that there rose up individuals there, where the indigenous society was instead used to living by a collective principle. Colonial fabrication was there: it imagined new individuals, born with France, who offered them a present and a future for the price of their past. Thus, they could be found in equal measure upon Algerian land, and the antecedence of the indigenes was erased. (Branche 2013, 204)

What interests me in the preceding citation is not only the fact that French colonization erased everything from before its implantation but also, and more significantly, the means it set in place to perfect this dispossession that victimized the indigenes. Among the means employed by the colonial master, the figure of the caïd figures prominently, since without him, one might say, it would simply have been impossible, if not extremely difficult, for colonial France to succeed in revising its temporal order. In *Les bandits de l'Atlas*, specifically, the caïd is the one who, in making use of his absolute power over the peasants, systematically erases the indigenes' anteriority in the land that he now governs according to his personal whims. It is also at the hands of the caïd that Brahim, the father of Hassan, the main character, just like his mother and his brother, finds death. Beyond maintaining an unjust order, the caïd incarnates the system of leadership through conferring upon himself unlimited rights over those under his charge.

In an article entitled "Le caïdat en Algérie au XIXe siècle" (The Caïdat in Algeria in the 19th Century 1992), Abderrazak Djellali informs us that the figure of the caïd is not an invention of French colonization, and that it already existed during the period of Turkish domination, a period when each caïd's charge was to supervise a specific aspect of social life. While the caïdat thus preceded French colonization, that colonization nevertheless gave a new inflection to this function. Consequently, Djellali notes, "la reconduction du système caïdal est liée à l'idéologie discriminatoire et raciale du colonialisme français d'où ségrégation entre européens et 'indigènes' sur les plans, politique, juridique et administratif . . . les caïds sont désignés non pas pour leur compétence mais pour leur audience et leur influence sur les groupes qu'ils doivent administrer, leur loyauté à l'autorité française, et les états de services rendus" "the extension of the caïdal system is linked to the discriminatory, racial ideology of French colonization where segregation between Europeans and 'indigenes' at the political, juridical and administrative levels . . . the caïds are designated not for their jurisdiction but for their hearings and their influence over the groups that they must administer, their loyalty to French authority, and the status of the services they have rendered" (1992, 40). The link is therefore established between the general administration of the colonized and the spoliation of the rural populations.

From that standpoint, the caïd in Algeria under French domination became a key element in the colonial system, assuring the effective deployment of the colonial economy all the while assuming for himself an economic power that was adjoined to his political power, crystallized in the decisions he made that affected the life of the peoples who were dominated and reduced to hard labor. The caïd as representative of the colonial order is depicted in *Les bandits de l'Atlas* in his full extent and all his vileness. He is the one who orders the punishing assault that ends in the immolation of the main character's mother and brother; he again is the one who orchestrates the assassination of the main character's father; and he is yet again the one who strips even his mother-in-law and half-sister of all their earthly goods that had been left to them by his father, also a caïd. The caïd is also expected to maintain, in the village community, an order that is already unjust, and he multiplies that injustice by maintaining for himself a horde of bandits who sow terror and desolation throughout. The institution of the caïdat as a relay within the colonial institution thus strengthens the mechanisms of submission and control in the rural Algerian world, summed up in the novel as follows: "Terre inaccessible, monde à part avec ses rites, ses traditions, ses lois, son code d'honneur. Monde archaïque, monde où les rapports de production émergent tout juste du féodalisme cruel, cynique, appliqué aux parcelles" "A land that is inacessible, a land apart with its rites, its traditions, its laws, its code of honor. An archaic world, world where the relationships of production emerge specifically from the cruel, cynical feudalism applied over the plots" (19). In such a context, it is not surprising that the construction of the invisibility of the peasants is manifested not only at the level of space but also at the level of bodies. The novel offers an interesting parallel between the control and the use of colonized bodies by showing how when these bodies were not useful in war (the text mentions those men who left for military service and for the most part never returned), they then become simple tools in the agricultural production that is meant for the glory of the colonizers and, to a certain degree, the caïds.

The reduction of peasant bodies occurs through several mechanisms of control by caïds. Whether it is a question of hard labor, impossible access to food, or even corporal punishment inflicted on the peasantry, the peasant body becomes "un corps autre" "an other body." There is no peasant body in Bounemeur's novel that is not linked to the idea of suffering. The bodies of peasants are bodies, so to speak, placed at the disposition of the colonial authority and its relay system, the caïdat, with those two entities holding absolute power not only over the mobility of these bodies, but also over their life and death. In *Les bandits de l'Atlas*, biopower means not only the ability to control or manage bodies, nor even only the ability to exploit them, but literally the power that defines the notion of sovereignty. In colonial Algeria, the novel suggests, sovereignty literally becomes the right to kill.[6] To kill off no longer corresponds to an extreme response of self-defense, and even less a punitive situation. At the hands of the colonists and the caïds, the right to kill acquires a permanent attribute and is administered in the most arbitrary manner. Not only does rural Algerian society assume the form of a prison, but it becomes the quintessential locus of a hierarchized surveillance, in the words of Michel Foucault for whom "disciplinary power was also organized as a multiple, automatic and anonymous power; for although surveillance rests on individuals, its functioning is that of network of relations from top to bottom, but also to a certain extent from bottom to top laterally; this network 'holds' the whole together and traverses it in its entirety with effects of power that derive from one another: supervisors, perpetually supervised." (1995, 176–77)

Foucault then adds that if it is true that the pyramidal organization of power confers upon it a "head," it is the apparatus as a whole that produces the "power" and arranges the distribution of individuals within the permanent and continuous field.

Organization of power in Bounemeur's novel in point of fact corresponds to the organization proposed by Foucault. At the top of the pyramid of power are the colonists (rich land owners, gendarmes, and other officials in the administration), whereas at the bottom are found the disillusioned peasants with the caïds just above them, invested with authority over the indigenes. Therefore, it is important to follow in the footsteps of Foucault and address the matter of the caïd who is considered superior to the colonized, from a social point of view, yet still inferior to the colonizers. As Abderrazak Djellali has clearly pointed out:

> Si par son pouvoir décisionnel et économique le caïdat appartenait de fait à la notabilité, néanmoins il évoluait socialement et politiquement en seconde zone du fait de l'idéologie coloniale fondée sur l'exclusion sociale. Considérés à l'instar de leurs coreligionnaires comme des gens à civiliser, les caïds n'ont pas pu s'intégrer à la classe dominante et évoluer d'égal à égal avec les européens. Leurs tentatives soit par "l'école républicaine" qui a ouvert ses portes aux loyaux serviteurs désireux d'acquérir un savoir moderne opposé au savoir traditionnel (apprentissage du Coran, hadit, charia) synonyme d'arriération, soit par les mariages mixtes qui sont restés très limites ou soit par l'acquisition de la citoyenneté, sont restées vaines.
>
> If by his economic power and his power to make decisions the caïdat de facto belonged to those of high standing, it nevertheless evolved socially and politically in a second zone due to the fact that colonial ideology was based on social exclusion. Considered to be like their coreligionists as needing to be civilized, the caïds were not able to integrate into the dominant class and evolve as equals with the Europeans. Their attempts, whether through the "Republican School" that opened its doors to its loyal servants who were desirous of acquiring a modern knowledge as opposed to traditional learning (studying the Quran, hadiths, sharia), which was synonymous with backwardness, or by mixed marriages that remained quite limited, or through acquisition of citizenship, were in vain. (1992, 44)

From the preceding citation, we easily understand why the caïd himself in Bounemeur's novel arranges the illicit, which he controls and protects, as a means of guaranteeing for himself a form of superiority and privileges that raise him above the peasantry without, however, placing him on the same level as the gendarme or colonial administrator. And doubtless he is conscious of the relativity of his power, since the caïd threatens to denounce his outlaw protégés if they disobey his orders to kill the peasants whose only crime is demanding minimal conditions of living. The doubling of surveillance evoked by Foucault is translated in the novel by the relay of control: the colonist controls the indigenes, but uses some of them, the infamous caïds, to control and discipline the rest of the countryside population. As for the novel's caïd, the narrator tells us that "sa cruauté était connue de tous. Son maître pouvait dormir sur ses deux oreilles. Pas un paysan n'échappait à son humiliation, pas un berger à sa trique" "his cruelty was known by all. Not a single peasant escaped humiliation from him, not a single shepherd escaped his cudgel (129)." Furthermore, beyond the paradigms of surveillance and punishment, we can say that the peasants of the Atlas found themselves inscribed in a state of permanent exception and were thus faced with a dictatorship, according to Olivier Le Cour Grandmaison:

> Si la suppression de la séparation des pouvoirs, la concentration entre les mains d'un seul homme- gouverneur général, mais aussi chef de bureau arabe- de fonctions législatives, judiciaires et exécutives, l'abolition de toutes les barrières légales susceptibles d'entraver l'exercice de la puissance souveraine et la disparition de toutes les garanties traditionnellement offertes aux individus par les constitutions démocratiques modernes sont autant de caractéristiques de la dictature, il ne fait pas de doute que le régime mis en place en Algérie au XIXe siècle, puis conservé par la Troisième République, a bien été une dictature.

> If suppression, separation of powers, concentration in the hands of a single man—the governor general, but also the Arab bureau chief—the legislative, judiciary, and executive functions, the abolition of all legal barriers that could hamper the exercise of his sovereign power and the loss of all guarantees traditionally offered to individuals by modern democratic constitutions are characteristics of dictatorship, there is no doubt that the regime set in place in Algeria during the nineteenth century, then preserved by the Third Republic, was truly a dictatorship. (2005, 228)

Furthermore, what is striking here is clearly less the division of control and power than the mechanisms that allowed for the creation of this scattered division of Algerian colonial society.

"Diviser pour mieux régner" "divide and conquer" is the basic tactic implemented by colonization, which through creating different subaltern categories with respect to rights and privileges assures extreme difficulty for any organization to mount a solid resistance to the colonial system on the basis of race.

For if the first division was made on the basis of race (whites vs. indigenes), for true efficacy, it had to be pursued at a level that would no longer be based on race, but rather on class. Thus, the creation of subalterns and their social disqualification in colonial Algeria rested on what Etienne Balibar and Olivier Le Cour Grandmaison have called a "racisme de classe" "racism of class," for

> si la racisation consiste notamment à imputer à un ensemble d'individus des caractéristiques négatives, souvent jugées inquiétantes et héréditaires, qui permettent son identification et son inscription au plus bas de la hiérarchie des hommes, force est de conclure que nous sommes bien en présence d'un "racisme de classes," les classes inférieures de la société étant pensées comme des races ou des quasi-races,

> if racialization consists notably in imputing negative characteristics to an entire group of individuals, often deemed disturbing and hereditary, allowing their identification and inscription at the very bottom of the human hierarchy, we must conclude that we are truly in the presence of a "racism of classes," with the lower classes in society being considered as races or quasi-races. (2005, 282)

In the context of a racism of class, the right to punish becomes the guarantee of security, and it is applied from top to bottom, that is, from the colonist to the peasant, by way of the caïd, but also from bottom to top, namely, from the peasant to the caïd, and even though it is rare, to the colonist because, as Bounemeur's novel indicates, "les bandits ne s'attaquaient aux colons qu'à l'occasion, parce qu'ils craignaient les poursuites et les forces inégales, conscients de ce qui les attendait" "the bandis only attacked the colonists occasionally, because they were afraid of being pursued and the unequal forces, aware of what waited for them" (103). This illustrates, moreover, the fragility of the caïdat as a social status, for the distinction is thus made by the peasants between caïds and colonists on the basis of the caïds' not having the same arena at their disposal as the colonists, and thus the peasants see that the *caïds* are themselves marginal despite their ephemeral and apparent centrality in the colonial system.

Hence, the colonial encounter inaugurated by the violence of French penetration into Algeria, as seen in the Bounemeur's novel, poses the central problem of human rights. In doing so, and in looking at the division of indigenes through distributions of power, the novel invites us to question the pertinence of the concept of human rights. Can we still believe in a universal declaration of human rights when some are reduced to their pure biological expression and subjected to sovereign power without any intervention? Can we only recognize a single humanity, one with a European civilization that dehumanizes the colonized "Other"? Every indication is that, "propre à la culture occidentale, la notion des droits de l'homme, malgré sa nécessité et sa sublimité, ne concerne que les corps juridiques abstraits et non des corps individuels réels, demandant à être guidés selon des comportements éthiques" "unique to Western culture, the notion of human rights, despite its need and sublimity, only concerns abstract juridical bodies and not the bodies of real individuals, asking to be governed according to ethical behaviors" (Rozenberg 2007, 29). Even more interesting is that awareness of this civilizational deception will push the marginal classes composed of peasants to choose the path of revolt.

The peasants in Bounemeur's novel choose radicalization and are true outlaws aiming to reestablish law and a return to justice. If it is true that colonization sought to impose a new temporal order unique to itself, it is also true that the novel's peasants seem to have observed that, as Aimé Césaire already pronounced in his magisterial essay entitled *Discourse on Colonialism*, "the colonialists may kill in Indochina, torture in Madagascar, imprison in Black Africa, crack down in the West Indies. Henceforth the colonized know that they have advantage over them. They know that their temporary 'masters' are lying" (2000, 32). The peasants of the Atlas realize, again with a nod to Césaire, that colonization is "neither evangelization, nor a philanthropic enterprise, nor a desire to push back the frontiers of ignorance, disease, and tyranny . . . nor an attempt to extend the rule of law," but rather the "projected shadow of a form of civilization which, at certain point in its history, finds itself obliged, for internal reasons, to extend to a world scale the competition of its antagonist economies" (33).

With racism of class having created a subaltern world that is cut in two, the poor classes must face two kinds of executioners: one who is familiar to them (the caïd) and the Other, the colonist, the stranger who has become the owner of their lands. Experiencing an interior exile, the peasants presented to us by Bounemeur are reduced to poverty and feel all the more the urgency for an insurrection because their existence is reduced to a choice between life (combat, resistance) and death (a passive waiting that can indeed be called a form of suicide). But in an even more interesting way, Bounemeur's novel suggests that at heart, if the racism of classes has created an awareness of marginality, the response to this dehumanization is not based upon a class struggle, but rather on the struggle for sovereignty over Algerian territory. From that perspective, *Les bandits de l'Atlas* presents two groups of rebels who, even though they differ in their reasons and motivations for dissidence, are alike in certain way, namely, in their refusal of the colonial *magister dixit*. About halfway through the novel, Bounemeur not only provides the necessary clues to the distinction between the bandits and the resistance, but in doing so he implicitly suggests that while the modes of action differ, we can establish a link between the two groups who oppose the order of colonial time. Bounemeur writes: "Les bandits sont le produit d'une crise économique et sociale au cours de laquelle ils s'érigent en révoltés pour leur propre compte, en groupe, individuellement, contre leur société régie par un patriarcat rigide et implacable, injuste, féodal dans ses rapports les plus infimes" "The bandits are the product of a socioeconomic crisis during which they have turned themselves into rebels on their own account, as a group, individually, against their society, which is ruled by a patriarchy that is rigid, implacable, unjust, feudal in its most minute relationships." And he continues: "Les résistants, eux, sont la conscience collective, représentant les aspirations, et les idéaux du peuple. Leur maturité se forge par étapes, en fonction de leurs expériences, de leurs idéaux, de la situation politique et des leçons tirées des étapes historiques nationales ou internationales" "Those rebels, they are the collective conscience, representing the aspirations, and the ideals of the people. Their maturity is created in stages, as a function of their experiences, their ideals, the political situation, and the lessons drawn from national and international stages in history" (102). At first glance, we are clearly facing two opposite trajectories. Nevertheless, if we consider that by wanting to signal the end of an unjust, feudal order imposed by an iniquitous society, the bandits recognize—in the novel—the collusion between their local executioners and those who are the target of the rebels, then it can rightly be thought that at heart, these two groups have the same objective, one based on what Andrée Michel has called the "conscience nationale" "national awareness." According to the sociologist, in fact, "les algériens, de celui qui exerçait une profession libérale au docker, avait conscience d'appartenir à un groupe dominé subissant la discrimination civique, politique, ou économique, quelle que soit leur place, dans la production . . . Pour le peuple algérien, la lutte contre l'exploitation exigeait avant tout la fin de la domination" "the Algerians, from the professional to the docker, were aware of belonging to a dominated group experiencing civic, political, economic discrimination, no matter their place, in production . . . For the Algerian people, the fight against exploitation required above all the end of domination" (1965, 208). We can see that the struggle for autonomy was not articulated around class interests but around the rejection of humiliation for a people who, despite the variety of rights that defined the members of that group, still remained completely under the yoke of the colonial political machine. Furthermore, Michel specifies that each layer of society played an important role in the struggle for national liberation, whether it was workers on strike in the defense of colonial freedoms, poor peasants who became combatants in the maquis, or even women, whose contribution to the war for independence has been the topic of several major studies.

Moreover, Benjamin Stora has brilliantly shown the limits of the Algerian nationalist movement, which failed to take into account the deep aspirations of the peasant society. Stora is also correct in mentioning, with regard to the political organization of French domination, that the peasantry, "sous l'égide française, survit une aristocratie indigène qui fait cause commune avec les Français, et donc certains, membres deviennent les administrateurs de la population rurale au nom de l'Etat français" (1986, 64) / "remained subject to the restrictive system set in place by the French administrative authorities. It survived an indigenous aristocracy that had made common cause with the French, and certain members of which had become administrators of the rural population in the name of the French state" (2001, 10). Finally, it is undeniable that, again following Stora's thought, the peasantry was faced with a double obstacle, namely, lack of training and the weakness of their level of education, and thus, in the end, if we look at the goal in the struggles for liberation for the peasants and poor classes, we could believe that rural society remained immune to the changes that the war of national liberation announced. In fact, as Fanon tells us, the national bourgeoisie is but the continuity, or the metastasized prolongation, of the colonial bourgeoisie. Nevertheless, for the purposes of my analysis, we must return to the very moment when the peasants made the decision to rebel against colonial injustice.

From the time they became conscious of their marginalization, the peasants were aware of the true intentions of colonialism and of the oppressive role of the caïds, who, in Adberrazak Djellali's words, "ne symbolisent plus que l'appauvrissement, l'injustice, la corruption. Ils deviennent synonymes de l'esprit du mal, [et] ce n'est pas par hasard si dans le langage populaire on qualifie les chefs de bandes de caïds" "only symbolized impoverishment, injustice, corruption. They become synonymous with the spirit of evil, [and] it is not by chance if in popular language the heads of gangs are called caïds" (1992, 45). That historical awareness, analyzed by historians, is what takes hold of Hassan, the protagonist of Bounemeur's novel, just as it does with a number of other peasants. Hassan, who at the beginning of his troubles attributes the deaths of his father, mother, and brother to those whom the author calls "bandits," quickly realizes in observing Boucetta, the head of the gang, that he was "ni un monstre ni un assassin, mais un homme comme les autres. Un paysan reconverti" "neither a monster nor an assassin, but a man like any other. A reconverted peasant" (138). In reality, it is hunger, poverty, illness, oppression, and torture—consequences of the colonial system—that cause the irruption of these "bandits," who must be distinguished from true bandits, those who are protected by the law and the colonial system, from the colonist to the caïd as well as the gangs under the protection of the caïd. As stated so well by Selom Komlan Gbanou, "les termes de 'bandits' et 'hors-la-loi' sont l'arme utilisée pour camoufler, aux yeux de l'opinion française et de la communauté internationale, les vrais enjeux du nationalisme algérien conduits par des structures politiques bien organisées" "the terms 'bandits' and 'outlaws' are the weapon used to camouflage, in the eyes of French opinion and the international community, the true states of Algerian nationalism engaged in by well-organized political structures" (2003, 81). To illustrate his points, the literary critic calls upon the 1987 work by Robert Barrat, *Les maquis de la liberté*, reissued in 2001 under the title *Un journaliste au cœur de la guerre d'Algérie (1954–1962)*. Barrat made the news in his day by calling attention to French popular consciousness that the caricature of Algerians as bandits, outlaws, and terrorists, beyond justifying brutal military operations called "pacification," aimed at covering up the emergence in the maquis of a conscious political claim made from the perspective of the historical process. As for the bandits, the novel tells us that some of these were men pushed by hunger to commit certain misdeeds. Others belonged to organized, armed bands, living on the edges of society. Their henchmen monitored the highways and kept them informed (106).

Thus, we see a true organization of banditry that rebels against banditry, and despite the reservations highlighted by Stora earlier, we can say that in the end, and likely for a variety of motives, the peasants who engaged in dissidence had something in common with the resistance of the Front de Libération Nationale (FLN). Both sets belonged to a same group that was subject to what Achille Mbembe called necropolitics, since it is true that "colonial occupation itself was a matter of seizing, delimiting, and asserting control over a physical geographical area—of writing on the ground a new set of social and spatial relations" (2003, 25). This common destiny of the "bandits" and the "rebels," united in their oppression and incarceration, furthermore easily explains why in Bounemeur's novel or even in historical reality, they are all found in the maquis, whereas the oppressed, they must unite their forces for the quest for freedom, dignity, and above all, honor.

From the dysphoric space that it was, the maquis becomes a space that serves to create a rejection of colonial temporality and a contestation of the right to punish, in that it guarantees the local insurgents a space for defense against penetration by the colonists' military.

Seen under this light, the maquis in which Hassan and other rebel peasants take refuge practically assures the same function that was assigned by Cilas Kemedjio to the back country in the novels of Mongo Beti, Jean Roger Essomba, and Maryse Condé. In fact, we can say that the maquis in *Les bandits de l'Atlas* is "une contestation contre l'édit colonial" "challenge against the colonial edict," given the understanding that "la loi coloniale pousse les résistants à une existence clandestine qui est une contestation radicale de l'édit colonial. La résistance interdite par l'occupation coloniale cherche refuge dans la forêt danse" "colonial law pushes the rebels into a clandestine existence that is a radical contestation of the colonial edict" (2003, 53).

In a way, we can even extend that thought and state that the characterization of the oppressed rebels as bandits had a positive role in the resistance. Returning to the thought of Selom Gbanou and to the functionality that Kemedjio attributes to the back country, we must ask ourselves if, in the end, the tactical withdrawal into the forest and the indeed often violent methods used by the insurgents didn't succeed in throwing the colonial administration off balance. To that point, Branche has shown that the war was not only a military war but also a psychological war that was sometimes heavily waged in the media and in the official reports of the French administration. For once, we could say, through their actions, the colonized escaped the intelligence of their masters who had come to bring them "civilization." Making use of a letter from a director of school in Algiers, Branche makes the following point on the topic:

> La population était surtout décrite comme "terrorisée" par les méthodes violentes des nationalistes, alors même que poignait, dans de nombreux documents, un net engagement de la jeunesse en faveur de l'affrontement, telle cette lettre d'un directeur d'école qui décrivait un "cortège d'enfants de 13 à 15 ans qui défilaient aux abords de l'école" en chantant un "hymne nationaliste" puis, s'arrêtant devant l'école, reprenaient leur chant en "l'accompagnant de gestes ne laissant place à aucune équivoque."
>
> The population was above described as "terrorized" by the violent methods of the nationalists, even though in numerous documents a clear engagement was shown by the youth in favor of the confrontation, such as this letter from a school director that described a "procession of children 13 to 15 years old who were marching at the edges of the school" singing a "nationalist hymn" and then, stopping in front of the school, took up their song again by "accompanying it with gestures that left no room for misinterpretation." (2013, 210)

From all evidence, since it is clear that there was a myth of total and complete adhesion by all Algerians to the independentist cause and that it continued to be maintained even in the days after the independences, it is then pertinent to note that the ages of the children mentioned in the letter used by the historian corresponds quite closely to that of Hassan in *Les bandits de l'Atlas*. Furthermore, it is also important to note that even if the struggle for liberation was first and foremost the history of an indigenous elite, children and peasants joined in the same spirit in the demand for justice, or more directly, for the autonomy that awaited them, and their demands were simply crushed militarily.

Clearly then, in this context marked by a configuration linked to separation and difference that is as much racial as religious and cultural, the indigenes who "ne connaissent qu'une législation exorbitante et discriminatoire qui les expose constamment aux instruments de violence de l'État colonial" "know only an exorbitant and discriminatory form of legislation that constantly exposes them to the instruments of violence of the colonial State" (Grandmaison, 231), these colonized will contribute their awareness of domination to finally organize to reclaim their humanity and break the chains of their dehumanization and, quite often, their bestialization. In *Les bandits de l'Atlas*, this will to break out of the vicious circle of necessity and expendability is appropriated by the peasants and their kind, which the administration labeled bandits. Hassan and his comrades in struggle, having withdrawn to the maquis for having struck the fatal blow to the colonial occupant through killing both the caïd, the local representative of the oppressor, and the French gendarmes, resemble in many ways that peasantry in whom Fanon perceived a revolutionary uniqueness. For him, "The peasantry is systematically left out of most of the nationalist parties' propaganda. But it is obvious that in colonial countries only the peasantry is revolutionary. It has nothing to lose and everything to gain. The underprivileged and starving peasant is the exploited who very soon discovers that only violence pays. For him there is no compromise, no possibility of concession. Colonization or decolonization: it is simply a power struggle" (2004, 23). This link to the forces Fanon speaks of has been so well understood by Hassan and his comrades in struggle that as the bandits he joins affirm: "Tu apprendras à te battre. La vie ou la mort, c'est Dieu qui nous les donne" "You'll learn to fight. Life or death, it's God who gives it to us" (142). Furthermore, in the chapters recounting the confrontation between the rebel peasants and the forces of terror composed of gendarmes and the caïd and his men, we read: "Nous nous battrons jusqu'au dernier . . . Nous, nous sommes prêts à mourir. Eux, ils ne veulent pas de la mort. Voilà notre supériorité et voilà notre chance" "We'll fight to the end . . . We are ready to die. Those guys, they don't want to die. That where we're better and that's our chance" (155).

The ending of Bounemeur's novel places a particular emphasis upon the success—albeit relative—of the peasant revolt up against the colonial authorities. Not only do the villagers who had been won over to the cause of the caïd and the gendarmes end up abandoning the battlefield, but the villagers accept the tortures and punishment inflicted by the family of the caïd who was killed by the rebel Hassan, rather than give any information for tracking down the fugitive. In this regard, moreover, Branche has cited the words pronounced by a caïd who died on the scaffold: "Je meurs innocent et ainsi mourront ceux qui accorderont leur confiance aux roumis et verseront leur sang pour les Français" "I die innocent and so will those who put their trust in Christians and spill their blood for the French" (2013, 212). We see that certain caïds, like the one mentioned above, despite having served to terrorize their coreligionists, leave a testimony that speaks to resistance, dissidence, and rejection of the colonial edict. That means beyond any doubt that despite any failure we can observe in the revolt of the peasantry in colonial Algeria, the meditation of the colonized upon their sorry human condition (which I call their *memento mori*) still often oriented them toward battle as a means to achieve a security that is not only physical but also social and political.

In general, such is the formulation of the response of the bandits/peasants to their stigmatization and their marginalization in colonial Algeria. With *Les bandits de l'Atlas*, and whatever can be said about the author's idiosyncratic choices or ideological positions, given that Bounemeur himself was a member of the national liberation army in Algeria, he succeeded in meeting a double challenge. First, his novel serves to remind us that sometimes it is from the edge, that is, from the periphery, that the necessary decisions and actions will come for the recentering of a population victimized by violence. In offering a reading that centers on people who are dominated, Bounemeur succeeds in placing within the collective imaginary figures who are often forgotten at the expense of nationalist leaders, such as the "honorable bandits." Second, from the philosophical point of view, and pertinent for today's societies where social insecurity, racism, and other forms of discrimination reign, Bounemeur leads the reader to meditate upon the words of Albert Memmi in his gloss on the dominated person: "*Lorsqu'un opprimé fait ainsi le tour de son oppression, elle lui devient invivable.* Lorsqu'un opprimé a entrevu la possibilité d'être libre et qu'il accepte d'en payer le prix, il est vain d'espérer encore la paix pour longtemps" (1968, 41) "When the oppressed has seen the extent of his oppression in this way, then it becomes unbearable to him. Once the victim of oppression has had a glimpse of the possibility of freedom, and agrees to pay the price for it, it is useless to hope for an enduring peace" (1968, 26). And even in recognizing the depth and importance of the thought of Mohammed Harbi, for whom discourse that looked at the revolution in Algeria as taking place thanks to an avant-garde peasantry was a means of neutralizing them (2008, 15), it still remains that *Les bandits de l'Atlas* gives voice to the vanquished and in that way makes a modest yet noteworthy contribution to filling in one of the numerous silences in Algerian history, both past and present.

NOTES

1. For an analysis of this movie from the perspective of genre, gender, and sexuality, see Anne Donadey "Gender, genre and intertextuality in Rachid Bouchareb's *Hors la loi*" *Studies in French Cinema*, 16.1(2016): 48–60.

2. See Jacques Rancière, *The Politics of Aesthetics*. New York: Continuum, 2004.

3. For a detailed study of indigenous rights in Algeria and the French Empire, see Olivier Le Cour Grandmaison, *De l'indigénat. Anatomie d'un "monstre juridique: Le Droit colonial en Algérie et dans l'empire francais."* Paris: Editions la Découverte, 2010.

4. For a discussion of the paradoxal citizenship of women in Algeria during colonization, see Marc André, "Algériennes: quelle citoyenneté? (Années 1930—années 1960)," *Clio. Femmes, Genre, Histoire 43(2016)*: 94–116.

5. The words "arabe," "musulman," and "indigènes" are all part of a typology of names used to designate the colonized figure in this analysis.

6. In his essay *Coloniser, Exterminer* (Fayard, 2005), Olivier Le Cour Grandmaison insists that there is a link between colonization and extermination and states that the permanent state of exception that was in effect in colonial Algeria until 1945 is synonymous to the colonial administration's power of life and death over the natives.

Chapter 2

The Immigrant Body as Body of Exception

EXILE, STATELESSNESS, AND INHOSPITALITY: ALBERT BENSOUSSAN'S *MIRAGE À 3*

Maghrebian literature as we know engages in a thematic complicity with the issue of migratory phenomena. From Driss Chraïbi to Iman Bassalah as well as Tahar Ben Jelloun, Rachid Boudjedra, Nabile Farès, and even Salim Jay, to mention only those authors, North Africa's writers construct their writing project around this important phenomenon, among other things. Human movement is a theme that is even more interesting and worth spending time on because it is quite topical right now, especially with respect to the feelings of fear provoked by polemical essayists such as Stephen Smith (2018) in calling it "la ruée vers l'Europe" "the rush to Europe" in his work of the same title. The issue under study here is therefore not new, especially if we look at the novelistic corpus of African writers in general, and of the Maghreb in particular. Nevertheless, for this reflection on the fictional coverage of the links between exile, statelessness, and inhospitality as a site for the quintessential manifestation of precarious lives, I will focus on the novel of a writer who represents a class of Maghrebian authors that are very often forgotten: Judeo-Maghrebian writers. I acknowledge the key role played by Guy Dugas in mediatizing and spreading Judeo-Maghrebian literature to which he has devoted, among others, two major texts in particular: *La littérature judéo-maghrébine d'expression française: Entre Djéha et Cagayous* (1991) and *Études littéraires maghrébines: Bibliographie critique de la littérature judéo-maghrébine d'expression française* (1994). Now, it is important to note that a brief survey of anthologies of Maghrebian literature shows that Judeo-Maghrebian texts (and specifically those of Bensoussan since he is the topic here) tend to be placed in a secondary role, when they are not simply ignored. Such is the case with the *Dictionnaire des auteurs maghrébins de langue française* by Jean Dejeux (1984) and even with Jamel Eddine Bencheikh's *Dictionnaire des littératures de langue arabe et maghrébine francophone* (2000), which make no mention at all of his work. Through his novel *Mirage à 3* (referred to as *Mirages* throughout my study), Bensoussan offers a vivid portrait, or rather a highly significant textual setting of exile, a notion that both describes and decries from the physical angle as well as the psychological perspective. The novel recounts the troubles of an Algerian exiled in France due to the brutal war that ravages his country and has forced him to flee. Suddenly, the problem of representation is presented, oscillating between images that haunt his imagination and the search for a national space. We observe that exile is one specific form of migration, which is not dependent upon the will of the subject, however, as Edward Said astutely pointed out in his essay *Reflections on Exile*: "Although it is true that anyone prevented from returning home is an exile, some distinctions can be made among exiles, refuges, expatriates and émigrés" (2000, 181). It is thus a case of more than a simple migration, and even while the flux might be the same, it is nevertheless important not to lose sight of the differences in motivations for departure. Thus, the following pages will concentrate on the manifestation of exile in Bensoussan's novel, by examining the linkage between the expatriation and the affirmation of identity. In other words, we will be approaching exile as an awareness of a divide and a writing of loss, by emphasizing the relationship between the imaginary and writing. In clear, I propose that exile is another form of marginality that calls for the interpretation of how the body if the exile is socially disqualified in the host society. Furthermore, I argue that by looking at the ways in which the exile tries to redefine a sense of belonging given his statelessness, one can draw a lesson with regard the precariousness caused by the relation between sovereignty and freedom of movement. How is the internal rupture between the character in exile and his world presented? How are the awarenesses of a loss and the strategies for self-definition and self-affirmation of the excluded subject articulated? What means do the writers use to name the unnameable and speak the unspeakable? And knowing that the experience of exile is often inscribed in a retrospective journey, we can also ask how the past and the present are perceived, along with the here and elsewhere. In other words, how is the tension between exile, history, memory, and identity resolved in the text?

Mirage situates the reader in an imaginary and a writing that structure the experience of exile around an anchoring point: the awareness of a loss and a divide. The main character in *Mirage* in fact experiences a crisis of not belonging that elicits within him a nostalgia where recollection and memory open up doors for him. We read from the very beginning of the novel: "Je désigne par là même ceux qui n'étaient pas de ce pays et composaient une modeste confrérie ou d'aigris ou de nostalgiques." "I thereby am referring to those who didn't belong to that country and made up a modest brotherhood either of the embittered or the nostalgic" (Bensoussan 1989, 9). This feeling of strangeness is affirmed all the more because the ostracism by which Daniel Ange, the main character, his wife Ruth, and all Algerians in France are victimized provokes a search for a native land. Moreover, Ruth is barely able to leave her house for the simple reason, as the novel explains, that she fears she will be reminded of her strangeness. To express her disgust and suspicion toward her new "fatherland," she uses an animal metaphor in calling her husband's premises a "gros nid d'aigles" "giant eagles' nest." The exile is thus seen as being at the mercy of the new land. Even more marked are Bensoussan's words that attribute traits of cannibalism to the adoptive country. The long passage illustrating that concept merits space here:

> Définitif est l'apophtegme selon lequel la patrie d'un cochon se trouve partout où il y a du gland. La relation de l'homme à sa terre est fondamentalement pain et sueur. L'exercice du travail entraîne l'homme dans le complexe système des rapports sociaux: il donne labeur, reçoit salaire, solidaire il se syndique, vote, paie cotisation, impôts, charges, il consomme sur place, fait prospérer et vivre la collectivité, à l'occasion il fait même don de sa personne, ce mangeur de glands devenant l'excellente chair à canon. Bref, il est un rouage essentiel, quoique infime, du grand corps articulé de la nation.

> The maxim saying that the fatherland of a pig is found wherever there are acorns is definitive. The relationship between people and their land is fundamentally bread and sweat. Carrying out work leads men into the complex system of social ties: he gives labor, receives a salary, uniting he forms unions, vote, pays membership fees, taxes, charges, he consumes on site, makes the collectivity prosper and live, often he even donates himself, this eater of acorns becoming the excellent fodder. In short, he is an essential cog, though an insignificant one, in the great organized body of the nation. (Bensoussan 1989, 39)

The evocation of exile as an essential element in the great organized body of the nation in the preceding citation is noteworthy for at least two reasons. First, the relationship established between the foreign body and the national body bears witness to the fact that the exclusion of the foreign exile is not totally assumed, in that his presence and his work become necessary conditions for the existence of the so-called nation. Regarding this, we can ask ourselves if the imperative to preserve the West from the masses coming from Africa, as found in Stephen Smith's study mentioned at the opening of this chapter, is not simply a form of hypocrisy, given that the national subject requires a depreciated life (that of the exile, the immigrant, or the foreigner) to confer upon himself the feeling that his own life is worthy. Second, this passage underscores the role of the borderland in which the foreigner lives. We could say that foreigners bestow a unity to the national group that is composed of non-foreigners who effectively have a right to the nation, and who exist for something more than the production of capital that guarantees the prosperity of the host country, which is nevertheless hostile to the presence of the foreigner. As Guillaume le Blanc shows:

> Il est essentiel à la nation que l'étranger ne soit pas purement et simplement exclu, un être du seul dehors, car alors c'en serait fait de la fonction nationale de la frontière: pour que la nation ait un *dedans*, encore faut-il qu'elle ne se contente pas de renvoyer *dehors* tous ceux qui n'appartiennent pas à ce *dedans* supposé de la nation; encore faut-il que des vies surgissent à la frontière, ni *dedans* ni *dehors*, à la fois *dedans* et *dehors*. Ainsi peut prendre sens le fantasme d'une intériorité nationale dont l'affirmation suppose l'identification de l'étranger comme ennemi potentiel.
>
> It is essential to the nation that the stranger not be purely and simply excluded, a being alone outside, for then that would be the end of the national function of the border: so that the nation has an *inside*, so it must not be content to send *outside* all those who do not belong to this supposed *inside* of the nation; it still needs lives emerging at the border, neither *inside* nor *outside*, both *inside* and *outside*. In this way the fantasy of a national interiority can make sense, whose affirmation supposes identifying the foreigner as a potential enemy. (2010, 19)

In confronting this exclusion that is doubled by an exploitation that borders on slavery, the feeling of foreignness can only give rise to a desire to go back. The gap for the creature in exile comes from the difficult affirmation of his identity, if it even still exists. That is likely the reason that Bensoussan's narrator lives "en arpentant péripathétiquement le chemin de [ses] souvenirs, le labyrinthe de [leur] mémoire commune" "by strolling peripathetically down the road of [his] memories, the labyrinth of [their] common memory." Truth be told, a human being can only truly flourish in society, for a solitary human can only make space for a tragic existence. From this perspective, exile is seen as a loss of landmarks, which in the case of space is a biculturality, understood as a double deployment of identity. Thus, what we observe in Bensoussan's novel is that the main character, who is of Algerian origin, is the site for the expression of several religious cultures. As the link with the author is understood by the fact that the novel has an autobiographical inspiration, his tale oscillates between Christianity and Islam, translating in that very way the chaos of identity. Not truly French, and henceforth not "really" Algerian, such is the state of Daniel Ange's identity. It is through an impalpable betweenness of identity that the character in exile is inscribed, coming from a culture that is now far away, yet being incapable of identifying with the culture of the host country. With their identity situated at the point of intersection of two worlds, the protagonists of *Mirage* suffer from "avoir traversé l'histoire sans la comprendre" "having traversed history without understanding it," according to the narrator. We can then say about this in-between state that Bensoussan's practice is located on two levels, the social frame, and the personal story, to reference Daniel Sibony (1997, 312). For example, the novel relates in the same passage the encounter between Eluard and Baudelaire on the one hand, and Egarim Gémira and Cheik Ben Hasmmadi on the other hand. This piggyback identity can also be read on the religious level inasmuch as according to Beïda Chikhi, "le religieux est à l'heure actuelle ce par quoi l'homme s'exprime le plus énergiquement" "the religious is at the present time the way mankind expresses itself most forcefully" (1996, 217). Therefore, all of Bensoussan's imaginative energy is poured into making his imaginary the locus of encounter between Islam and Christianity. Thanks to this biculturality, Mohamed can stand side by side with God (and not Allah) and Saint Matthew (Bensoussan 1989, 130–31). What is challenging here is less the discourse on religious matters than the encounter, which I find doubly interesting for being able to see that a writer with a Jewish background, and molded by Islam, can effect that intersection with Christian references. It seems to me too that there is a highly significant dimension of the intercultural in Bensoussan's prose, a truly multicultural space. Which does not, however, eliminate the denunciative tone in the text.

The exile then proceeds through an idealization of the lost country, an idealization that becomes a defensive rejection of reality and the land of exile. Since everything is but solitude and a void around him, to define himself, the exile ineluctably turns to alterity, the concept defined by Michel Laronde as being "à la fois rapport de complémentarité, à la fois collective et individuelle" "both a link of complementarity and both collective and individual" (1993, 20). And when this "acculturation," or rather this assimilation, is ineffective, the exile refuses to identify with the Other, therefore failing to enter into the foreign space to become an integral part of it. That, in point of fact, is the choice made by the hero of *Mirage*, who opts for a regression and a fixation on the past. The search for the ideal, mythical homeland takes on the shape of a nostalgia for the past and origins, a desire to return, and a phobia of the space of exile, that is, the host country. That space is tragic, a locus of division and mourning. The writing of alterity in this case proceeds by differentiation (the Other opposed to the "I") rather than by assimilation (a similar Other, not much different from the "I"), according to Daniel Henri Pageaux (1994, 65). The foreign reality is thus seen as inferior to the culture of origin. The novel allows the symbols and images of the desert, along with the labyrinth and the semic opposites such as here/there, and before/now to emerge as a backdrop. In *Mirage*, we note in fact a rejection of reality by the exile and his manifest refusal to identify with France, the host country. In search of a territory that will be soothing and calm, the exiled being is in perpetual movement and therefore constructs his own space by deconstructing that of the Other, just as it is true that alterity is the prism of self-representation. However, displacement can ward off a spatial fixation and degenerate into distraction, instability; in short, it can become endless wandering. The characters in *Mirages* confront this wandering, and we come to realize through close examination that their instability is stable and their distraction is but a vain attempt to succeed in defining their identity. Now, if wandering is fruitful and salutary for Giambatista Viko, the protagonist in *L'errance* by Georges Ngal, what Bensoussan recounts is rather the source of the torments. The exile's perigrination through spaces, through "les coordonnées topographiques de l'action imaginée et contée" "the topographical coordinates of imagined and recounted action," to use Henri Mitterand's words (1980, 192), is essentially sterile. Since the space of exile is different from the space of the native land, the exiles' relationship to space becomes conflictual, and their migrations toward better spaces are ultimately sterile. Like Yalann Waldick in Driss Chraïbi's *Les boucs* (1955), the protagonist of Bensoussan's *Mirage à 3* thought he had found "over there" to be a better "here." In a word, the exile has the sense of living in a dream, with everything around him but an illusion. Everything has counted for nothing, and the narrator of *Mirage* has well understood that, because speaking of Algerian exiles in France, he affirms: "Tous réunis au bord du jardin promis et refusé, et tous souffrants et tous tourmentés" "All gathered together at the edge of the promised and refused garden, and all suffering and all tormented" (16–17). Furthermore, Bensoussan resorts to a metaphor to show the crowning mirage of exile, namely, the inaccessible paradise: "Le ciel descend sur ma fenêtre. Pourquoi n'arrive-t-il jamais au bleu. Le voilà blanc, le voilà gris . . . mais bleu, il n'est jamais bleu" "The sky comes down on my window. Why is it never blue? It's white, it's gray . . . but blue . . . it's never blue" (67). In fact, Bensoussan's main character will come to know several women during his exile, but the result will always be the same. Because the mirage always yields to a determinism, the will to break the spiral of exile will prevail. Thus, departure is necessary, but "serait-ce là enfin le territoire promis à leur décadence?" "Would it finally be the land that was promised to their decadence?" (146). We come to understand the writer's methodology in working through a conflicting construction. Beginning from a negative landmark, he gradually sets his sight upon a positive landmark to make a bitter assessment of exile. Given that exile is made up only of mirages, the search becomes an endless starting over for yet another place, a permanent search that translates into departure. In short, the novel reveals that the only thing that can be found in exile is mirages. And this failed enterprise of identification pushes the exiles into their final entrenchment.

The narrator questions the notion of nationality, then defines the homeland as the land of ancestors, before speaking of the impossibility, or rather the refusal, of protagonist Daniel Ange to become one with the land of exile, or with the women who have come from it: "il ne serait jamais capable de pénétrer dans cette femme . . . ni de féconder la terre de l'exil" "he would never be capable of penetrating this woman . . . nor of fertilizing the land of exile" (1989, 163). This is truly the case of an exile that, as Maurice Blanchot says, "prend la forme concrète de l'existence vagabonde à laquelle glisse le jeune étranger, exilé de ses conditions de vie, jeté dans l'insécurité d'un espace où il ne saurait vivre ni mourir lui-même" "takes the concrete form of a vagabond existence to which the young foreigner slips, exiled from his conditions of life, thrown into the insecurity of a space where he cannot live or die by himself" (1978, 155). Blanchot's explanation can explain the memories that fail to resolve the question of identity but at least ensure a role of tenacity and hope, in the sense that memory helps "renouveler en nous-mêmes des résonances de cette contemplation de la grandeur" "renew in us the resonances of this contemplation of grandeur," according to Bachelard (1967, 168). As will be seen, the loss behind exile is an absence, of which simple awareness unleashes recollections and nostalgias in the person in exile. Ambiguity is then experienced in an obsessional way by the exile who is forced to resort to other arguments to construct his disordered, fragmented, and tainted identity.

Having left countries that are now far away and now being subjected to the space of France, Bensoussan's characters are torn between a "here" and a "there," poles that are the two antipodes of identity. Belonging to diverse cultures leads to a malaise for these exiles. Identity is situated at the juncture of two worlds, both poorly known, poorly understood, and often even ignored, so that the path of reconstitution follows the path of alterity, which is "à la fois rapport d'opposition et rapport de complémentarité à la fois collective et individuelle" "both a relationship of opposition and relationship of complementarity that is both collective and individual" (Laronde 1993, 20). Identity is therefore doubly envisaged from an individual and a collective perspective. The novel in fact leads us to a reading of constructions that can be said, as in the writing of Greimas (1966), to be either opposites or binaries from the semantic point of view. And in fact, here we can cite the opposites of here/there, before/now, pain/ease, sorrow/pleasure.

Furthermore, it can be said that in the text, the image of the sky and the metaphors from nature (desert, animals) help structure the exile's void. Furthermore, the organization of the work allows for the appearance, transversally, of the tears, the tragic imprisonment, but also and especially the loss, illustrated notably through the loss of the son in Bensoussan's novel. Henceforth, if we accept the idea that the family is an institution in the sense that it "joue le rôle primordial dans la transmission de la culture" "plays the primordial role in the transmission of culture," as indicated by Jacques Lacan (1988, 13), we can then readily understand that the death of Daniel Ange's son, added to exile, explains the weight of emptiness in which exiles live, which pushes them to institute an axis of time that will create a bridge between the present and the past, aiming ultimately at reaching oblivion. But before achieving this oblivion, it is important to be able, and above all, to remember.

For Hegel, to be means precisely to have been. This definition of the present through the past seems most important in that it establishes a basis for and justifies the notion of memories. The understanding of the past as therapy for the exile thus supposes going back to an era that is over and done with, timewise. But it must be said that this past undoubtedly conditions the present, for to understand it is precisely to escape its grip and torment. Remembering is what in fact generates the feeling of aloneness and uprooting. That relationship is quite subtle in *Mirage,* where memory precedes the oblivion that each time carries away the memory only to preserve it. Long stored away, the impossibility of memory, or oblivion, becomes a victory. Following Paul Ricœur (2000, 536), we can say that the writing of *Mirage* is located in the trajectory of "forgiveness." By forgiveness, we mean acknowledgment of culpability and reconciliation with the past. In following that conclusion, Bensoussan's novel includes a horizon, one of an appeased memory, and in a certain way the horizon of happy oblivion. The horizon is then the locus of intersection for the roads to forgetting and pardon. The balance between memory and forgetting is quasi-verifiable in *Mirage.* If there is an erasure of tracks in *Mirage* and if despite everything, memory is effective, forgetting appears to be beneficial, given that at the same time, and paradoxically, some traces remain. The past illuminates the future. It is the point of departure for reflections by which the characters explore their being, through the effort of remembering and fighting against forgetting. Yet, at the same time, the novel offers a forceful experience of time. Consequently, the link between the exiled characters and history is a significant anchoring device in Bensoussan's novelistic writing. The narration is seen to be almost entirely at the service of an attempt to reconstruct history. On one level, the diegesis functions as what François Hartog (2003) calls the Ancien Régime of historicity. Time is perceived as the end result, an aging with respect to the moment of enunciation. The history of the past predominates at the beginning of *Mirage.* The characters only think about their identity through their relationship to the past. The unfolding of scenes of memories and the evocation of the faraway native land seem to respond to the writer's project—whether avowed or not, whether conscious or unconscious—of writing, or rather rewriting, history. The future thus derives from the past, and the recollection of events that have occurred is linked to that Ancien Régime of historicity. The text includes, in a symbolic manner, an interior voyage and a determination on the part of the characters to clarify their existence by resorting to history, understood as the sum of past events that fill their lives. There is a definite fascination with the past, undoubtedly for a long-ago past—one that is opposed to the recent past, because as the exiles are powerless when faced with the truth of the past and caught between memory, oblivion, and recollection, their history comes back to them and becomes recentered at the moment it is experienced.

Where in the first case, "ancient" history was relative to the son of the hero of *Mirage,* the new history will be founded upon a past in which the actors are still living. The novel thus assumes the form of a historical document, so to speak. But it is precisely the matter of a history of the present, a "presentism" defined by François Hartog (2003, 28) as a tendency to sacrifice, if we ascribe to Dominique Maingueneau's representation, the "visée durative" "long-term goal" in favor of the "visée ponctuelle" "immediate goal" (1981, 22). The first is wider while the second is less so. That is, it is a singular experience of time in which the engendering of historical time is suspended and a contemporary experience of time reigns, whereby the present itself now furnishes its history. Thus, we see the events of the Algerian war being evoked from the perspective of the "present." Even if the past is evoked, it is done so only as a function of a set of criteria that fall precisely within the moment of enunciation, that is, as a rupture in time with the deeds that are evoked. The past perfect yields its place to the contemporary. The changes and modifications of history do not resist the time that has passed, and so the past contributes to the understanding of the present and only the present, without any ambition of looking to the future. Likewise, that tendency changes course in that it is the present that counts and it alone has the potential to understand the past.

Ambiguity is created even further in this experience of time, and Hartog does do a fine job of underscoring the understanding that futurism (domination of the future point of view) is already in itself a presentism. This nuance indeed cloaks the writing of exile. In fact, the impossibility of a successful return to the past leads the characters to "futurize" the present. Furthermore, we can read in the writer's imaginary that the present is the ultimate instant for the definition of identity. As if to escape the obsession with the past, the characters in *Mirage* appear to devote themselves to living only in the present moment. Here, a quotation from the philosopher Marcus Aurelius is invaluable: "Si tu te sépares de toi-même, c'est-à-dire de ta pensée . . . tout ce que tu as fait ou dit dans le passé, tout ce qui dans le futur te tourmente, tout ce qui échappe à ton libre arbitre, si tu sépares [de toi-même] le futur et le passé, si tu t'appliques à vivre seulement la vie que tu vis, c'est-à-dire seulement le présent, tu pourras passer tout le temps qui te reste jusqu'à ta mort avec calme, bienveillance, sérénité" "If you separate yourself from yourself, that is from your thought . . . everything you have done or said in the past, everything that is tormenting you in the future, everything that escapes your free will, if you separate [from yourself] the future and the past, if you make an effort to live only the life that you are living, that is, only in the present, you will be able to spend the rest of the time you have up until your death, with calm, benevolence, serenity" (Hartog 2003, 121–22). In *Mirage,* Daniel Ange chooses not to be concerned with the "before" or "after," but only with the "now." Such is the prevailing principle in his adulterous relationship with Maria, who rightly reproaches him for focusing only on the imminence of his actions. He renounces all projects, choosing therefore a sort of pleasure in the moment of action. He realizes that his past no longer makes sense, and refuses to believe in any future; his whole life can be summed up as a feeling of the present. Wandering is consequently seen as emanating from the culmination of this presentist penchant. If I define errancy as a perpetual movement from one space to another, and tourism as the discovery through travel to a hitherto unknown or little-known space, then these two concepts can be seen as analogous. The difference, it should be noted, is that errancy, unlike tourism, is in most cases an inexorable and incontrovertible solution. We can see the suggestiveness in the novel's closing with yet another departure. And if we add to that the attenuation of time, we can indeed venture to conclude that presentism sheds a light on Bensoussan's writing, as in the final analysis it rejects the past and the future by acknowledging the history of, and in, the present. Strategies are therefore created to manage the impasse of finding oneself distanced by marginality and suffering its adversities.

The act of artistic creation represents a moment of appeasement for the uprooting. The essential creative gesture consequently illustrates one of the vital moments in the process of self-affirmation, and in its maintenance. This interpretation of the reading is all the more plausible because at the heart of the diegesis we find characters who explicitly reveal a writing project meant for pouring out their sorrows and resisting adversity. Writing helps the exile in his quest to go beyond fear toward hope, with the proper support for the descent into hell. Through words, the writer envisages the reconstitution of an existence that has been fragmented by time and history. Writing, books, constitute the essential locus for evasion and finding reassurance. If survival has meant having to experience killing and if affirmation of survival requires killing entire masses in the novels of Elias Canetti and José Maria Arguedas (Mildonian 2002), in Bensoussan's novel that survival and affirmation are based upon artistic creation, and more precisely writing. In *Mirage,* where despite his social function that has little to do with literature, the work's central character is strongly fixated on the desire to write, a desire that obsesses him and that he keeps alive. For Daniel Ange, if paradise is impossible, if Eden is promised but denied, then writing appears to be for him the moment of understanding a history that he has lived without understanding. Aware of the impossibility of going back in time, the exile liberation through the act of writing, or at the very least a passage to a land of spiritual, physical, and psychic harmony. The blurring of Bensoussan's narration can explain this urgency of writing. We are from the very beginning in the presence of a narrator who finds himself both outside the narration and an Other. Thus, there is a kind of doubling, as seen when we read: "Et alors il m'ouvrait son âme tourmentée. Et cette histoire peut commencer" "And then he opened up to me his tormented soul. And this story can begin" (Bensoussan 1989, 9). There is a need for testimony through writing and thus the narration is a forceful obsession for Bensoussan, to the point that the three movements constituting the framework of his text are handled by three different procedures, to which we can add that of the primary narrator. Returning to the text, the reader quickly notices the primacy conferred upon writing. The wife of the novel's main character is his wellspring, his muse for his writing, the text tells us. In fact, the act of writing carries with it the re-creation of the individual, assures survival, and legitimizes existence: "J'écris, j'écris pour exister, pour être, être ici, en ce lieu avec quelque raison, justifier ma présence, la désabsurdiser. J'écris pour amasser autour de mon corps à l'ancre, de ma main posée sur la table d'écriture, tout le sable de mes rêves, l'humus de mon jardin secret, le poids d'encre de mes nuits" "I write, I write in order to exist, to be, to be here, in this place, for some reason, to justify my presence, to take away its absurdity. I write to gather about my anchored body, with my hand placed on the writing table, all the sand of my dreams, the earth in my secret garden, the weight of ink in my nights" (114). Writing likewise functions as a catharsis for the exile in the sense that it allows his reconciliation with his deep being. Poetry thus favors the evasion and survival of its author. It is so vital that through writing, the exile who has become the artist "se protégerait du monde où agir est difficile, en s'établissant dans un monde irréel sur lequel il règne souverainement" "could protect himself from the world in which to act is difficult, by establishing himself in an unreal world over which he reigns with sovereignty," to use the words of Blanchot (1955, 57).

Blanchot makes it clear that through their work, artists not only protect themselves from the world but from the demand that pulls them outside of themselves. Thus, writing tries to close in on the loss that is born of the exile. It is dramatized by trying to fill the void and it reinvents the individual, and certainly Bensoussan seems to have truly understood this: "J'écris pour me créer, à défaut de terre, de territoire légitime, un parc en droit et en acte, une chasse à moi seule réservée, pour me bâtir une nue-propriété" "I write to create, for lack of land, legitimate territory, a park, legal and active, a hunting spot that is for myself alone, in order to build myself a place of bare ownership" (Bensoussan 1989, 114), and he can always conclude in the voice of his hero: "Rien n'est perdu, mon amour, il nous reste la parole" "Nothing is lost, my love, we still have words" (141). Significantly, the act of writing is a response to exile, a position of outrage. For his inability to regain his native land, the exile turns to writing to create a solitary and imaginary world that does not exist in reality, but only in his mind. This writing is not only meant to be creative but to justify and protect. It flows in the clearest possible way so that the poetry recreates the man in exile by trying to reconstruct all that lies within him, but which are now only a vestige. There is no doubt, the poet in his godless days has come to tell of better days ahead. We could in these circumstances compare the cathartic function of literature in Bensoussan's works to that of painting in the works of Abdelwahab Meddeb (1986). By understanding that there is no writing without language, we shall see that language is also a motive for resistance in withstanding the test of exile, and indirectly an element for the construction of identity. Cultural awareness is like linguistic awareness, defined by Jean-Marc Moura as "la place de la langue dans la conscience de l'écrivain" "the place of language in the writer's consciousness" (1999, 42). Faced with a lost land, the writer tries to save his language. The main character in the novel affirms this awareness of the centrality of language in his deepest being: "J'ai perdu la langue arabe" "I've lost the Arabic language" (Bensoussan 1989, 93). Consequently, to avoid a Tower of Babel, where incomprehension and lack of communication would predominate, his enunciation adopts specific forms that seek to absorb and fight, or rather to colonize in his own turn, the dominant culture. From this perspective, enunciation in *Mirage* addresses the issue of the exile's linguistic consciousness through the four levels outlined by Moura (1999, 44).

First, the work constructs its own enunciation by rejecting the dominant models from the metropole—France and Algeria in this case. Then, the context of the enunciation is inscribed in a "tradition autochtone" "autochtonous tradition" through specific linguistic usages that the work manifests: the novel is sprinkled with Arabic words and expression. Then in doing so, the work creates a "poetics" that joins specific formal traits of the language. One clear illustration of this is seen in all the syntactic ruptures at play in *Mirage*. Negations are used in place of affirmation and Bensoussan even employs a negative modality, deconstructing the tool of negation. In the same vein, passages in the novel become the perfect sites for the burial of grammar rules and constructions of phrases. The lexicon strives for the register of family talk, sometimes using slang: "en voyant la gueule qu'il fait" "seeing the face he's making" (Bensoussan 1989, 39). Beyond this deconstruction of code, the author resorts to a linguistic in-betweenness to gain control of the French, appropriating and domesticating it by giving it a voice in his language. Thus, instead of affirming himself through submission to French, Bensoussan calls upon Arabic oral sources that he imposes upon his enunciation in French. For example, on page 90, the author speaks of *fatmahs* and the *Ouled-Naïls* without translating the terms, as if these words were part of the vocabulary of the first-language speech. With the text situated at the border of two languages, "l'une de ces langues, celle de la passion en retrait, est l'objet perdu tout trouvé qui stimule l'anamnèse et le désir d'écrire, de rattraper ce qui s'est dérobé, ou alors de fantasmer sur ce qui est en retrait dans une position traumatique et s'amenuise pendant que l'autre grandit" "one of the languages is that of a retired passion, the lost object that has been found that stimulates anamnesis and the desire to write, to catch what has been hidden, or to fantasize on what is held back in a traumatic position and is dwindling as the other one grows" (Chikhi 1996, 152).

Furthermore, the author of *Mirage* chooses, along the same line of reasoning as in working with and on language, to close the novel with an expression from the Breton language "Kenavo" "Goodbye" (Bensoussan 1989, 164). We can deduce, then, that *Mirage* is a francophone text that could be situated in the realm of Moura's concept of postcolonial *mouvance*. But we must not lose sight of the fact that Algeria and France had a colonial relationship, and there is mention of the war of Algeria in the novel. Despite that important enterprise of "survival," the void remains within the person of the exile. Thus, the novelist's plot depends heavily on mirage, as the title indicates, and the entire text is but a legacy of errance. Nevertheless, the tribulations are not completely resolved through writing. Once set in motion, the main character's project of writing will never take definitive shape; Daniel Ange's manuscript is rejected and draws the wrath of the administration. The novel is also an invitation to reflect upon writing in exile. Is writing in exile more painful than writing in one's homeland? Confronting this failure, exiled heroes continue their exploration in a search for their identity through the territories of the original act. In addition to the act of writing, sex appears as another tool used by the main character in his effort to deal with the emptiness of exile.

Resorting to eroticism becomes a privileged medium of the psychosomatic description of the exile. Furthermore, psychoanalytic analysis leads back to the mother of the hero of *Mirage*. Throughout his exile, Daniel Ange in fact knows three women, each one playing an important role in his life. We know, for example, from what we are told in the text, that Ruth is the shore in his uprooting, and his source of inspiration. Maria, his partner, is the sexual legitimization of his life. But the role of sexuality quickly turns from being a simple object of stability to the very justification of his being and aspiration. Between his spouse, his lover, and his beloved, the novel's main character is constantly on the move, in the end transcending the physical aspect of the sexual act. Sexuality is henceforth oriented toward origins.

Sexuality is brought to bear in the writing of exile as a sedative added to writing that seems unable to compensate for the torments of the identity crisis. It is the exile's attempt to create for himself a paradise like the one he has forged in his mind and that he achieves through the sexual act, despite its mythical nature. Sex is then perceived as a passport that can facilitate, in fact assure social mobility within the tragic space of imprisonment. Trapped in the urgent need for personal reconstruction (of identity), the exiled individual inscribes sexual life within a social logic of constructing the "I." It can be clearly seen that the subject searching for personal landmarks and desiring social insertion seeks to establish a bond with the Other, a bond in which he inscribes the basis of his existence. We thus begin to see a "réseau sexuel" "network of sex" being woven into the text, where social assurance and tranquility are sought through a "sexualité extériorisée" "exteriorized sexuality," that is, the link between one ego and multiple others. Sex seems to secure an assurance for the exile, all the while distancing him from the fear of death. Bensoussan orchestrates a knowing mix of sex and religion, and we do know that those two realms explore origins. Either he is searching for an explanation of origins through belief, or religion structures the sexual act. More than effecting the encounter between Christianity and Islam, he justifies sex through the religious: "je sens tes . . . contre mon, oui, oui, pénètre, prends, prends moi, tout est à toi . . . Saint Matthieu a dit: tu entreras par la porte" "I feel you . . . against my . . . yes, yes, come, take, take me, I'm all yours . . . Saint Matthew said: you will enter through the [narrow] gate" (Bensoussan 1989, 130–31). If it is true that the merging of the Bible and the Quran symbolizes an erasure constituting "un point de mélancolie dont les conséquences psychopathologiques dans la production romanesque des Arabes sont infinies" "a point of melancholy whose psychopathological consequences in the novelistic production of Arabs are infinite" and that the religious is effectively the means by which people most fervently explain themselves in our times (Chikhi 1996, 78), then we can understand that in Bensoussan's writing, what is at question is what can be called *regressum ad uterum* (return to the womb).

Both the resort to religion and sexuality, added to the need to return to the womb all exemplify the status of the exile as *homo expendibilis*, deprived of social and civil protection and whose body has been kept at the periphery of society. The author's imaginary is obsessed in this sense by the growing feeling of childhood as the site of peace and tranquility, whence this desire to return to the protective womb. The obsessive image of the female sex appears indeed to betray the maternal myth. The narrative functions in fact like a confrontation of the horrors of life in exile, with the subject anthropomorphizing his suffering and thereby renouncing any projection into the future, so that there is no longer a presentist aspiration, but the desire to return to a state of childhood, or more specifically to the protection of the mother's womb, the desired seat of paradise made mythical through distance and the implacable tragedy of exile. This desire to return to an infantile stage is attested to in the text at more than one instance. For example, after a sexual scene, the hero of *Mirage* cries out: "J'ai retrouvé mes vingt ans" "I feel like I am twenty again" (Bensoussan 1989, 99).

And if we consider along those same lines that each sex act is in itself a reduction of age or a rejuvenation, then we can conclude that the hero's repeated attempts translate an unconscious desire to retrieve the fetal condition, not through an Oedipal desire but through the need to escape physical and mental disintegration, a disintegration moreover suggested by the narration as being the true fate of exile. If exile destroys, it is all the more legitimate to try to rebuild, to be reborn, since birth is not possible except by returning to the womb. Sexuality analyzed in that way certainly proves a desire to testify to the experience of exile. It is at once the royal road to insertion, the feeling of assurance, the moment of relaxation, and the reason for regression to protection and tranquility. With Bensoussan, there emerges an emphasis on the period of childhood and its joys. This rather astute textualizing of the sex act by the novelist is important inasmuch as it conclusively contributes to the search for identity. Finally, with respect to the Bensoussan's writing of exile, we can say, along with Giuliana Toso Rodinis, that "la sexualité pénètre [dans le texte] avec violence comme élément complémentaire de la vie, de ses jeux démentiels et de ses rares bonheurs" "sexuality penetrates [in the text] with violence as the complementary element of life, its outrageous games and its rare happinesses" (1994, 99). Besides, in writing, sex is itself constructed as a land of asylum for the exile. Exile is then experienced as the sum of adversities against which resistance takes shape according to paradigms that appear to be parallel while also being complementary. In response to this impasse, which keeps the exile outside the picture, other voices rise up to tell of the troubles of the undiscoverable and inaccessible nation. *Mirage* gives the sex act a place of honor in the treatment of the concept of identity quest, as showed above in the analysis of sexuality as a sedative to loneliness. Like Orpheus descending to the Underworld, Bensoussan, through the person of his character, appears to go off in search of his origins. This notion is all the more plausible because we know that the author is a Frenchman from Algeria, of Jewish origins and of Moroccan and Spanish heritage, and that his novels are in some ways autobiographical. We could say that this writing is obsessed with the intensification of childhood as the ultimate moment of pleasure. The women who find their way into Daniel Ange's bed end up seeming like his mother: he is thus in search of his mother, lost during the war. Hence, the imaginary return to the nation of origin, albeit at the philosophical, imaginary level. And this leads to the construction of an imaginary nation that depends on forgiving and forgetting.

The identity conflict unfolds in several times, and it can easily be said that the spiritual quest as a means of assessment seems embedded in a void. By scrutinizing the imaginary where exile is the referent, we will be able to disengage the line of separation between palpable and concrete rejection, on the one hand, and perceivable rejection, on the other hand. The latter is based on silence, one manifested in the mission assigned to writing, that of filling the void. The recurring metaphors of desert and silence bear incredible testimony to the presence and weight of the void. Here, we are dealing with an ecstatic silence and a liberating emptiness. We are dealing with a narrative text that supports the construction of a space where the final elaboration of the word is affected through silence. In *Mirage*, the reader is vaguely fixated on the details of dates. The chronological landmarks appear as "197," "April 29," and it is only on page 127 that we have two precise dates, 1977 and 1978, which—I must emphasize—only appear once. Paradoxically, while this constant void distances the word, it simultaneously draws it in, in a very specific way.

The writing of exile finds the greatest manifestation of its void in the encounter with opposites that are otherwise considered contrary and deemed incompatible. Chikhi analyzes this void, which she calls "inaugural" in Maghrebian literature, and sees in it "la poétisation du vide [qui] aurait donc une 'fonction réparatrice.' Elle correspondrait à la l'élaboration d'un parcours théorique . . . vers une plénitude du sens total, absorbant le non-sens initial qui a affecté le sujet" "the poeticization of the void which then serves the 'function of repairing.' It would correspond to the elaboration of a theoretical pathway . . . toward a fullness in the complete sense, absorbing the initial non-sense that affected the subject" (1996, 70). That means that it is crucial to make the distinction between the sterile void and the fertile void, that is, the one in which we might find the highest intelligibility in the search for identity. For that we can follow Chikhi and question whether Bensoussan's writing borrows, unconsciously or consciously, the traits of Chinese taoism. We can truly observe in the texts that the mind disintegrates to ultimately dissolve in time. And the identity of the exile seems to fashion itself from this moment on into a noumenal reality, in creative energy and exaltation of nature. To deepen our understanding of silence in this writing of exile torn between impotence and conquest of the world, I take into account the concepts developed by Blanchot on the link between creation and death. For him, it is a matter of a "happy death." In effect, in his analysis of Kafka's letter of December 1914, he notices that Kafka establishes a deep relationship between art and death, writing: "Pourquoi la mort? C'est qu'elle est extrême. Qui dispose d'elle, dispose extrêmement de soi, est lié à tout ce qu'il peut, son pouvoir est extrême. L'art est maîtrise du moment suprême, suprême maîtrise" "Why death ? Because it is extreme. Whoever controls it, has complete control over the self, is bound to all that he can do, is power in the extreme. Art is mastery of the supreme moment, supreme mastery" (1955, 110). This citation advocates for the need for the artist to be able to experience death.

But this is a matter of a death in which the dialectic of good and evil is found turned around. Comparable to Hegelian wisdom, and still following Blanchot, this felicitous meaning of death works toward the discovery, in death, of an extreme negativity, of "la mesure de l'absolument positif" "the measure of the absolutely positive." By this reasoning, the question of the freedom to die attains its profound meaning only in exiled writing, given that "toutes les échappatoires ont été récusées" "all loopholes have been removed." In the end, the hero of *Mirage* only knows mirages. Thus, if we bring Blanchot's statement to Bensoussan's novel, we can then understand that Bensoussan proceeds through silence, as Blanchot states: "Il se retranche du monde pour écrire, [et il écrit] pour mourir dans la paix" "he withdraws from the world to write, [and he writes] to die in peace," before concluding: "Maintenant, la mort, la mort contente, est le salaire de l'art, elle est la visée et la justification de l'écriture. Ecrire pour périr paisiblement" "Now, death, happy death, is the wages of art, it is the goal and the justification of writing" (1955, 113–14). Since the exile does not exist and because he is subjected to a universe that refuses to legitimize his existence, it is truly only from the moment of his death that he exists, if we ascribe to the notion that only death gives power and sense of action, in a word, life, what is true. Through the narration of exile, death is not only made possible but is exalted. When death is desired and accepted, the artist attains the absolute.

Finally, the void and silence of writing in exile can be approached from the perspective of Paul Ricœur, especially through forgetting and forgiveness. Ricœur, in fact, distinguishes between the duty to forgive and the impossible duty of forgetting. In his words, "L'oubli et le pardon désignent, séparément et conjointement, l'horizon de toute notre recherche. Séparément, dans la mesure où ils relèvent chacun d'une problématique distincte: pour l'oubli, celle de la mémoire et de la fidélité au passé; pour le pardon, celle de la culpabilité et de la réconciliation avec le passé" (2000, 536) "Forgetting and forgiveness, separately and together, designate the horizon of our entire investigation. Separately, inasmuch as they each belong to a distinct problematic: for forgetting, the problematic of memory and faithfulness to the past; for forgiveness, guilt and reconciliation with the past" (2004, 412). His exegesis seems to me all the more pertinent and applicable to Bensoussan's novel because it reveals the complex relationship between memory and forgetting. In this sense, to remember means to forget. Ricœur stresses that it is not a matter of forgetting through erasure, but a forgetting that makes memory possible. The void can therefore take account for a forgetting that is legitimate since it does not silence evil, but speaks it in a "soothing" manner. For the philosopher that means showing how it is possible to preserve "dans son intégrité la frontière entre amnistie et amnésie à la faveur du travail de mémoire, complété par celui du deuil, et guidé par l'esprit de pardon" "in its integrity the border between general pardon and amnesia in favor of the work of memory, completed by that of sorrow, and guided by the spirit of forgiveness" (Ricœur 2000, 619). It is in the sense of that assessment that we read *Mirage* at the end of the day, for it truly seems that the silence, death, and errancy to which the characters are subjected are part of the trajectory of writing that places oneself outside "[le] cercle de l'accusation et de la punition" "the circle of accusation and punishment" to envisage, after the happy death Blanchot speaks about, a happy memory "dans le régime de l'échange" "in the system of replacement" that is so dear to Ricœur. We can then state that it is a question of a paradoxical space of exile, for the links between forgetting and memory are seen no longer in terms of opposition but rather of complementarity. Ricoeur's conclusion on this subject is more edifying: "Leurs [l'oubli et le pardon] itinéraires respectifs se croisent en un lieu qui n'est pas un lieu et que désigne mieux le terme d'horizon. Horizon d'une mémoire apaisée, voire d'un oubli heureux" (2000, 536) / "Their respective itineraries [forgetting and forgiving] intersect at a place that is not a place and which is best indicated by the term 'horizon': Horizon of a memory appeased, even of a happy forgetting" (2004, 412).

In general, we can say that Bensoussan's novel is an invitation to reflect upon the condition of non-belonging that characterizes subaltern, invisible, and unheard lives of exiles whose hope for a better future fade when confronted with a denial of solidarity that then makes the exile a shadow. Through displacement, the topographical dimension of exile is supremely important, for it is from that starting point that solitude acquires all its meaning. With the exiled character now deterritorialized, his space is articulated around an interminable intermediary. The position adopted toward the land of exile is a result of the atmosphere of rejection that he confronts. Thus, finding himself reduced at the border, he chooses life at the edges. In *Mirage*, this choice of marginality can be read through rejection of the host country. If his homeland, defined by the author himself as the land of his father in a succession of generations, cannot be found, and on the other hand the country of exile is hostile to his ability to thrive, the hero then refuses any form of belonging to France. Solitude therefore follows the pathways of lamentation, and he prefers to exclude himself from a society that he finds, moreover, repugnant. Later, he describes himself as a citizen without a city, banned to the antipodes of his native land all the while emphasizing solitude as the single true homeland of the exile. For the eternal stranger, only solitude allows for calm and tranquility, for the promotion of a space for remembering and reconciling.

Inasmuch as the body of the exile belongs to no space of socialization at the end of the day, due to his status as eternal stranger in the host country as well as his distance from his native land, it poses the very problem of marginality. The exile's life, as seen in Bensoussan's novel, is reduced to an abnormal life: troubles, nostalgia, torment, idealization of the native land, but also the search for a problematic identity—these are the parameters that sum up the existence of exiles and illustrate perfectly the thought of Fabienne Brugère and Guillaume le Blanc:

> Les exilés d'aujourd'hui sont les expulsés de demain. Ils ne sont plus seulement des êtres partis de leurs terres, ils deviennent des individus en trop qui doivent partir au plus vite de nos terres. L'exilé d'hier pouvait encore avoir la promesse de l'ailleurs, il est désormais cet être maintenu au-dehors, contre lequel il s'agit de faire frontière.
>
> Today's exiles are tomorrow's deportees. They are no longer beings who have left their lands, they have become too many individuals who must depart from our lands as soon as possible. Yesterday's exile could still have the promise of an elsewhere; he is now this creature kept outside, against whom we must establish a border. (2018, 51)

As we have seen, the insertion of the exile into foreign space falls within an aporia, so to speak. Bensoussan's writing about the marginal condition of his protagonist Daniel Ange therefore seems to echo Edward Said's characterization of exile: "Exile is life led outside habitual order. It is nomadic, decentered, contrapuntal; but no sooner does one get accustomed to it than its unsettling force erupts anew" (2000, 186). *Mirage à 3* provides valuable witness to the interest in a writing of fracture, one that sets in motion a subject marked by the stigmata of his status as a foreigner and examines the road to self-discovery with respect to the Other. At the same time, we perceive in this novel a writing of cosmopolitanism, for we indeed can see that the characters mingle in a host community, without withdrawing into themselves. This, in turn, poses the question of inhospitality as a condition of the acceptability of the symbolic killing of the exile. If the hope of returning to life after the torment of exile is doomed to failure, it is also perhaps because today's modern societies seem to be closed in on themselves. Consequently, the foreigner is no longer the "Other" against whom the gates of solidarity are locked, but instead the creature who, because of his status, carries within him the seeds of destruction for the host society. In that context, the path for hospitality that Brugère and Le Blanc sum up in the three verbs of "rescue, welcome, and belong" gives way to a hostility manifested by stigmatization, rejection, and quite often deportation. Therefore, the condition of the exile allows us to see the fragile aspect of the body of the Other, as well as the precarity of the existence of those who, because they are considered foreigners, cannot belong to the national body, which paradoxically needs their presence to legitimize and validate itself in a national space that is shut off from "strangers." If the apprehension of the real and the definition of a national space seem to be read as a mirage, it is because *Mirage à 3* is an eloquent testimony of the imprisoning nature of the space of exile, and quite simply a textualization of the fate of humankind in the time of the global village: displacement.

OTHERING THE IMMIGRANT BODY: MEHDI CHAREF AND FAWZIA ZOUARI

Between October and December 1983, the descendants of African immigrants burst upon the French scene in a march for equality and against racism, now renamed and better known as the "Marche des Beurs" "March of the Beurs." This march, which began in Marseilles and ended with a resounding entry into the city of Paris, followed an alarming fact, the increase in racist acts targeting French citizens of immigrant heritage, to use an expression much in vogue in the linguistic repertory of identity construction in contemporary France.

If it is true that at the time this demand for visibility shook France, it is even more important to emphasize that forgetting, silence, and indifference appear to have been the responses from French society to this demand, which was also taken back up by small groups whose only objective was to satisfy their own particular interests,[1] to the detriment of the appeals based on justice and equality formulated by the leaders of these crisis-stricken youths. Fifteen years later, in 1998, a newspaper item hit France and inflamed Parisian attitudes: two young Algerian girls were left to die of hunger, and one did die while the other, her sister, was saved only at the last minute. Still with regard to the African diaspora in France, in 2005, that is, about twenty years after the 1983 march, young people of African immigrant heritage in France made a spectacular return to the scene and created an impression on France's collective consciousness with urban riots whose results and uniqueness distinguished them from all the other riots France had known during the preceding years. And just like two decades earlier, the French government's response could be summed up as silence, aside from the repression that came into play as the "miraculous weapon" for restoring order, without France ever making an effort to understand the profound causes of these manifestations of violence. It is therefore quite clear that the issues raised at the beginning of the 1980s resurfaced thirty years later, a bit as if the affected populations were a mass that was considered even more inexistent because their numerous calls for help had garnered no response other than silence and repression. It is important to note that if it is true that the urban riots of 2005 already revealed the problem of contested citizenship, and no longer African immigration alone, it is still true that the French citizens are heirs of (post)colonial African immigrants to France.[2] Based on that observation and building on the scholarship that exists the African diaspora in France, in this part of my study, I propose to offer evidence of the contours, reasons, and a possible explanation for the rejection that at first victimizes the immigrants, and then their offspring—who are no longer properly speaking immigrants, but born on French soil. To do so, I will begin with a reflection on space as the operative element of junction and disjunction, from the slums of the 1960s to the temporary housing that followed. Such a reading will allow me to determine how *Le thé au harem d'Archi Ahmed* (1983) by Mehdi Charef and *Ce pays dont je meurs* (1999) by Fawzia Zouari, even though published at an interval of fifteen years, resonate by being read as a poetics of despair for an entire generation of *sans—parts* who have been stigmatized and left behind because of their origins.

"Convaincu qu'il n'est ni arabe ni français depuis bien longtemps" "Convinced now for quite some time that he is neither Arab nor French," Madjid, the protagonist in Mehdi Charef's novel, defines himself as the "fils d'immigrés, paumé entre deux cultures, deux histoires, deux langues, deux couleurs de peau, ni blanc ni noir, à s'inventer ses propres racines, ses attaches, se les fabriquer" "son of immigrants, lost between two cultures, two histories, two languages, two skin colors, neither white nor black, left to invent his own roots, his connections, to create them for himself" (1983, 17). Thus, is the stage set at the opening of *Le thé au harem d'Archi Ahmed*, and it speaks volumes not only of the condition of immigrants but of the condition of their children at the beginning of the 1980s in France. This novel by Charef, a pioneer of what was to become known as the literature of the banlieue, recounts the adventures of a group of youths in the city, with particular emphasis on their difficulties in trying to fit in, or thinking about themselves as totally separate chapters in the history of the French nation. *Ce pays dont je meurs* by Fawzia Zouari, for its part, is the story of an Algerian family that finds itself in Paris, and whose tribulations in trying to fit in end with the disintegration of the family, and ultimately death. But how do we understand this situation of marginality that results from a deterritorialization of characters and their installation in a space that is basically dysphoric? The answer to this question is rather simple. It is because in reality and at the source, we find the movement undertaken by African immigrants of French colonies to the metropole, whether in search of a better future or often also seeking to serve

France and protect the interests of the mother country, an issue for which Rachid Bouchareb offered perhaps the most poignant fictional representation in his film *Indigènes/Days of Glory*.

Recalling history is not without its uses, as it allows us to emphasize two important factors for understanding the situation of young people of African origin such as Madjid, the protagonist of *Le thé au harem d'Archi Ahmed*, and Nacéra et Amira, central characters in *Ce pays dont je meurs*. First, in Charef's novel, we see a stigmatization of immigrants of African origin and of their offspring, despite the fact that other European immigrants and their children escape, so to speak, the category of immigration, at least in the official discourse and daily treatment supposedly reserved for one and all. Next, and in consequence of the first observation, everything happens, in effect as if, incapable of confronting its colonial acts, France decades ago launched into an enterprise of systematically scrubbing history, if not simply celebrating its colonial grandeur,[3] by implementing an amnesia that is quite often justified under the pretext of respect for the laws of the Republic and the necessity of protecting it from a barbarian invasion, or rather from the rise in communitarianism, to use a favorite term in the rhetoric of segregation found in today's France.

Ce pays dont je meurs opens with a macabre spectacle, and through prolepsis reveals police and firemen bringing out two sisters on a stretcher, one already dead and the other in critical condition. At the heart of this situation, we learn throughout our reading of the novel, is a condition of solitude and an inability to be accepted by the host society, France. One detail deserves emphasis, however: if Nacéra is in the same situation as Madjid, Charef's character, Amira, who ends up allowing herself to be fed, was born on French territory. This specific point is important inasmuch as it will permit me to highlight, through my reflection, the blurring of the borders between immigration and citizenship that today seem to characterize the perception of "the colonial Other" in contemporary France. Basically, I could say, the body of the citizen who is an heir of postcolonial immigration and the body of the immigrant who has recently arrived upon the shores of France from Africa appear to be marked by the seal of banishment, to the point that both bodies seem to merge together and become what Mohamed Sidi Barkat has called "corps d'exception" "bodies of exception" (2005), that is, bodies whose recognition and political-ontological integration into the nation remains an impossibility.

Such in fact is the context in which the major characters of Charef et Zouari, whose tribulations can be summed up as the consequences of an oscillation between invitation and rejection, a movement that, we might say, summarizes quite well the condition of the immigrant in French society in the aftermath of World War II. We can then say that the misery propelling the migratory flux of African immigrants to France is equally found at the end of their journey in French society, where the dreams they have built up come crashing down brutally. But what is even more important than the fact of failure is indeed the living conditions of these immigrants and their children. In her documentary entitled *Mémoire d'immigrés: l'héritage maghrébin*, by giving voice to immigrants and specifically to the generation of the fathers, Yamina Benguigui revealed how immigrant workers were reduced to the pure expression of their bodies (the body becomes both the locus of inscription of a social condition and the unique means of emergence for the inhabitants of the slums and temporary housing) but also promised a return to their native land once their task had ended.[4]

Clearly, the immigrant is necessary as a production force, but at the same time, the presence of the immigrant is not desired by the host country. Furthermore, as Abdelmalek Sayad observed with regard to this presence that was not a precursor to a future in France:

> Toute présence étrangère, présence non nationale dans la nation, est pensée comme nécessairement provisoire, alors même que ce provisoire pourrait être indéfini, se prolonger indéfiniment, ce qui donne de la sorte une présence étrangère durablement provisoire ou, en d'autres termes, une présence durable, mais vécue par tout le monde de manière provisoire, assortie aux yeux de tous d'un intense sentiment de provisoire.

> Any foreign presence, a non-national presence in the nation, is thought to be of necessity temporary, even when this temporary period could be indefinite, prolonged indefinitely, which gives a sort of strange presence that is permanently temporary, attached in everyone's eyes to an intense feeling of provisionality. (2006, 164)

It is likely because of this perception of foreign presence as provisional that in *Ce pays dont je meurs*, for example, the narrator insists on what can be called the indifference that greets the presence of her family in France. It is an indifference that is also a mechanism of public construction of the immigrants' invisibility, whereas they by definition constitute a visible minority. Zouari's narrator illustrates this situation in a reply to her younger sister, who allows herself to die, refusing to face the rejection of her immigrant family, and even worse, her own rejection, one that is all the more incomprehensible because she was born in France and thus is a citizen, though without doubt reduced to the category of immigrants. In a poignant passage, Nacéra speaks to her sister Amira in the following words: "Tu n'existes pas ma sœur, tu n'existes pas pour ces gens là. Seule l'idée qu'ils ont de toi existe. Quel que soit ton physique, on te jugera selon ton nom. Tu seras comme moi, un halo à la crinière crépue, toute Amira que tu es. Comprends-tu, maintenant, que tu n'es pas française ?" "You don't exist, sister dear, you don't exist for those people. The only thing that exists is the idea that they have of you. No matter what you look like, they'll judge you by your name. You'll be like me, a halo with a fuzzy head of hair, whatever you think you are as Amira. Do you understand, now, that you aren't French?" (Zaouri 1999, 126).

In that same way, the description of the city where the immigrant workers live in *Le thé au harem d'Archi Ahmed* allows this feeling of inexistence to seep through, emplified through the immigrants' living space: "Des travailleurs latins, nord-africains, y logent, dans cette cité gérée par l'employeur. Ils vivent là comme des bêtes, à l'écart de la ville, entre les travaux de l'autoroute, la voie du chemin de fer et le port de Gennevilliers, dans ce camp de travail entouré d'un haut grillage" "Latin workers, North Africans live there, in that housing complex managed by their employer. They live there like animals, separate from the city, between road construction sites, the railroad tracks, and the port of Gennevilliers, in the work camp surrounded by high fences" (Charef 1983, 77). Madelaine Hron (2005) and Anna Kemp (2016) have already written on the pathological dimension of immigrant bodies in literature (Hron) and on what Kemp calls "the politics of pain" and its literary contribution to the fortune of writers who set themselves up against the French Republican tradition. While agreeing with Hron's and Kemp's analyses, I will focus rather on showing how, from the irruption of sorrow and pathology, the immigrant body is one that is made "Other" but is paradoxically placed at the disposition of the French Republic. We must moreover stipulate along with Charef and Zouari that we are not speaking here about illegal immigration, but in fact about an intentional immigration, one that is encouraged and very often desired. What creates a problem, I believe, is that this immigration, which the host country insists on perceiving as provisional, in Sayad's words, is at the same time an immigration without which France both during and after the two world wars would have been entirely different.

My thesis then is that these immigrant bodies are held and inscribed in a contradictory position, between being needed and being discarded. It is in fact useful, to grasp the reach of my thought, to begin with the thinking of French philosopher Jean-Luc Nancy on the assemblage of bodies, which allows me to qualify the migrant's body as a dead body even before its entry into the world. I therefore propose that in the context of the immigrant's invitation-rejection by France, we are dealing with a revival that is unheard of and certainly deformed in the scene of Christ's encounter with Mary Magdalene, to which Jean-Luc Nancy has given a remarkable philosophical interpretation in his work *Noli Me Tangere* (2003). There is a clear relationship between Christ's meeting with Mary Magdalene and the repeatedly violent encounter between Africa and France. Just as the couple Jesus/Mary Magdalene is characterized in hagiography by violence or desire, indeed the other two, the Africa-France couple, share in that same contradiction, in both senses. The West is a passion for Africa, in both senses of the word passion, and inversely, Africa is France's temple of desire. This view allows us to understand the circumstances in which Madjid's father in Charef's novel is reduced to an almost vegetable state after a work accident. Since that accident, his father "a la même éternelle expression dans le regard, un mélange de vide et de lointain . . . le papa a perdu la raison depuis qu'il est tombé du toit qu'il couvrait. Sur la tête" "has the same eternal expression on his face, a mix of emptiness and the faraway . . . the father had lost his reason since he fell from the roof he was working on. On his head" (1983, 41). A similar circumstance is seen with the father of the young girls in Zouari's novel, a victim of an accident, a fall of six meters that left his vertebral column broken. And as the narrator says: "Nous vîmes mon père sortir de l'hôpital sur un fauteuil roulant, nous comprîmes le malheur qui venait de nous frapper. Il nous restait à mesurerl'extrême fragilité de notre condition" "We saw my father come out of the hospital in a wheel chair, and we understood the tragedy that had struck us. All we had to do was gage the fragility of our condition" (Zouari 1999, 55).

Based on the state in which the fathers of immigrant families find themselves in those two novels, we could certainly agree with the thinking of Nancy in the above-quoted passage. For him, the character of Mary Magdalene is made for disrupting, in both senses of the word, the religious legend. Along with that interpretation, I would ask the question of what type of resurrection is portended by this ambiguous link between France and its immigrants of African origin? For if the Jesus-Mary Magdalene coupling is comparable, in Nancy's thinking, to the France-Africa couple, could it also be that the existence of African immigrants in France is made for disrupting the sense of French identity? In Benguigui's documentary, we observe that already at the time of the wave of immigrant workers who came to France, that is, around the beginning of the 1950s, there was the acute housing problem for these workers who had come from the French colonial empire in Africa. Beyond being literally deprived of rights and being controlled by the French government, those immigrant workers were reduced to living in temporary housing and in other shanty towns, before being progressively displaced to the suburbs that we know today. Later, through the practice of family reunification, the families of immigrant workers joined them in France, creating another groundswell that was from the very beginning seen as undesirable and with which France was forced to come to terms.[5] Faced with the dialectics of invitation and rejection that I mentioned earlier, and doubtlessly due to the rapid spread of the image of the immigrant as a threat to national integrity in the minds of so many French, there was a progressive implementation of what

Pascal Blanchard and Nicolas Bancel have called "les nouveaux espaces de l'exclusion" "the new spaces of exclusion": the banlieue, "devenue, à travers les médias, les films, les discours politiques, une *terra incognita*, et un espace quasi-ethnique . . . lieux appréhendés comme des enclaves au sein de la République, des 'points noirs,' des espaces à reconquérir ou à pacifier" "having become, through the media, films, and political discourse, a *terra incognita*, and a quasi-ethnic space . . . loci seen as enclaves within the heart of the Republic, 'black spots,' spaces to reconquer or to pacify"(1998, 81).

The description of the shanty towns in *Le thé au harem d'Archi Ahmed*, just like the representation of the space inhabited by the immigrant families in *Ce pays dont je meurs*, is revealing in the ways that space, as a marker of existence, translates the shunting of first, the populations who have come from Africa, then their offspring. For if we start from the principle that space only exists if it is filled, then the existence of these individuals who populate this space will be a function of the ways in which they behave there, as well as of the modalities of their presence inside that place. Charef's narrator describes where Madjid and his parents live as being "le plus cruel des bidonvilles de toute la banlieue parisienne. Des vraies *favelas* brésiliennes, le soleil en moins, sans la musique endiablée pour crier au secours" "the most inhuman of the shanty towns of any Parisian banlieue. True Brazilian *favelas*, minus the sun, and no boisterous music to cry for help" (1983, 115), in which "les enfants jouent avec une petite graine d'insouciance dans la misère, dans la boue, sous la fumée dense et épaisse que crachent le cheminots" "children play with a small grain of carelessness in poverty, mud, under the dense, thick smoke that the railroad workers spit out" (117). Even though describing an apartment in Paris itself, Zouari's narrator emphasizes the unhealthiness and decaying of the HLM building in which the family has chosen to live. We can see that the slum, just like Zouari's Paris, is the quintessential space of humiliation and failure. In one way, we could say that the *cité de transit* (transitional housing areas), meant to be a temporary place, was not only built in a unique and permanent place of immobility (for some of these transitional housing places were surrounded by barbed wire), but its logic was prolonged in what are today called *banlieues*, mostly populated by African immigrants and their children. And if today's banlieues are to all appearances less "surveillées" "monitored," it must still be noted that the transitional housing units were quite often managed by former soldiers who had returned from Algeria and were deemed the most suitable for monitoring these foreigners, given that they knew these indigenes, as Benguigui's documentary reveals.

In terms of the treatment of immigrants and their children, Nacira Guénif-Souilamas has identified it with a prolongation of colonial logic: "Le parallélisme entre le traitement colonial des colonisés et le traitement des Français d'ascendance coloniale renvoie à la même matrice essentialiste et normative:

elle consiste à ne reconnaître que le semblable et à rejeter la responsabilité des dommages et dénis subis sur ceux qui en sont les victimes, parce qu'ils sont marqués du stigmate d'une différence indélébile" "The parallelism between the colonial treatment of the colonized and the treatment of French of colonial ancestry boils down to the same basic, normative matrix: it consists in only recognizing what is similar and rejection the responsibility for damage and denials experienced by those who were its victims, because they are marked by the stigma of an indelible difference" (2005, 212). We thus note in both Charef's shanty towns and Zouari's Paris a cohabitation that is even more problematic because the various race relations are predefined by a group of predeterminations and configurations resulting from a set of popular images inherited from colonial stereotypes. Charef inscribes the racial relations in his novel at the center of a perpetual tension, as witnessed by the different scenes that allow us to see how the Arab is constructed not only as a permanent danger but as a social misfit.

From the very opening pages of *Le thé au harem d'Archi Ahmed*, with the description of the *cité* as a deathtrap, the author offers a highly instructive scene. The encounter between Madjid and Levesque, who is white, bears witness to the fact that the mere perception of the Others is sufficient: the elevator smells of urine, and Madjid observes that if white people's dogs are used as deterrents against these Maghrebians who urinate in the elevators, for Levesque "c'est les Arabes qui pissent dans l'ascenseur et dégradent le bâtiment" "it is the Arabs who piss in the elevator and destroy the building" (1983, 12). With respect to the troubled cohabitation of races on the one hand and the functional values of dogs in the novel on the other hand, the narrator points out that these whites—owners of German shepherds like Mr. Pelletier—are already poised for provocation, ready to release their dogs to discipline these undesirable "foreigners" who have been installed in a common space through the force of fate and the irony of history: the dog's owner shows off, gloats, and the animal replaces the police and becomes an agent of control and repression. In *Ce pays dont je meurs*, I would say that beyond the relegation already mentioned, the character Amira personifies in every way this fracture between "native" French, as they say, and their compatriots who were born of African immigrants.

Reclusive, anorexic, and nervous, Amira only comes to understand the extent of her depression when after the death of her father, she finds love in the arms of Nicolas, a "vrai français" "true Frenchman," as would be said in the context of the novel. Unfortunately for her, struggling with her Algerian roots in her attempt to do away with the wound, the irony of fate strikes: "Alors que ma sœur n'aspirait qu'à une chose, être française jusqu'à la pointe de ses pieds, son Nicolas n'avait qu'une envie: trouver en elle l'Arabe obéissante, une langoureuse houri qui céderait à ses caprices et comblerait ses fantasmes" "Where my sister aspired to one thing only, being French from top to bottom, her Nicolas had only one desire: finding in her the obedient Arab, a langorous *houri* who yielded to his whims and fulfilled his fantasies" (Zouari 1999, 126). Although a French national, Amira seems to be perceived only under the prism of her origins. Her boyfriend Nicolas's fantasies do not fail to recall the colonial period, which was characterized by what can be called the regulation of prostitution. Borrowing from Christelle Taraud (2003), we can say that just as with the regime of the *indigénat* in the colony, in France too Amira is a victim of a sexual violence that is based on a politics of exception practiced by her French lover who sees her only as "l'arabe obéissante" "the obedient Arab," or better yet, to use Taraud's expression, "la fille soumise" "the submissive girl." This allusion to colonization, just like the comings and goings between France and Algeria in the novels by Charef and Zouari, merit some time for reflection so that we can understand the logic that subtends the continuity of a practice of segregation, from the colonies to the metropole.

To do so, let us return to a detail from *Le thé au harem d'Archi Ahmed* mentioned earlier: the dog and its role in the control and repression of young descendants of immigrants in Charef's novel is interesting for at least two reasons. First, it recalls the role of dogs on slave plantations, as remarkably brought to life by Patrick Chamoiseau in his novel *L'esclave vieil homme et le molosse* (1997) [The old man slave and the mastiff], but second, as a consequence, it suggests a deep analogy with the slum or with the Paris of immigrants, not only in the colonial space, where to discipline and punish was the rule, but likewise in the slave habitation. The origins and modes of operation of that long night of despair and banishment in which immigrants and their children living in transition buildings and slums are submerged, just like their descendants in today's banlieues, have been brilliantly summed up by Achille Mbembe in his study *Sortir de la grande nuit*:

> La scène primordiale de cette brutalité et de cette discrimination a été la *plantation* sous l'esclavage, puis la *colonie* à partir du XIXe siècle. De manière tout à fait directe, le problème que posent le régime de la plantation et le régime colonial est celui de la fonctionnalité de la race comme principe d'exercice du pouvoir et comme règle de sociabilité. Dans le contexte d'aujourd'hui, convoquer la race, c'est appeler à une réflexion à propos du *dissemblable*, de celui ou celle avec qui l'on ne partage rien ou très peu de ceux ou celles qui, tout en étant avec nous, à côté de nous ou parmi nous, ne sont, en dernière analyse, pas des nôtres. Bien avant l'Empire, la *plantation* et la *colonie* constituaient un "ailleurs." Elles participaient du "lointain" et de l'étrangeté—d'un au-delà des mers. Et c'est presque toujours en tant qu'extrêmes limites qu'elles apparaissent dans l'imaginaire métropolitain. Aujourd'hui, la *plantation* et la *colonie* se

sont déplacées et ont planté leurs tentes ici même, hors les murs de la Cité (en banlieue).

> The primordial scene of this brutality and this discrimination was the *plantation* under slavery, then the *colony* beginning in the nineteenth century. In quite a direct way, the problem posed by the regime of the plantation and the colonial regime is that of the functionality of race as a principle for the exercise of power and a rule of sociability. In today's context, to call upon race is to call for a reflection regarding the *dissimilar*, of the one with whom we share nothing or very little, all while they are with us, next to us, or among us, but, in the final analysis are not of us. Well before the Empire, the *plantation* and the *colony* constituted an "elsewhere." They were part of what was "distant" and strange—of a place beyond the seas. And it almost always in extreme limits that they appear in the metropolitan imaginary. Today *plantation* and *colony* have been displaced and they have planted their tents right here, outside the walls of the Cité (in the banlieue). (2010, 94)

It could not be any clearer that not only have the plantation and the colony—or at least the logics that determine their organization and management—been displaced and are now to be found in the hexagon itself. And what is even more interesting is that the dog on the plantation and the dog in Charef's novel seems to have gone from animal to human, while the inhabitants of these impoverished quarters seem to have made, at least from the appearance of the treatment that is reserved for them, the reverse voyage. These urban pariahs of which *Le thé au harem d'Archi Ahmed* and *Ce pays dont je meurs* speak are in reality nothing other than these animals that the Republic keeps muzzled, with their pleas left in silence and simply ignored. In explaining this situation, Mbembe questioned the possibility of characterizing the situation in contemporary France as "Palestinization":

> This treatment and these forms of humiliation, which were once tolerated only in the colonies, are now resurfacing in the metropolis itself, where, during sweeps and raids in the *banlieues,* they are applied not only to aliens—illegal immigrants and refugees—but increasingly to French citizens of African descent or the descendants of former African slaves. In other words, a conflation is occurring between colonial modes of control, treatment, and segregation, the treatment in metropolitan France of men and women judged undesirable, and the treatment of citizens considered to be second-class simply because they are not "French of pure stock" or "of white race." (2009, 51–52)

In other words, as long as France is not seen as maintaining colonies on its territory, the paradigm of Palestinization indeed can remain pertinent and worthy of clarification. In fact, it is important to underscore that the riots of Fall 2005, in their own way and one decidedly more decisive than the "March of the Beurs" in 1983, reveal a war of representation about France's past and present.

The major problematic arising from this clash of ideas is in fact to know whether the reference to imperial heritage is valid to interpret, understand, and explain the racial discrimination that victimizes young immigrants and French of immigrant origin, such as those in the fiction of Charef and Zouari. As remarkably demonstrated by Florence Bernault (2009), the colonial paradigm has been the object of disagreement among historians of contemporary France. As Bernault emphasizes, though confronted by some of her colleagues who believed that there had to be a stop in using the alibi of race and even rehabilitating French colonialism in the spirit of the law of February 23, 2005, discussed earlier, thus refuting any significance of the use of the colonial model as an analytical framework, there were nevertheless those—beginning with the publication by Nicolas Bancel, Pascal Blanchard, and others, of *La fracture coloniale* (2005) and *Zoos humains* (2002)—who did point to the need to subject history as a discipline to a serious reckoning of France's colonial past. Bernault clearly shows in her article how the tension resulting from these two positions helped create the sometimes amnesiac or apologetic discourse on colonial violence. She evokes by turn the position of the French government, which was to encourage, if not oblige historians to revisit, or even to revise France's colonial past to validate its grandeur; the position of the young feminist militant Houria Bouteldja and her "Appel des Indigènes de la République" "Call to Indigenes of the Republic"; and the outlooks of thinkers such as Pierre Tevanian, Saïd Bouamama, Jean-Loup Amselle, and Achille Mbembe, to cite only those, from which she draws a pertinent conclusion for the analysis that I am proposing in this chapter.

While for Bernault there is a need for an accounting of the colonial syndrome as a means to explore and understand the precarity of Afro-descendants in contemporary France, it must also be said that the novels of Charef et Zouari are no exception. If the allusions to Africa in *Le thé au harem d'Archi Ahmed* are quite subtly made in the often-nostalgic comparison between the country of origin and the host country, or in the emphasis on stereotypes inherited from colonization and whose trappings are Arabic and black, they are very explicit in *Ce pays dont je meurs*. A long passage from Fawzia Zouari's novel deserves to be presented here:

> Donc, nous n'étions plus à l'école de maman, censée diffuser les enseignements par magie, mais à celle, fanfaronne, de la République. Nous y apprenions tout, sauf le monde arabe. Nous y entendions les récits les plus extraordinaires, à l'exception du passé de nos parents et de l'histoire de notre pays. Des guerriers

harnachés, il y en avait bien s<u>û</u>r, mais autres que ceux qui ornaient le salon de grand père Lazrag. Il y avait les héros de Zola et Flaubert que nous pouvions aimer sans prétendre nous identifier à eux. Il y avait la beauté des sites et des monuments français qu'il convenait de louer, tout en reconnaissant qu'ils ne nous appartenaient pas. Nous entrevoyions les perspectives les plus folles, hormis notre avenir d'enfants d'immigrés. Nous égrenions les prouesses technologiques de la France, ses grands progrès industriels et son économie fleurissante d'après-guerre, sans mentionner l'immigration massive qui en assurait la prospérité.

Thus, we were no longer schooled by Mother, handing out assignments magically, but by the swaggering Republic. We learned everything there, except Arabic. We heard the most extraordinary stories, with the exception of our parents' past and our country's history. Sure, there were warriors in armor, but different from those that hung in the living room of Grandpa Lazreg. There were the heroes of Zola and Flaubert that we could love without claiming to identify with them. There was the beauty of French places and monuments that were worthy of praise, all while recognizing that they didn't belong to us. We glimpsed the wildest prospects, apart from our childhood as immigrants. We were permeated with France's technological prowesses, its great industrial progress, and its flourishing postwar economy, without any mention of the massive immigration that assured that prosperity. (85)

The above passage highlights the mechanisms for the erasure of history and thus of France's colonial memory, and at the same time, the malaise created by a school of thought that stood out by its lack of a common history for France and its colonies. The awareness by immigrants and their descendants that their history has gone silent even as they are endlessly faced with references to their origins, just like the silence on the contributions of African immigrants to the history of France, in fact, is the recipe for an explosive cocktail. The consequence of such a state of affairs, as Benjamin Stora recently warned, will be the rise to power of a "besoin d'histoire" "need for history" (Stora 2007). Caught in the trap that François Dubet called "la galère" "the galley," and subjected to public construction of their invisibility, which is even more paradoxical because they are precisely a visible minority, the youths described in the Charef's and Zouari's novels are forced to invent strategies for survival while awaiting recognition by a system to which they belong in their own right, but which constantly humiliates and penalizes them. These young characters in the novels in many ways resemble the unorganized, excluded, rage-filled youths described by Dubet in *La galère*: "Ils sont peu intégrés, ils se sentent exclus et ils sont enragés parce que la domination subie n'a pas de sens" "They are unintegrated, they feel excluded and they are enraged because the domination that they experience makes no sense" (1987, 95). The exclusions that in fact victimize Madjid, Amira, and Nacéra push them to protect themselves from a hostile outside world and at the same time place them in a situation of marginality that, Dubet says, "désigne l'action par laquelle des acteurs à la fois exclus et désorganisés créent une sociabilité plus ou moins volontairement isolée qui leur permet de survivre et de se protéger" "designates the action by which the actors, both excluded and disorganized, create a more or less voluntarily isolated sociability that allows them to survive and protect themselves" (1987, 100). These observations by sociologists then make the outbreaks of violence, drugs, and delinquency in *Le thé au harem d'Archi Ahmed* more intelligible, just as they shed light on the suicide chosen by the young girls at the center of *Ce pays dont je meurs*.

French society in the novels therefore appears as a kind of jungle inside of which only the strongest will survive and succeed. The poetics of despair in Charef and Zouari calls to an ethics of survival. And that explains the propensity of the young people in these two works for delinquency and sex. For deep down, these young people are asking for nothing more than the right to exist. The formulation of the right to exist that I am using here is taken from Lydie Moudileno, who in a remarkable article returns to Jean-Paul Sartre's *La Nausée* (1938) to hold it up as a mirror to Lucio Mad's *Les trafiqueurs* (1995) to illustrate that the Sartrean preface to *La Nausée* is largely derived from stereotyping. Thus, for Moudileno, the Sartrean preface

> se met en place un discours par lequel l'existentiel, en tant qu'angoisse et spéculation à partir de cette angoisse, relève d'une conscience strictement occidentale. Par contraste, l'être-dans-le-monde du noir, c'est sa négritude, qui relève, elle, de l'Être et d'un rapport non problématisé au réel. Parce qu'ils sont par essence, culture, race ou autre, en dehors, les Nègres de Sartre constituent, si ce n'est une autre espèce, en tout cas des exceptions à la problématique existentielle. Comme les morts, comme les personnages du roman, comme aussi cet insecte que Roquentin écrase entre ses doigts [dans *La Nausée* (1938)], "ils se sont lavés," selon Sartre, du "péché d'exister."

lays out a discourse the existential, as well as anguish and speculation from this anguish, comes under a strictly Western consciousness. By contrast, for the being-in-the-black-world, his negritude is part of Being and of a nonproblematized relationship with the real. Because they are by essence, culture, race, or something else, something outside, Sartre's Blacks constitute, if not another species, at least exceptions to the existential problematic. Like the death, like the characters in the novel, and just like that insect that Roquentin crushes in his fingers [in *La Nausée*, 1938], "they have been cleansed," according to Sartre, of the "sin of existing." (Moudileno 2002, 86)

The notion of pleading for the right to exist, in my opinion, sums up the novels by Charef and Zouari and is set as a counterpoint to the permanence of despair and oblivion. The two novels are structured around the promotion of the idea that there are human categories that share in what is common: that is, those who are visible, who have a right to speak, and on the other hand, the mutes, whose visibility and right to speak are challenged. Consequently, we are given every indication in these novels that the most profound aspiration of French immigrant youths is to exist, to no longer be invisible, mute, silenced.

On the whole, then, what is problematic and heuristic in the cartography of misery displayed in these novels, is less the physical characteristics of the spaces of these immigrants and the axiological values attached to them by the narrators, than the stigmatization of these immigrants who become undesirables, recluses, in short, *sans-parts*, whose only worth is in the productive capacity of their bodies. These immigrants are aware of the injustice that strikes them, that surrounds them, and they deplore their living conditions. Two conclusions stand out. The first conclusion: In Charef's and Zouari's novels, the body of the immigrant becomes a quintessential "corps d'exception" "body of exception," an alterity on the inside, similar to the body of the colonized which Mohammed Sidi Barkat presents as a body without reason, thought to be dangerous, included in the social body as someone excluded, a victim of the suspension of the principle of equality (2005). We are therefore confronting a reduction of the immigrant body to its mere biological function, with the immigrant body being both necessary for the production of capital as well as paradoxically being able to be put to death without ever being able to staking a claim to having rights. The repressive society with which these African immigrants are confronted resorts to a stigmatization of descendants of Africa that is based on their bodies, and more specifically on the color of their skin.

The repressive and segregationist society in question here is also what Guénif-Souilamas has called the "gouvernement des corps" "government of bodies," with the bodies of the descendants of North African immigrants in France constituting veritable "objet[s] d'un investissement fantasmatique qui renoue avec l'aliénation et la soumission imposés à leurs grands-parents ou leurs arrière-grands-parents" "object[s] of a fantastical investment that is tied to alienation and the submision that was imposed on their grandparents or great-grandparents" (2005, 204). We can then easily understand the conditions where the socially disqualified youths of the French *cités*, like those in *Le thé au harem d'Archi Ahmed* and *Ce pays dont je meurs*, continue to oscillate between visibility and invisibility, muteness and silences, and whose poetics of despair swing endlessly between Eros and Thanatos, between the omnipresent pleasures of sex seen in these novels, along with their corollaries (alcohol, prostitution, theft), and the death that results from security measures preaching repression, or suicide, a recourse for immigrants or citizens traumatized by stigmatization, or the self-destructive violence in which France's young people find themselves, cornered between hope and imprisonment. Second conclusion: The hatred of foreigners, their banishment, their stigmatization, and ultimately their social disqualification, beyond making these immigrants "urban pariahs," brings the question of globalization back to the center of the debate and causes us to question whether today's globalization respects the right to circulate and the right to exist.

We have seen, at any rate, that the North African immigrant—invited to France and immediately labeled undesirable, where his body is subject to exertion without any retribution, the immigrant worker who literally becomes the figure of the new slave—is banished from society, that is, both from the interior and the exterior. This immigrant is already dead in his lifetime; for he is put to death even before being judged, and in a certain measure, because of his African origins, he is declared dead even before he is born. From this perspective, the subterfuges of the colonial authorities are played out in the metropole in the postcolonial period, and the immigrant becomes the obsession of a French society that appears to immunize and protect itself quite carefully against plague and leprosy, to borrow from Michel Foucault's thoughts on biopolitics. To face this state of affairs, so that finally the inclusion of the immigrant and the immigrant's heirs might be possible in full French citizenship, a complete reinvention of today's politics is necessary, according to Étienne Balibar, who calls for us to

> trouver par l'expérience les *lieux de la fiction* et selon qui, le statut des étrangers dans la "nation" ou la représentation de la différence entre nationaux et étrangers—une telle abolition ne serait pas seulement la fin des différences qui font la civilisation, elle priverait de sens la notion essentielle d'hospitalité—mais qu'il s'agit de faire passer d'une fonction de discrimination à une fonction de réciprocité, et d'ouverture locale sur les solidarités et les conflits de l'espace global.

> find through experience the loci of fiction and according to which the status of foreigners in the "nation" or the representation of difference among nationals and foreigners—such an abolition would not only be the end of differences that create civilization, they would take away the meaning of the basic notion of hospitality—but it would mean going from a function of discrimination to a function of reciprocity, and a local opening up to the solidarities and conflicts of the global space. (2002, 15)

To change the status of the foreigner from a function of discrimination to a function of reciprocity, to respect the law so that there is no more "humanitarian reason," to restore to immigrants their status as human beings with access to citizenship and the right to exist—these seem to me to be the implicit objectives of the requiem for these immigrants who are remarkably fictionalized by Mehdi Charef and Fawzia Zouari.

NOTES

1. Recall, for example, the clever political and media distortion of the march through association with SOS-Racism.

2. See Charles Tshimanga, Didier Gondola, and Peter J. Bloom (eds) *Frenchness and the African Diaspora*, Bloomington: Indiana University Press, 2009; Hervé Tchumkam, *State Power, Stigmatization and Youth Resistance Cultures in the French Banlieues: Uncanny Citizenship*, Lanham: Lexington Books, 2015.

3. A recent illustration is the Law of February 23, 2005, which aimed to celebrate the accomplishments of colonization and revive imperial glory, both as a duty for the nation and as a normative orientation for academic researchers.

4. The migrants that were expected to return do not include the harkis who are part of this history, however, marked by the stigma of the war. For further discussion of the plight of the harkis, see Vincent Crapanzano, *The Harkis: The Wound that Never Heals*, Chicago: University of Chicago Press, 2011.

5. See, for example, Gilles Kepel, *Banlieues de l'Islam*, Paris, Seuil, 1987.

Chapter 3

Women Body, Pathological Body

THE FEMALE BODY AS PATHOLOGICAL BODY: DISQUALIFICATION AND BIOPOLITICS IN *LA JEUNE FILLE ET LA MERE*

The question of women's writing or of the representation of the woman is a persistent preoccupation of the African imaginary. Sometimes presented as an object or a silent player in history, sometimes as a character deconstructing hierarchy and accepted social standards, woman, for the most part, remains this singular figure around whom the fiction is deflected, for better or for worse. Unlike Odile Cazenave (1996) who theorizes that it is with women writers that woman truly begins to invade the world of francophone fiction in Africa, I would suggest instead that with texts like *Les bouts de bois de Dieu* (1960) by Ousmane Sembene, the female subject was already a salient feature in fiction. Of course, the matter of Penda, the leader of the railway workers' strike in that novel, being a prostitute and paradoxically the one whose courage permits the aggressive resistance to the colonial order is highly suggestive in that she represents an atypical figure. That paradoxical position of the female subject is moreover even more emphasized in novels from the Maghreb, likely because of the region's anthropological repertory and the difficulty that is sometimes experienced by departing from certain religious and traditional values. It is precisely the core of these tensions between traditional values and the will and ambitions of the female subject that is taken up in Leïla Marouane's *La jeune fille et la mère*.

Published in 2005, this short but difficult novel is a fictionalization of two parallel but similar destinies, those of a mother and her daughter. In this work, Leïla Marouane recounts, with an often-disconcerting realism linked to hypotyposis and detailed descriptions, the misadventures of Djamila, the daughter of a modest family in the south of Algeria, struggling with herself and society, including her family—because she has dared to explore her sexuality, the point of departure for the events that lead to the conflict that will witness the emergence of the rebel's fate. But beyond a reflection upon woman's condition, I will also show that Marouane's *La jeune fille et la mère* is a novel for which we can say that, ultimately, the fate of the woman is an effective pretext for showcasing the fate of Algeria as a whole up as faced with the destructive forces of the infernal spiraling of the (post)colony. First, I will show how the representation of woman in Marouane's novel forms part of an interrogation of what I call the empire of subalternity and biopower. Then, I will attempt to show that the transgressions made by the woman in the novel are hugely based on the elements of Algeria's colonial past and the nationalist struggles that the country has experienced.

The Empire of Subalternity and Control of the Female Body

La jeune fille et la mère by Leïla Marouane recounts the tribulations of a mother and her daughter, both caught in the snare of patriarchy. As a victim of colonial violence, the mother makes it her mission to ensure that her daughter has a different fate, in short, that the daughter achieves a freedom of which she, the mother, has been deprived. From this perspective, the novel can be taken as a writing on the female condition. Still, it goes beyond questioning male domination: the novel opens up a space of remembrance through analepses, and these narrative anachronisms enlighten the reader about women's contributions to the liberation of Algeria. Thus, to the problematic of the status of women is added the status of Algeria as a whole in face of the embodiments of colonization: despoliation, violence, denial of humanity.

By analyzing the modalities of female representation by way of the concept of biopower, this section aims to demonstrate that the female body in the circumstances presented in Marouane's novel is a mirror of the national condition faced in the burdens of colonization. In *Black Body: Women, Colonialism and Space*, Radhika Mohanram already signaled that "there is a metonymic link between the veil, Algerian women and Algeria itself, in that the colonization of Algeria is equated with the unveiling of its women" (1999, 73). Likewise, in *Transfigurations of the Maghreb: Feminism, Decolonization and Literatures*, Winnifred Woodhull argues that "the cultural record makes clear that women embody Algeria not only for Algerians in the days since independence but also for the French colonizers who conquer them militarily, control them administratively, study them as sociologists, ethnographers, and historians, and represent them in both high and popular forms of art and literature. In the colonialist fantasy, to possess Algeria's women is to possess Algeria" (1993, 16). Building on Mohanram and Woodhull, I will show that the female body in Marouane's novel functions as a metaphor for the national body, thus giving the fiction a triple function: as a site for symbolic mediations, a novel of female revolt, and a writing of Algerian memory. According to Valérie Orlando, the francophone Maghrebian novel is a powerful repertory of the struggles and representations of the North African woman. As we see in her study, not only does the novel of women in the Maghreb serve as the site of vindication for the call to justice, but it also ensures, in a way, a position of individuation, with the story of a single woman serving for similar stories of hundreds of other women. Orlando's observation presented below will provide the starting point for my own reflection:

> Through their narratives Maghrebian Francophone authors such as Leila Sebbar and Assia Djebar have sought to analyze the shortcomings of the complex social and political arena of the Maghrebian woman. Negotiation between social, racial and gender spheres are a constant battle for the Maghrebian woman, whether she lives in exile or in her home country. It is through writing that these authors study their own history as well as that of hundreds of women who have no voice or sociopolitical recourse in their respective societies. (1995, 15)

As we can see, there is no Maghrebian female literature that is not a militant literature, whether the author is in exile or in the native land. This perceptive finding is especially valid in understanding Marouane's *La jeune fille et la mère* because in itself the title, as a paratextual element, invites the reader to easily comprehend the topic of the text. In fact, with this title, Marouane positions herself alongside writers whose works serve as hallmarks of a titrology that privileges objects, like the great figures of Maghrebian literature such as Driss Chraïbi (*Les boucs*, 1955), Assia Djebar (*Les alouettes naïves*, 1967), and Rachid Boudjedra (*L'escargot entêté*, 1977). As such, the syntagm "la jeune fille et la mère" suggests a similarity either by trait or fate, an analogy made clear here by the use of the coordinate conjunction "and," which has an additive value for two elements of the same kind or same function.

In Marouane's novel, beyond being of same kind or having the same function, the girl and the mother clearly share in the same troubles, which are uniform in their nature but varying in terms of their deployment, as well as their motivations. It is the marginal condition of the female such as it appears in the fictional world that leads the Algerian novelist to take up her pen. With manifestations of the objectification of women being so often given the shape of an inventory of moments of subalternity, I will proceed in a different fashion, by showing instead how space, religion, and biopower (control of bodies or power wielded over the body) participate in this novel dealing with the exclusion of the female character. The work in fact opens with the narrator being shocked at the appearance of her father as she is making love in a public garden with the village cabinet-maker, and a bit like a detective charged with unraveling a mystery, she imagines the reasons for her father's presence in this location since it was "ni son chemin habituel ni son lieu de prédilection" "neither his usual path nor his preferred location" (11). As her thoughts swirl in her mind, the narrator admits that because of the powers invested in her father by men and religion, the reasons for his presence in this public garden at that precise moment, whatever they may be, change nothing in his fate. It is also true, as Beïda Chikhi says, that "le religieux est à l'heure actuelle ce par quoi l'homme s'exprime le plus énergiquement" "the religious is at the present time the way that humans express themselves most forcefully" (1996, 217), and Marouane significantly inserts the religious factor within the very opening of her novel. Thus, we learn through the voice of Djamila, the narrator, that the circumstances of her father's shocking discovery of her "ne changerait en rien sa décision de se débarrasser [d'elle] au plus vite, plus vite qu'il ne l'avait lui-même prévu, et de la façon la plus légale qui soit. Devant Allah et devant les hommes" "would change nothing in his decision to get rid of her as quickly as possible, faster than he himself had ever foreseen, and in the most legal way. Before Allah and before men" (11).

From its very opening lines, then, the novel thus posits in a striking way that it is not so much religion that is the problem, as such, but the manner by which it is interpreted by men to perpetuate patriarchy and to keep women in submission. With regard to the interpretation of religion and its application to a problematical distribution of time and space, of the spoken word and silence, the narrator informs the reader that her father, as a male, had a concubine, without that being the slightest problem at all. In other words, women's submission in society is presented in the text as based on a very male, arbitrary manner in the application of sacred texts, which results in the position of the father of the family as the "Envoyé" "Envoy" of God on earth (29), as Djamila puts it.

Already at this stage, there is a clear relationship established between the religious and the political, around the idea of the "partage du sensible" "distribution of the sensible" theorized by Jacques Rancière. For him, the idea of the "distribution of the sensible" comes down to "a delimitation of spaces and times, of the visible and the invisible, of speech and silences, that simultaneously determines the place and the stakes as a form of experience". "Politics," Rancière adds, "revolves around what is seen and what can be said about it, around who has the ability to see and the talent to speak, around the properties of spaces and the possibilities of time" (2004, 13). Seen from Rancière's perspective, it is clear that the fictionalized space is a gendered space inasmuch as if men are situated next to visibility and the spoken word, women on the other hand are reduced to an invisibility accompanied by silence. But in returning to Chikhi's observation cited above, it is important to point out that religion is but a pretext used to predetermine the places occupied by the different sexes on the social ladder. As Fatima Mernissi observed in *Women and Islam*:

> If women's rights are a problem for some modern Muslim men, it is neither because of the Koran nor the prophet, not the Islamic tradition, but simply because those rights conflict with the interests of the male elite. The elite faction is trying to convince us that their egotistic, highly subjective and mediocre view of culture and society has a sacred basis. (qtd in Smail Salhi 2003, 31)

We can see that men thus manipulate sacred texts by giving them a wholly personal interpretation, to maintain their secure ascendancy over women, a domination that goes to the point of controlling their sexuality. The following passage in the novel is quite revealing about this ascendancy: "Comme l'exigeait la coutume, et ma future belle famille, il me fallait un certificat de virginité, délivré en trois exemplaires par un gynécologue 'assermenté'" "As demanded by custom, and my future in-laws, I needed a certificate of virginity, provided in three copies from a duly certified gynecologist" (2005, 125).

The regulation of female sexuality that is evidenced by the mention of a certificate of virginity attests to what Fatima Mernissi understood as the socialization of sexual intercourse. She writes: "Islam socializes sexual intercourse through the institution of marriage within the framework of the family. The only legitimate sexual intercourse is between married people." (1987, 59). Having had sexual intercourse outside of marriage, Djamila is therefore guilty of transgression in the eyes of her father. This situation that gives men absolute power while condemning women to obedience and submission perhaps finds its most radical expression in the power of repudiation enjoyed by men. In any case, the narrator's mother will be repudiated by the father after his discovery of his daughter engaged in the act of sex. Woman's virginity henceforward becomes the condition of honor and even of the presence of the mother in the conjugal household. In fact, the repudiated wife is systematically condemned to a fate of wandering, as it is well understood that even her family would no longer want anything to do with her, as we find with the mother of the narrator of *La jeune fille et la mère*. Repudiated and thus persona non grata, she returns to a hellish life, given that she had previously married the narrator's father against her will and in the absence of any desire as well. This deplorable female situation is as much a part of the youth of the mother of Djamila, the narrator, as it is in the life of her daughter. Choosing to narrate retrospectively, Marouane returns to the mother's past, where we learn that as a fifteen-year-old minor, she had narrowly escaped rape by the colonial soldiery, being stripped naked in front of her own father who himself had been heavily beaten and tortured. Except that, because of religion, marriage is impossible between her as a Muslim and the French officer who had saved her from the rape, and to whom her father had promised her, the father tried to marry her off forcefully to the family farmhand before she could escape. Her mother, that woman who was so determined to acquire knowledge, would thus see herself now reduced to a life of wandering that would take her from the marriage of which the daughter gives the rawest possible account.

For the mother who is "effrénée dans son élan de s'affranchir des maîtres comme elle les désignait avec ironie" "frantic in her desire to free herself from masters, as she had ironically called them," marriage is basically nothing other than "une histoire de sexe" "about sex" (23), and according to her daughter, the mother's fate can be summed up as "une alternance de grossesses, de fausses couches, de coïts forcés, de répudiations et de taches ménagères. Une vie débilitante à souhait" "alternating between pregnancies, miscarriages, forced sex, repudiation, and household chores" (13). In terms of female status, we can readily understand that it derives from an antagonism between men and women, where the woman would be happy to be a simple sounding board for male desire, not just simply "un dépôt de spermatozoïdes, un nid à avortons" "a repository for sperm, a nest for little runts" (24), to use Djamila's mother's words.

More instructive for understanding the modalities of female representation in *La jeune fille et la mère* is the manner in which patriarchy, and by extension society, organizes control over the female body, which is paradoxically sacralized and desacralized. I am speaking here of "desacralization" rather than "profanation" because, as I will show later, profanation in this text and the philosophical interpretation I give it are rather a liberating of the female subject, so to speak. Returning to the subject of control over the female body and the mechanisms employed for a biopoliticization of the female body, the novel can be said to be brimming with scenes that are sufficiently evocative of the way women are controlled, with their bodies becoming pure objects given over to control, caprices, and abuses by fathers and husband. The fictional space for the female sex, by definition a prison, is thereby essentially dysphoric, and progressively becomes a kind of camp inside which the bodies of prisoners or detainees are marked. The gender of the Other is so marked in *La jeune fille et la mère* that we agree with Michel Bozon in saying that "la sexualité de l'autre est souvent utilisée dans la construction des stéréotypes . . . qui disent à leurs manières les rapports qui existent entre les peuples, en même temps que les rêves ou les hantises d'une époque" "the sexuality of the other is often used in the construction of stereotypes . . . which speak in their own ways of the relationships that exist between peoples, as well as an era's dreams and obsessions" (2002, 85). In Marouane's imaginary, in fact, the female body clearly appears to be left to the disposition not only of male subjects but also of the agents of the colonial order, the colonial soldiers. The colonization of North Africa, beyond the spoliation of its resources, constructed entire populations as objects of the will and desire of the colonial master, and doubly so the women. As Christelle Taraud shows in *La prostitution coloniale*, Maghrebian women of that period passed from male domination to colonial domination, with one of the first "inventions" of the French Army in Algeria being its regulation of prostitution, thus delivering North African women to all the abuses and fantasies of the French military. French soldiers in North Africa appropriated in effect "le droit du coït" "the right to sex," which Taraud defines as "le produit d'un discours de domination, de restructuration et d'autorité sur l'Afrique du Nord" "the product of a discourse of domination, restructuration, and authority over North Africa" (2003, 317). Hence, we understand that the female North African body became a privileged site for the exercise of male power, and colonial power. As Frantz Fanon argues through a discussion of the veil in his essay *A Dying Colonialism*, possessing an Algerian woman meant possessing Algeria itself, to which one might add that penetrating the Algerian woman equated penetrating and dominating the land itself. Accordingly, Fanon enounces the political doctrine defined by the colonial administration: "If we want to destroy the structure of Algerian society, its capacity for resistance, we murst first of all conquer the women; we must go and find them behind the veil where they hide themselves and in the houses where the men keep them out of sight" (1965, 37–38)

Furthermore, the invocation of the veil in the novel is indicative in this regard, and the veil in the passage cited below assumes a paradoxical function in that while it is meant to hide the female body, here it could certainly serve as a weapon of combat. To show this aspect, it will suffice to spend a bit of time on the words of Djamila's grandmother to her mother: "Tu t'y habitueras, lui disait alors sa mère. Si bien que l'idée de traverser la ville sans le voile te semblera un cauchemar, et tu verras bientôt combien c'est agréable et confortable de voir sans être vue" "You'll get used to it, her mother then said. So much so that the idea of crossing through city without a veil will seem like a nightmare to you, and you will soon see that it is preferable and comfortable to see without being seen" (2005, 15). In the same way, the father's decision to deprive the girl of her jewels, cut her hair, or even cover her with blows, is all an effective part of this exercise of paternal or marital power that makes the body the receptacle of the most extreme desires and the most extreme frustrations. Even worse is the inspection of the girl's vagina after her father surprises her having sex in the garden. The minute, detailed narration of the trip made by Djamila and her father in the middle of the night to the home of the old woman so that this would-be gynecologist can verify the young woman's virginity is gripping.

In presenting this scene, and several others, such as attacks by a group of old women who drag Djamila from her life into a forced marriage, Marouane achieves a tour de force that must be emphasized, that is, the introduction of a noteworthy nuance, namely, that the subalternization of women in Algerian society is not uniquely and systematically an act by men. Even considering the distinct functionality of Djamila's brothers, we must admit that unlike in the many clichés, there are men in Maghrebian society who are eager for women's liberation, in other words, men who oppose in different ways the torturers of women. Moreover, the narrator's mother, herself carried away by the permanence of current practices, was particularly insistent that her daughter remain a virgin, even though she never used the word "virginity": "You lose it (she never said the word), you lose it, and that's the end of us, it's the end of everything, you lose it and your father throws us out into the desert, you lose it and your brothers and sisters will be orphans left to the mercy of vampires. You lose it, and I'll cut your throat" (40). Beyond invectives and imprecations, the mother, just like the old woman of the slums I just mentioned, succumbs to the systematic control of her daughter's vagina, and her daughter's refusal was all her mother needed to erupt in anger: "Mais s'il arrivait que je veuille me dérober à l'inspection du fond de mon vagin, qu'elle auscultait munie d'une loupiote à piles, à la recherche de la fameuse membrane pratique qui m'humiliait, qui me mortifiait . . . ma mère hurlait, se déchirait les joues, s'arrachait les cheveux par touffes, prenant Dieu, ses prophètes et les saints de la terre à témoin" "But if I wanted to escape from the deep inspection of my vagina, for her to examine me with the aid of a battery-operated light, in search of the infamous practical membrane that humiliated me, that mortified me . . . my mother howled, tore at her cheeks, pulled out clumps of her hair, calling upon God, his prophets and earthly saints as her witnesses" (41). In a word, we could say that through Marouane's pen, the female, even more than the male, becomes a fierce and dogged guardian of the temple and traditions that devalorize women. Seen from this perspective, Marouane can be considered a female writer who contributes to the project of "recasting postcolonialism," a theoretical and analytical pedagogy that Anne Donadey beautifully circumscribed in her essay, *Recasting Postcolonialism* (1991). The disciplining of the young girl's body leads to a permanent traumatism for the young girl, because, reduced to her body, she is a victim of self-hatred: "Je ne savais alors que faire de mon corps ainsi exposé, ni comment détourner le regard de mon procréateur de ma nudité, un regard dont je n'ai pas saisi l'expression, qui allait s'ancrer telle une écharde dans ma mémoire, me donnant toutes les peines du monde pour l'en déloger" "I didn't know what to do with my body exposed in such a way, then, nor how to turn away the gaze of my procreator away from my nudity, a look whose expression I couldn't grasp, but which was going to be anchored like a splinter in my memory, giving me all kinds of torment in order to dislodge it" (26). This reduction of the female person to her body, or better, to naked life, whether by the colonial society or the defenders of tradition, sets the female at the center of a paradox in which the aporia that results is challenging. It assures the perpetuation of the family and watches over the household tasks, but its function of procreating or giving life positions it under the seal of authority, of giving death that society applies to it with no recourse to appeal and in whatever manner it likes.

The idea of the camp is therefore posited as the consummate matrix of space in which women, including the daughter and mother, evolve—a biopolitics par excellence. The strategies of both the patriarchy and the colonial power toward women thus can be seen as measures of enclosure and control, and that are also a ban on women. So much so that we can draw from the thought of Judith Revel about French suburbs and apply it to the space in Marouane's novel. Indeed, in analyzing what she considers "la vie en milieu précaire" "life in a precarious environment" in the French suburbs, Revel takes up a reading given by the Italian philosopher Giorgio Agamben, and offers her thesis that "dans les banlieues françaises, la métropole est devenue l'espace où s'appliquent désormais en même temps les deux grands paradigmes historiques de gestion des hommes décrits par Foucault, celui de la lèpre, et celui de la peste" "in the French suburbs, the metropole has become the space for the occurrence of the two great historical paradigms for human management described by Foucault, that of leprosy and that of the plague" (2007). In fact, the analogy between French suburbs and Algeria given by Marouane is excellent, for in either situation, it is a question of bare life. Leprosy and the plague seem to be the pathology—in every sense of the word—that characterizes the young girl and her mother who are victims of biopolitics and evolve within a prison that takes on the appearance of a camp. Now just as Agamben wrote, "Inasmuch as its inhabitants have been stripped of every political status and reduced completely to naked life, the camp is also the most absolute biopolitical space that has ever been realized—a space in which power confronts nothing other than pure biological life without any mediation" (2000, 40.1). The question of biopower and its corollary of the reduction of the female to an object will, however, will be answered in the pages of *La jeune fille et la mère*. As we shall now see, Marouane articulates female liberation in the liberation of Algeria's national territory from the grips of colonial forces.

(Post)colonial Order and Female Transgression

In *La jeune fille et la mère*, the similarity between the trajectories of women and the country is striking. Everything occurs as if the woman is a metaphor for the nation, with the fate of one bearing a strange resemblance to the other.

For a novel that is unburdened by stylistic procedures and rhetorical figures, we can almost say that Marouane's fiction rests entirely upon a metonymy. In admitting that the target of the colonial invasion was the colonization of the country being colonized, we understand that behind the focus on the female figure, a reflection upon a national space indeed stands out. Just like the women in the novel, the Algerian territory experienced rape and subjugation. Furthermore, the colonial prostitution I spoke about earlier corresponds in the clearest of ways to that common fate shared by women and their country. That the unruly soldiers whose malicious mission is to force the national space into submission to the diktat of a metropole take charge of the organization, indeed the institutionalization of prostitution, reveals that colonization was not only a control of lands and resources but also a dehumanization of humans, and most particularly of women who came into a political economy of consumption, just as I demonstrated earlier concerning biopower and control over female bodies. Thanks to the intrusion, or rather to the return to the mother's story in the tale of Djamila's tribulations, Marouane underscores the question of Algeria's liberation, the problematic of freeing the national body from colonial guardianship, so to speak. It is also very important to remember that this is the same mother who was destroying her body.

The novel informs the reader that women made an effective contribution to anticolonial resistance. I have already mentioned the scene of the attempted rape of the narrator's grandmother by French soldiers, a scene in which the violence inflicted by the French military is analogous to that, cruel and deadly, which the French army deployed in attempts to crush the Algerian rebels during the war of liberation. In fact, the madness into which Djamila's mother descends, has roots going back to her childhood, when Algeria was under full occupation. I have also said that this madness pushes the mother to a violence that will victimize her daughter. Basically, the mother's obsession is to guarantee for her daughter a future that she herself had dreamed of and that will vanish before the reality of facts, and that explains the variety of strategies she employs, ranging from verbal sparring to the use of force and the simulation of madness: "Ma mère avait tenu à ce que mon destin soit celui d'une femme libre. Elle me voulait instruite, ma mère, elle y croyait dur comme fer, à mon avenir d'érudite, elle se persuadait que j'irais loin, à l'université et au delà, sur la lune, ou sous les mers, là où, la tête haute, je ne serais à la merci de personne" "My mother was determined that my fate would be that of a free woman. She wanted me educated, she had an unfailing belief in that, she persuaded herself that I would go far, to university and beyond, on the moon, under the seas, where, with my head held high, I would be at no one's mercy" (12). The phrase "à l'université et au delà, sur la lune, ou sous les mers, là où, la tête haute, je ne serais à la merci de personne" can be interpreted as a poetic rendition of hyperbole, in the sense that the expressions parallel the violence expressed earlier. This mother who fights for a better future for her daughter is in fact nothing other than a former combatant engaged in the struggle for her country's independence. The parallel between the national body and the female body is all the more striking when we discover that without training, without prior military training, even if it is only in fiction, Djamila's mother "était prête à mourir pour la souveraineté de son pays, et sa propre liberté, [et devient] du jour au lendemain l'agent de liaison le plus couru de la région" "was ready to die for her country's sovereignty, its own freedom, and overnight became the foremost liaison officer in the region" (16). The identification, or rather confusion, between the female body and the country is even more significant because "tout comme ce pays, j'ai besoin, moi, de vivre sans chaînes et sans camisole, j'ai besoin d'air et de liberté" "just like this country, I myself needed to live without chains and without a strait jacket, I needed air and freedom" (16), as the narrator's mother exclaims. This all takes place as if the national consciousness motivates, or provokes, female awareness of the self and her status, or vice versa.[1] This parallel between the woman's body and the land is reminiscent of Anne Donadey's discussion of Edward Said's *Orientalism* and the sexual metaphor. Donadey writes: "Said used sexual metaphors to insist on the link between sexuality and the power of colonial conquest. . . . Taking the land and taking the women become two parallel activities intimately connected in the male colonizer's psyche" (1991, 105). More recently, Natalya Vince has rendered the same parallel through the expression "embodying the nation" as she reflects on the relation between Women, walls and the boundaries of the nation. In any case, it is what makes Djamila's mother's trajectory stand out, since she fled a forced marriage with the help of other women on their family farm and saw herself taken in by rebels who organized in secrecy and lived in the maquis. Let us note two things before moving forward. The first is this solidarity among women who have always been part of the resistance against any invasions, and the second is the breakdown of the barrier between men and women in the face of colonial invasion. That is exemplified by the fact that in times of conflict, "les hommes . . . s'aperçurent de l'existence des femmes, de leur bravoure surtout, et entreprirent de les recruter. Le père le plus récalcitrant ne pouvait alors s'opposer à la requête des héros" "men became aware of women's existence, especially of their bravery, and took to recruiting them. The most recalcitrant father could not then oppose a request from heroes" (16). And it is likely in recalling the role played by women during the Algerian national resistance that we come across one of the main features of the originality of Marouane's novel resides, since it is a priori a novel on the condition of women. The transgression of the (post)colonial order is also seen, in the novel, in the transgression of the patriarchal order imposed by men who reduce women to motherhood and household chores.

And yet, as Danièle Djamila Amrane-Minne recalls, women have played a determinant role, even if it is left out of accounts of Algeria's national resistance, except in examples like those of the son of Gillo Pontecorvo, *La bataille d'Alger*, where the role played notably by Hassiba Bent Bouali, Djamila Boupacha, and Zohra Driff in the struggle against the forces occupying Algiers during the famous "battle of Algiers" is featured in a central way. Amrane-Minne writes on the topic of the active participation of women in the resistance, and about the ways in which, in the context of the struggle, the border between men and women was blurred:

> Terrible repressive measures were taken against both men and women indiscriminately. One woman in the *maquis* out of five was killed during battles. The women fighting in urban guerilla warfare were practically all arrested and had to be subjected to the same torture as the men, and like the men, some women also died. Members of the national resistance who were in charge accepted taking risks, and punished men and women equally for collaborating with the enemy. Collaborating with the enemy was punishable by death for men as well as for women. During the war, women were active in all the fields of battle. They often found it difficult to make themselves be taken seriously, but once that had overcome the suspicions their presence aroused, they were fully accepted. Joint fighting by men and women, whether in the *maquis* or in small armed groups in the cities, definitely achieved good results. (1999, 67)

Only, and in spite of this active part taken by women during the war of liberation, it so happened that once decolonization was achieved and independence acquired, women were relegated to a marginal place. Gilbert Meynier makes the following observation:

> Pendant toute la guerre, le FLN répandit l'idée que les femmes étaient libérées par la Révolution. Dès lors qu'elles furent censées avoir conquis tous les droits, on passa insensiblement à l'idée qu'elles n'avaient plus rien à réclamer. Dans sa vision populiste unanimiste, et toujours prêt à utiliser des compétences qui pussent renforcer sa clientèle, Boumediene proposa de designer une femme au CNRA mais il ne fut pas suivi. Insista-t-il d'ailleurs beaucoup ? Le FLN ne fit jamais aboutir le projet d'organiser spécifiquement les femmes dans une association faisant suite à l'UFMA de la période MTLD.

> During the entire war, the FLN spread the idea that women were freed by the Revolution. As soon as they were said to have acquired all their rights, people went imperceptibly to the notion that they had nothing more to demand. In his unanimist populist vision, and always ready to use skills that could reinforce his clientele, Boumediene proposed to designate a woman to the CNRA, but this

proposal was not followed. Was he really asking that much? The FLN never realized its project of specifically organizing women in an association following up the UFMA [Union of Muslim Women of Algeria] in the period of the MTLD [Movement for the Triumph of Democratic Liberties]. (2003, 318)

We are dealing, then, with the woman who is victimized, in a certain way, by the failures of the FLN to give the female sex the freedom she was promised and that she expected as she engaged in the nationalist struggle for her country's independence. In a social context taken up by fiction and characterized by a metonymic vision of the young girl whose "identité est ramenée à son hymen. Son destin, ainsi que celui de toute sa famille, sont définis par rapport à sa préservation" "identity leads back to her hymen. Her fate and that of her whole family are defined with respect to its preservation," where "le corps de la jeune fille ne lui appartient pas mais est confisqué au profit d'intérêts plus important touchant sa famille et le cercle social dans lequel elle évolue" "the young girl's body does not belong to her but is confiscated to the more important benefit of interests touching her family and social circle in which she evolves" (2014, 300). Again, referencing Ayadi, we understand the madness that ensues after the revolt of Djamila's mother when she stands up against her husband's positions in open defiance. It is thus because she experienced turbulences related to the history of her country that the mother dreams of a better future for her daughter. That dream will be broken by the fact that, in the image of the rest of Africa, the suns of the independences will not shine, tarnished as they are by the conditions in which African countries accede to independence, and by the ways in which independence is but a substitution of one torturer for another: "les combattants dont tu parles, vieille folle, ne sont plus. Ils ont été remplacés par des transfuges et des traîtres qui se moqueront de toi et de ta révolution" "the combatants you're talking about, stupid old woman, no longer exist. They have been replaced by defectors and traitors who mock you and your revolution" (104), says Djamila's father to her mother during a fight—this mother, an engaged fighter whose bravery earned her the name of Joan of Arc of the Hills, "l'illettrée devant qui les hommes se prosternaient" "the illiterate woman before whom men bowed down" (14). Like the women of Algeria discussed by Zahia Smail Salhi, Djamila's mother is a woman who is tired of waiting to achieve the promises of female autonomy and freedoms, and understands that similar to those who are like her, "the women of Algeria had come to understand that no one else would help them seek emancipation. They knew that they would have to create their own movement, to fight the violation of women's human rights" (2003, 31). Conscious of this necessity of taking her fate in her own hands like every Algerian woman, the narrator's mother was to believe in and implement a number of strategies, true war plans for retrieving her dignity in the face of patriarchy as well as her torturers, for she was conscious that she would never be free "si les hommes, [s]on père, [s]es oncles, [s]es frères, [s]es cousins, [s]es voisins ne l'étaient pas" "if men, her father, her uncles, her brothers, her cousins, her neighbors were not" (2005, 17). Among those strategies is one of physically assaulting her daughter Djamila and disfiguring her, thereby deploying a true ruse of war, a powerful subterfuge to make her escape the threat of a forced marriage that hovers over her, and thereby carrying out a "violence [qui] deviendrait alors un passeport pour la liberté" "violence that would then become a passport to freedom," as noted by Ayadi. In the novel, the inaugural moment of the breaking of the chains of silence is found in the scene where the mother brutally opposes the plan for her daughter's marriage and brutally and without any further proceedings sends away the group of women who have come to lead her daughter off to marriage. Added to this transgression of the father's authority are the transgressions of the young girl Djamila and the women's organization lending strong hands to those rebelling against the colonial forces. Together, these instances of rejecting the established order and of overturning the powers that be help validate the redemption that follows the fall of women and the country, in that well-known duality. Thus, in giving her life in the hope of saving her daughter's life, the narrator's mother, by her sacrifice that is analogous to the sacrifice she made for her country's sovereignty, is the consummate example of the character who makes possible the identification of the female body with the national body.

It therefore becomes clear that beyond the female figure, the inscription of the female body in Leïla Marouane's *La jeune fille et la mère* is a metaphor for the national body. The occupation and pillaging of the national territory are shown in the mirror of the biopoliticization of human relations and thus the control of the female body to illustrate the relationship between women and the nation, to provide evidence of transgression as an operative mode and to assess the autonomy of the female character, as well as the sovereignty of national space. Thus, through her novel, Marouane triggers an unleashing of memory against forgetting, a forgetting that "reste l'inquiétante menace qui se profile à l'arrière-plan de la phénoménologie de la mémoire et de l'épistémologie de l'histoire" (Ricoeur 2000, 536) / "remains the disturbing threat that lurks in the background of the phenomenology of memory and the epistemology of history" (2004, 412). By permitting a return to colonial memory in Algeria through an anamnesis, Marouane underscores the contributions of women in the struggles for independence so that no one overlooks them. In summation, we can say that the writing of *La jeune fille et la mère* places its author at the very heart of the third period of defense of the national culture as identified by Frantz Fanon in *Les damnés de la terre,* in that Marouane "se transforme en réveilleur de peuple" "transforms herself into someone who awakens the people" by offering a writing that is a "littérature de combat, littérature révolutionnaire, littérature nationale" "literature of combat, a revolutionary literature, a national literature," because she felt "la nécessité de dire [sa] nation, de composer la phrase qui exprime le peuple, de se faire le porte-parole d'une nouvelle réalité en actes" "the need to speak her nation, to compose the words that express her people, to make herself the porte-parole of a new reality in acts" (211–12). Through these conditions of production for liberating the Algerian woman through her novel, Marouane simultaneously rewrites the story of the liberation of Algeria, her native country.

And now we can conclude that *La jeune fille et la mère* is a novel of both female revolt and a historiographic project that focuses on the narration of a nation, Algeria. From that perspective, we can postulate that through her novel, Marouane invites us to consider and reflect upon the condition of woman during colonization, and in a more significant and interesting way, after Algeria's accession to independence. By fictionalizing Djamila's mother, Marouane seems, if not to invite reflection, at least to raise the reader's interest in the fact that, as remarkably observed by Gilbert Meynier:

> En 1962, tout était en place pour que les femmes rentrent dans le cocon de leurs foyers d'où la parenthèse de la guerre de libération les avait fait sortir. Globalement, la surabondance des déclarations et des actes virilisants, à quelques exceptions près, ne fit pas vraiment du FLN un parangon de révolution féminine. Les femmes ne furent jamais, ni dans le discours, ni dans la pratique du FLN, prises en considération pour elles-mêmes. Mais, si bien des femmes durent s'incliner et accepter de se resserrer dans le carcan masculin, la guerre, par ou malgré le FLN, leur avait tout de même ouvert des horizons. Pour elles, la nouveauté de l'événement était telle que rien ne fut plus comme avant.
>
> In 1962, everything was set for women to enter the cocoon of their households from which the parenthesis of the war of liberation had brought them out. Globally, the glut of declarations and virilizing actions, with just a few exceptions, did not make the FLN a paragon of female revolution. The women were never, either in the FLN's discourse or practice, taken into consideration for themselves. But, if many women had to bow and accept being kept in the shackles of males, the war, by or despite the FLN, had nevertheless opened horizons. For them, the novelty of the event was such that nothing was ever the same again. (2003, 19)

In a certain way, the Algeria that acceded to independence somehow continues to perpetuate the social and sexual divisions that were in place during colonization. With respect to women's bodies, it is interesting to note that

Marouane establishes a parallel between the rape of the narrator's mother and the profanation of the narrator's own body, which is made clear in the process of control and discipline imposed by the father figure. As the body of the Algerian woman did not belong to herself during colonization, so that body was struck with stigma after the independences. Alf Andrew Heggoy (1974) observed early on that the limitation of the role of women took a decisive turn through the presence of imperial France. In that context, the female body was doubly disqualified: first through racialization, then through sexualization. It could even be that the explanation for the Algerian woman being kept in the position of subaltern is a consequence of colonization, if we accept the analysis offered by Meynier:

> Encore une fois, et comme tout au long de l'histoire de l'Algérie coloniale, le colonisateur traquait le jeu: l'émancipation perturbait le reflexe communautaire patriarcal et, à ce titre, elle était instrumentalisée par les français en arme contre le patriotisme algérien, tant il est vrai que les femmes ont toujours été un enjeu durant la période coloniale. Pour le FLN, la France ne pouvait que vouloir entraîner les musulmanes dans la bassesse des mœurs et la destruction de leur honneur.

> Once again, and as throughout the long history of colonial Algeria, the colonizer played the game: emancipation upset the patriarchal community reflex, and thereby it became an instrument for the French to use against Algerian patriotism, as it is true that women were always an issue during the colonial period. For the FLN, the only wish France had was to lead Muslim in their wayward morals and to the destruction of their honor. (2003, 312)

It therefore clearly appears that to the civilizational imperative that victimized Algerians of both sexes, we can add an imperative to civilize the Algerian woman by teaching her to respect "sa place" "her place," just like the indigene was formerly subjected to the injunction of silence and obedience. The body of the Algerian woman, from mothers to daughters, as Marouane suggests, is ultimately the object of a fantastic investment on the part of men: first the colonizers, then Algerians, the new masters of the country and the de facto holders of selective rights of the individual. That is undoubtedly the definitive message of *La jeune fille et la mère*, which encourages us to reflect upon the use of the female body in a context where, as the narrator's mother says in addressing her daughter as if she were speaking to her own mother who had once been the victim of colonial barbarity: "Ah, si tu savais ce qu'est devenue ta fille, ta guerrière, la jeanne d'Arc redoutée par les hommes et par les femmes . . . Hélas, ma mère, de nos jours les révolutions ne profitent plus qu'aux lâches" "Oh, if you knew what became of your daughter, your warrior, the Joan of Arc feared by men and women . . . Alas, mother, in our time, revolution only benefits cowards" (157). In thus showing the reduction of the Algerian female to her body from the colonial period to the aftermath of the independences, Marouane pulls back the veil from the woman who, like the peasant, unfortunately remained the impoverished heir of Algerian national resistance, the ultimate consequence of an authority that opted for a governing of bodies and that decided to transform the lives of citizens into precarious lives, doubly excluded from social and civil protections. In so doing, Marouane contributes to the restitution of voices that have long remained silent, in short, to an unveiling of all those courageous women who made enormous sacrifices for the liberation of Algeria, in the recognition that, as expressed by Mildred Mortimer in her conclusion to an article that appeared in 1999, "as the fiftieth anniversary of Algerian independence draws near, some voices remain stifled, but silence is being broken, so that healing may occur and the heroic actions and sacrifices of Algeria's women combatants may be fully recognized at last" (1999, 115).

Violated Bodies, Women in Revolt: *Le Chatiment Des Hypocrites* between Madness And Vengeance

In *Histoire de l'Algérie depuis l'indépendance* (2004), the historian Benjamin Stora points out that at the beginning of the 1980s, the official history of Algeria was largely constructed upon the creation of landmarks, the mythification of official history. Emmanuel Alcaraz, another historian, recalls that in Algeria there had been a kind of fabrication of national memory of the war of independence led by Algeria against the colonial occupier, France. For Alcaraz, the self-legitimation of Algerian power rests upon a true "rituel politique, à l'intersection du politique et du religieux, [dans lequel] le pouvoir se met en scène et opère une recharge sacrale en affichant sa proximité avec le sang des 'martyrs' qui fonde la légitimité politique en Algérie. Les dirigeants se posent en héritiers des 'martyrs'" "political ritual, where politics and religion come together, and where authority enters the picture and creates a sacred recharging by displaying its proximity to the blood of the 'martyrs' who established political legitimacy in Algeria. The leaders set themselves up as heirs of the 'martyrs'" (2013, 26).

A link can be established between the thought of Alcaraz and Stora, for whom the establishment of landmarks to construct the legitimacy of official history has not only effaced any pluralistic approach but has also produced a lapse in memory (91). It is through this perspective that the Algerian State has taken control of religious institutions and nationalized Islam. And by way of consequence, as Stora powerfully reminds us, it has created a condition of crime and permanent insecurity inasmuch as the political movement of Islam was born out of Islam's refusal to submit to the State.

In the ensuing organized disorder and the fabrication of a memory lapse, one of the major categories of Algerian society whose role has been struck by this lapse in memory is the category of women. The laws imposed upon women—for example, the prohibition against marriage to a non-Muslim, the absolute necessity for a legal guardian, the maintenance of polygamy—are contrary to the Constitution of 1976, which proclaims equality before the law. Thus, Stora emphasizes, "de nombreuses associations de femmes, en particulier les combattantes de la guerre de libération, considèrent que ce code constitue une régression significative par rapport aux mutations effectives qui se sont produites depuis l'indépendance, dans le rapport entre les sexes" "many women's groups, in particular those who fought in the war of liberation, consider that this code constitutes a significant regression with respect to the actual transformations that have occurred since independence, in the relationship between men and women" (2004, 94).[2] Benjamin Stora's observation is echoed by Anne Donadey who points out that "in a society where space—real and imaginary—was divided along gender lines, women were, for the first time, called on by the male leadership to participate actively in the armed struggle. However, after the war was won, women were sent back to the private space of the home" (2001, 1).

Such, in fact, is the context in which, in the days following Algeria's independence, woman was to be faced with a marginalization whose effects would be destructive both to her and to the man who becomes her torturer, leading therefore to the disintegration of Algerian society. For, in fact, numerous women are victims of maltreatment, abuse, and frustrations; but while certain women resign themselves to this social disqualification and accept its consequences, others achieve recognition through a stance of refusal. Fictionalizing this refusal to be marginalized is consequently even more poignant as the boundaries between reality and fiction are blurred in novels of solitary or collective revolt.

That is notably the case with the Algerian writer Leïla Marouane, whose real name is Leyla Mechentel and whose novel *Le châtiment des hypocrites* (2001) is my focus in this section. Through a reading of the novel that focuses on the use of the body, I will attempt to show that the narration's posture of rejecting a patriarchal order is split between madness and vengeance, by emphasizing the ways that Fatima, the main character, descends into a kind of madness to slake her vengeance, the sole condition for purifying her body that has been sullied by her captors. In the end, I will show that through murder, woman commits the essential gesture that allows her to be reconciled with herself and to mark a rupture from a universe that is fundamentally hostile to her.

Le châtiment des hypocrites is likely the Algerian woman's novel that exposes with the greatest of clarity, details, and depth the violence that characterizes the revolt of raped women. Fatima Amor, also known as Miss Kosra, the main character of the novel, is kidnapped one morning by three men who "avaient besoin de ses services pour leurs compagnons, là haut, dans les montagnes" "needed her services for their companions, up in the mountains" (2001, 17). Taken hostage, imprisoned, and kept for what can be called the fundamentalists' general staff, she is raped and mutilated throughout several months. The opening of Marouane's novel says much about the precarious nature of the lives of women in an Algeria where, as I mentioned in the introduction, French colonization appears to have given way to another form of hegemony, the domination of women by men. It is therefore quite useful to recall that Fatima is selected for this kidnaping because, as we learn in the novel, "elle était femme, à visage et mollets découverts, un surcroît de taille, elle devait jour après jour penser un nouvel itinéraire, trouver une nouvelle ruse pour, c'était bien le cas de le dire, brouiller les pistes" "she was a woman, with an uncovered face and calves, with a nice shape, [and] day after day she had to figure out a new route, find a new means to, it must be said, cover her tracks" (13). Covering her tracks was necessary because of the laws imposed on Algerian women that Fatima found to be especially contradictory to the religion because, she said to herself, "le Prophète encourageait les femmes à se faire belles, à s'habiller de soie et d'or, à s'enduire longuement, lui-même se parfumait, rougissait sa barbe au henné, ses lèvres à l'écorce de noix" "the Prophet encouraged women to make themselves beautiful, to dress in silk and gold, to lather themselves with lotions, and he himself used perfume, dyed his beard with henna, colored his lips with bark from nuts" (15).

Following a conversation that fails to sway the determination of her rapists, Fatima, like any woman subject to masculine domination, experiences the worst moments of her existence: with her virginity taken from her through rape, torture, bodily harm, incarceration, and mutilation are to be the lot of her existence in captivity. Fatima's abduction appears thus to sanction a transgression of the religious laws that expect the rape of a woman. In a sociopolitical environment marked by Islam's refusal to submit to the State, everything in fact seems to occur at this level as if through a sort of deviation from combat: while waiting to set the central Algerian State in disorder, the Islamist fundamentalists who abducted and tortured Fatima had decided to demonstrate their power through sexual domination insofar as penetrating women by force was meant to affirm their power and authority in a symbolic manner. Thus, penetrating women without their consent came down to inculcating an incontestable order of male domination, and consequently of subjecting women to obeying them and showing a scrupulous respect for orders given by men. We see that female marginalization proceeds from a control over the woman's body as it is subjected to the temper of the male subject who, like a sovereign in political philosophy, exerts power over life and death (Mernissi 1987, 1991). Through her kidnaping, Fatima Kosra, who is not yet called Fatima Amor, is thus placed at the mercy of the commander of the fundamentalists, by means of a separation that in some way sacralizes the female body as it removes it from common use to instead place it in the sacred sphere of control of the Islamist fundamentalists, who impose upon her an imaginary space in which she is but a mere toy. From that viewpoint, we could compare the detained Fatima to a slave with special status, for she is simultaneously excluded from and included in humanity, as a woman who is not herself properly human but who allows the terrorists to be human beings, if we follow along with Giorgio Agamben's thoughts on the special status of slaves. We could then say that, subjected to the constraints of the central Algerian authorities against whom they dissent, the fundamentalists in Marounae's novel cannot feel themselves as alive, free, and powerful unless they forcefully subject women to their own needs. In this line of thought, Fatima Kosra corresponds perfectly to the special status slave described by Agamben, the slave who "although excluded from political life, has an entirely special relation with it. The slave in fact represents a not properly human life that renders possible for others the *bios politikos*, that is to say, the truly human life" (2015, 20). From the preceding citation, we can draft a reconfiguration of intersex relationships in postcolonial Algeria by borrowing from the figure of the slave, the figure par excellence of the enactment of the individual relationships of domination and subjection.

Seen in this light, the woman, represented here by Fatima Kosra, becomes, in the hands of the Islamist fundamentalists who have abducted her, the perfect metaphor of that slave who, while excluded from political life, is included within it insofar as her existence validates and legitimizes the lives of the terrorists, who at the same time become the perfect double of the master in the dialectic of master and slave. I shall return to the hermeneutical pertinence of the figure of the slave a bit later, but I want to point out that Fatima is all the more a slave in the hands of her masters (the fundamentalists) as the use of her body is perfectly unproductive, and therefore escapes an interpretation related to work, inasmuch as the involuntary sexual work imposed upon her through rape—just as her work in captivity of caring for the medical needs of the terrorists wounded in armed conflicts—is not defined by the work that she produces (she is doubly necessary, but expendable), but by the use of her body as it is made available to the terrorists, without any mediation. This specific use of Fatima's body by the terrorists, given its lack of productivity, does not then seem to explain the fact that through the submission of women, a submission that aims in any case to reinforce the line of fracture between males and females, and by the very same act, a world is created that is not determined by the phallus, but by a vision of the world organized as a division of sexual organs that attribute to the phallus the expression of virility and thereby institute an authority that is meant to be exclusively masculine. Thus, Pierre Bourdieu is likely correct in affirming that

> [if] the sexual relation appears as a social relation of domination, this is because it is constructed through the fundamental principle of division between the active male and the passive female and because this principle creates, organizes, expresses and directs desires—male desire as the desire for possession, eroticized domination, and female desire as the desire for masculine domination, as eroticized subordination or even, in the limiting case, as the eroticized recognition of domination. (2001, 21)

Sexual relations, which according to Bourdieu evolve into a relationship of domination, are indeed at work in Marouane's novel. But just as I briefly alluded to earlier, what is striking in the narration of *Le châtiment des hypocrites* is that while it appears to be beyond recognition as eroticized domination, possession of women reflects the inability of the male terrorists to affirm their virility, and thus their control, in gaining power over the Algerian State that they are battling. To be clear, the displacement of the sacrificial figure of the State to the female seems to indicate the collapse of the terrorist cause and thereby suggests two hypotheses. First, it is impossible to speak of "sacrificial violence" insofar as the act of violence (abduction, rape, mutilation) is no longer aimed at the executioner (those who hold political power) who was supposed to be destroyed, as Jesse Goldhammer demonstrates so well in a gloss on sacrificial violence: "Sacrificial violence used to establish new forms of power must be capable of auguring both purity and abjection, which correspond to the Old Regime's king and executioner respectively" (2005, 204–5). Second, the break from the forbidden precedes the destruction of the limits of the human condition. In acknowledging along with Dennis Jeffrey that "les interdits ont pour fonction de préserver au cœur des communautés humaines les limites indispensables aux fonctions essentielles de leur survie tout en préservant ce qui fait l'humanité de l'homme" "what is forbidden serves the function of preserving, at the heart of human communities, the indispensable limits of the basic functions of their survival while preserving what makes of humanity human beings" (2003, 204–5), it is then fitting to ask if transgression of the forbidden by the terrorists who torture women in Marouane's novel doesn't place the sacrificing characters at the limit of what separates humans from animals. The difficulty in responding with exactness to this question leads me to consider the words of René Girard:

> Le rapport entre la victime potentielle et la victime actuelle ne doit pas se définir en termes de culpabilité et d'innocence. Il n'y a rien à "expier." La société cherche à détourner vers une victime relativement indifférente, une victime "sacrifiable," une violence qui risque de frapper ses propres membres, ceux qu'elle entend à tout prix protéger.
>
> The relationship between the potential victim and the actual victim must not be defined in terms of culpability and innocence. There is nothing to be "expiated." Society seeks to turn to a relatively indifferent victim, a victim that is "sacrificable," a violence that risks striking its own members, those whom it seeks to protect at all costs. (1998, 13)

Thus, we find in *Le châtiment des hypocrites* what Girard calls an "irrational violence," given that basically the first victim, that is, the true target of the object of sacrifice (the controlling State), remains beyond the grasp of the one who takes on the sacrifice. We then find ourselves in the very center of an aporia relative to the sacrifice, to the meaning and the stakes that surround its execution. This interpretation also indicates that at the heart of the social revenge that frames the Algerian society described in Marouane's novel, the victimization of women goes far beyond the simple framework of masculine domination and can be seen as a proof of the failure of the fundamentalists who turn toward women as sacrificable victims, if we apply Girard's thought in this context, a violence that is in fact be meant for the potential victim, the Algerian state. Fatima is thus nothing more and nothing less than a traumatized woman when at last she is freed.

The trauma of which Fatima is victim, beyond the stigma of rape, is repeated in a social and cultural context within which, the anthropologist Abderrahmane Moussaoui writes, "les victimes de ces violences sexuelles ont elles-mêmes contribué, à leur corps défendant, à renforcer cette 'amnésie collective.' Elles se sont longtemps abstenues de dénoncer ces crimes qui les ont dévastées, de peur de s'exposer à une stigmatisation sociale redoutable et ruineuse" "the victims of these sexual violences have themselves contibuted, against their will, to reinforce this 'scollective amnesia.' They long abstained from denouncing these crimes that devastates them, for fear of exposing themselves to a formidable and ruinous social stigmatization" (2016, 89–90). Clearly, the inegalitarian organization of the society from which Marouane's novel draws its sources creates a situation in which the rape victim is also made to feel guilty by the social group of which she is a member. For this reason, it is extremely difficult to imagine life after the rape, given that, as

Abderrahmane Moussaoui quite suitably recalls in an extract that deserves to be presented in its entirety, the criminalization of the victim leads to the impossibility of a justice that could protect female victims of rape:

> Au lieu de l'agresseur, inaccessible, c'est la victime qui occupe la place de suspect. Elle doit répondre aux interrogations sur les conditions qui ont fait d'elle une victime; des conditions qu'elle est supposée avoir facilitées d'une manière ou d'une autre. Le silence et le déni dominent donc. La difficulté est double: une justice qui refuse de se saisir d'un dossier en l'absence de preuves fournies par le plaignant; une victime murée dans le silence. "En Algérie, c'est à la victime de fournir les preuves de son agression contrairement à d'autres pays, où la justice se saisit du cas," précise la directrice d'Amnesty International Algérie. Autre difficulté soulignée par Fadhila Chitour, médecin et représentante du réseau Wassila, en charge de la protection des femmes victimes de violences en Algérie: la première erreur de la législation algérienne est "de ne pas définir ce qu'est le viol." Quant à l'agresseur, il suffit qu'il accepte d'épouser sa victime, selon l'article 236 du Code pénal, pour échapper à la justice.
>
> Instead of the aggressor, who is inaccessible, it is the victim who occupies the position of suspect. She must respond to interrogations on the conditions that made her a victim, conditions that she is supposed to have facilitated in one way or another. Silence and denial thus predominate. The difficulty is two-fold: a justice that refuses to take hold of a dossier in the absence of furnished proof by the plaintiff; a victim walled in by silence. "In Algeria, it is the victim who must furnish proof of the aggression, unlike in other countries, where justice handles the case," specifies the director of Amnesty International Algeria. Another problem underscored by Fadhila Chitour, a medical doctor and representative of the Wassila network, charged with the protection of women who are victims of violence in Algeria: the first mistake of the Algerian legislation is "not to define rape." As for the aggressor, all he must do is agree to marry his victim, according to article 236 of the Penal Code, to escape the hands of justice. (2016, 94–95)

What clearly stands out from the preceding quote is that not only is the victim positioned as being at fault for having experienced an offense, but the heinous act of violation is no longer considered an offense once the victim who has been sexually abused without her consent is taken as a spouse. This state of affairs crystallizes the legal process at the end of which one could agree that the State, the guarantor of the law, as the legislator, legitimizes and removes any penalty, so to speak, for the rape of women. For in reality, if the victim needs to prove that the offense was committed, it is clear, as I pointed out above, that the woman is thus reduced to her naked life, that is to say, to her pure, outright biological expression. Even worse, in this precise context, the

Algerian woman becomes the figure par excellence of the slave whose death was not considered a homicide. And Fatima's itinerary is so similar to the reality described in the above quotation that it could be said that the relationships between fiction and reality tend to blur the line between the real and the imaginary. The novel is furthermore unequivocal on this point, for "craignant d'affronter les hommes de sa famille, de devoir rendre compte de ces dix-neuf mois écoulés, se dérobant aux questions de sa mère, ces questions en corrélation avec l'honneur du patio, et l'intégrité de l'hymen—autant se laisser esquinter la jugulaire que son capital virginité—elle décida prolonger sa disparition" "fearing to affront the males in her family, of having to account for the past nineteen months, evading her mother's questions, these questions related to the honor of the courtyard, and an intact hymen—better to damage the jugular than one's capital of virginity—she decided to prolong her disappearance" (2001, 27–28). This can equally explain why Fatima "regretta son obstination face aux admonestations de sa mère et de ceux qui se targuaient de prodiguer de sages conseils. Ca te coûte rien de fourrer un foulard dans ton sac, tu le passeras sur la tête le moment venu" "rued her obstination when confronted with the admonishments of her mother and of those who boasted of proferring wise counsel. It costs you nothing to stuff a scarf in your bag, you can put it on your head when the time comes" (16). The preceding quotation translates the sentiment by which, as the victim that she is on the point of becoming, the woman will blame herself for having through her own obstinacy encouraged the occurrence of her abduction. Consequently, Fatima will seek refuge in shelters for women in trouble, in makeshift buildings, thus abandoning the child that is the fruit of the repeated rapes she endured, and also making the decision to take refuge in prostitution. On this point, it is important to emphasize that colonial prostitution indeed gave way to postcolonial rape, with the result that the victim, incapable of obtaining justice, is reduced to turning to prostitution if she chooses to avoid suicide, incapable of facing the stigmatization held by a society that appears to have literally legitimized rape, thereby exposing the woman either to suicide or to a survival that adopts the very ways of the criminality that has victimized her. We are then not surprised to see that the victim who is thus abandoned and finds herself without any support from State or family, can succumb to madness, as her own tormentor, or else by joining madness and criminality, as would be the case with Fatima in Marouane's novel.

But how are we to understand that the victim becomes the tormentor? Through what prism can we propose a new reading of the murder as the capital scene in *Le châtiment des hypocrites*? Finally, what philosophical lesson does Leïla Marouane's novel postulate in terms not only of the woman but indeed of any human being placed in a position of victim, where his or her body is profaned by an unjust order where men and political authorities are the guardians who transform politics into biopolitics, that is, who reduce political life into naked life that is so often sanctioned by death and obliteration? Finally, it is important to know whether it is possible for Marouane's heroine, through a means other than vengeance, to close the parentheses opened by the rape, reinforced by the threat of repudiation, all enshrined in a world inside which "la rectitude politique commande de bannir la vengeance; pourtant celle-ci constitue le fondement même de la justice officielle qui en est l'une des formes les plus perverties: ses critères obéissent aux impératifs de l'époque, aux classes dirigeantes et aux niveaux hiérarchiques auxquels appartiennent les victimes et les coupables" "political rectitude commands the banishment of vengeance; yet that itself constitutes the very basis of the official justice which is one of its most perverted forms: its criteria obey the imperatives of the time, the ruling class and the hierarchical levels to which the victims and the guilty belong," according to Suzanne Robert (1999, 16) in her remarkable reflection upon vengeance.

Nevertheless, before reaching that point, when Fatima is out walking one day in the streets of Algiers, she unexpectedly comes across Rachid Amor, a school friend whose wife she will become after a marriage that will take her from Algeria to France. On that migration, it is necessary to point out the remarkable article by Maria Vendetti, who based her interpretation of *Le châtiment des hypocrites* on the tension between Paris and Algeria, offering a most interesting reading of Marouane's novels in general and the one I am analyzing in particular, focused on the pathology that arises from the inability of Algerian immigrants to become integrated in France. According to Vendetti, with respect to *Le châtiment des hypocrites* and *La vie sexuelle d'un islamiste à Paris* (2007), "what defines the characters' descent into madness and incoherence is the refusal of physically inscribed laws on to the 'foreign' immigrant body and the telling of stories that stems from the pathology created by flawed or outright denied integration into French society" (2006, 132–33). There is thus a significant link between madness, immigration, and integration that for Vendetti constitutes the significant basis of Marouane's imaginary, or at least in the two novels she analyzes. While this perspective is absolutely pertinent, I would prefer to take another path in interpreting the social disqualification found in *Le châtiment des hypocrites*. For in fact, it seems that the novel's action would have been exactly the same if we can imagine Algiers as the sole space of the fiction. Clearly, I am postulating that the turning point of the narrative thread is the abduction, rape, and mutilations experienced by Fatima Kosra, and that the exodus to Paris is but another alternative that could have in fact been a displacement from the city of Algiers to a village, or even from Algiers to another Algerian city. While Vendetti offers a pertinent reading, it is indeed possible to postulate that Paris is but another place, a place of exile, one that will never succeed in curing Marouane's main character of the wound inflicted upon her in Algeria. For that reason, I will insist rather upon a descent into hell that causes the disintegration of the violated woman, frees her from her demons, but all while setting her up in a permanent spatial, mental, and identitary no-place.

Janes Evan (2009) and Nevine El Nossery (2012) have amply commented on the traumatic dimension that holds sway over the fictional space in *Le châtiment des hypocrites*. For my part, I shall focus on vengeance as a weapon that allows Fatima to break the chains of silence and once again find her ability to regain her pride after having experienced an assault, an ability that was taken from her by the State and the tribunals who are supposed to stand for the law and protect her from her torturers. In fact, when Fatima is liberated and chooses wandering rather than a return to her family, she is completely subjected to the psychic disorders that Julia Kristeva has called abjection in *Les pouvoirs de l'horreur*:

> Il y a dans l'abjection, une de ces violentes et obscures révoltes de l'être contre ce qui le menace et qui lui paraît venir d'un dehors ou d'un dedans exorbitant, jeté à côté du possible, du tolérable, du pensable. C'est là, tout prêt mais inassimilable. Ça sollicite, inquiète, fascine le désir qui pourtant ne se laisse pas séduire. Apeuré, il se détourne. Ecœuré, il rejette. Un absolu le protège de l'opprobre, il en est fier, il y tient. Mais en même temps, quand même, cet élan, ce spasme, ce saut, est attiré vers un ailleurs aussi tentant que condamné. Inlassablement, comme un boomerang indomptable, un pôle d'appel et de répulsion met celui qui en est habité littéralement hors de lui.
>
> In abjection, there is one of those violent and obscure revolts of the human being against what is menacing him or her and seems to him or her to be coming from the outside or from an exorbitant inside, thrown against the possible, the tolerable, the conceivable. It is there, close yet inassimilable. It appeals, worries, fascinates the desire that nevertheless does not allow itself to be seduced. Frightened, it turns away. Repelled, it rejects. An absolute protects it from hatred, it is proud of that and holds to it. But at the same time, nevertheless, this impetus, this spasm, this leap is attracted to an elsewhere as tempting as it is condemned. Relentlessly, like an indomitable boomerang, a pole that calls and repels places the one who is inhabited by it literally outside himself or herself. (1980, 9)

Kristeva's reflection seems to completely summarize the psychological posture of the main character in Marouane's novel. It would seem quite accurate to think that, between the paradoxical movement of attraction and repulsion, Fatima corresponds perfectly to the subject caught in the state of abjection, with respect to the different oscillations that victimize her throughout the entire novel, and which can be summarized in a specific stance. A violent and obscure revolt is brewing within her against any threats, which is observed in her flesh (Evans) and which places her literally outside of herself (Kristeva).

This stance is all the more uncomfortable as Fatima is constrained to take refuge in a madness whose complexity Nevine El Nossery explains in the following terms:

> Si ce trouble mental est le résultat du traumatisme qu'elle a refoulé pendant plusieurs mois, il est aussi dû au fait que Fatima se trouve au confluent de plusieurs idéologies contraires. D'une part, elle revendique une identité, la seule possible pour elle du fait qu'elle est exclue du groupe auquel elle est censée appartenir, comme étant une "individue," d'autre part elle reste marquée par les règles assignées par sa société traditionnelle concernant la bonne conduite d'une femme musulmane et son confinement dans la sphère privée. N'ayant personne à qui parler de son malheur, ni sa famille, ni la société qui l'a rejetée, ni même son mari qui ne veut rien savoir de son passé et qui semble plonger dans son ego, Fatima garde dans son sac un journal intime, dans lequel elle consigne ses conquêtes sexuelles comme pour emprisonner l'absurdité de la vie et de sa mémoire.
>
> If this mental disorder is the result of a trauma that she has suppressed for many months, it is also due to the fact that Fatima finds herself at the cross-section of many contradictory ideologies. On the one hand, she seeks an identity, the sole one possible for her because she is excluded from the group to which she is supposed to belong, as an "individual," and on the other hand, she remains marked by the rules assigned by traditional society regarding proper conduct for a proper Muslim woman and her confinement in a private sphere. Having no one to talk to about her unhappiness, neither her family nor the society who has rejected her, nor even her husband who refuses to learn about her past and who seems plunged inside his own ego, Fatima keeps an intimate journal inside her purse, in which she lists her sexual conquests as if to imprison the absurdity of life and of her memory. (2012, 166)

Crazed by the violence she has experienced, Fatima decides to take control of the abjection that pervades her and tears her apart. By prostituting herself, she uses the object of her troubles (her vagina) to try to set things straight. She transforms herself from a life-giving midwife into a giver of death, by each time removing a piece of the sexual organs of her "clients," thus assuring herself that she is not only depriving them of the phallus that guarantees their superiority, but she also takes away their ability to subject another woman to their sexual desires without the woman's consent. In the words of Jane Evans, it is a matter of taking away from these men "their social significance as procreator and protector of the opposite sex; for those men inclined to commit violent sex with women, she ensures that the latter will not be made pregnant against their will" (2009, 197).

The punitive mission Fatima takes on will reach its climax when, five years after her marriage, she decides in her turn, like the fundamentalists who replace their potential victim (the State) with easily sacrificable victims (women), to replace her tormentors (the fundamentalists) with any male human being (the men to whom she offers her body, and finally, her husband). Thus, in the final scene of the novel, she drugs and rapes her husband, then electrocutes and burns him in a scene that is described with an extraordinary violence: "À mon retour, l'aube pointait, et mon mari était plus que purifié. Il était cuit. Irréversiblement cuit. Lorsque je l'ai découpé, pas une goutte de sang n'est venue poisser le parquet qu'il venait de fabriquer" "When I returned, dawn was breaking, and my husband was more than purified. He was burned. Irreversibly burned. When I cup him up, not a drop of blood stuck to the parquet flooring he had just created" (2001, 219). Threatened with repudiation and having returned to her native land, the site of the manifestation of her first trauma, Fatima appears to begin to cure from her madness and her abjection through the murder of the husband who, because he himself was a convert to radical Islam, reminded her of her tormentors.

The originality of Marouane's novel, in my opinion, is articulated around the problematic of vengeance. And to fictionalize this vengeance, it is remarkable that Marouane chooses, in a work dominated by Islam, to make use of a biblical intertext to thereby indicate the pertinence of the reading I am proposing: "À trente trois ans, l'âge de cet Autre qui lui aussi, et contrairement à ses projets, inspira haine et crimes ses adeptes, écumant et consommant les mâles, errant comme une vagabonde, elle [Fatima] rencontra Rachid Amor" "At thirty, the age of this Other who also, and contrary to his plans, inspired hatred and crimes for his followers, fomenting and consuming the males, wandering like a vagabond, she [Fatima] met Rachid Amor" (2001, 29). The comparison between Fatima and Christ in the Bible, or rather the closeness of their ages and the differences in the mission of each, is interesting for at least two reasons. First, Marouane seems to subtly emphasize the reasons for which Fatima responds by opting for vengeance rather than the completion of her mission, like Christ. Next, and as a consequence of the first observation, in acknowledging with Christian theology that Christ was on a mission and that his death would save lives, Fatima neither has a mission nor is she endowed with some divine power that might allow her to accept with pride and courage her own "crucifixion." This brief, seemingly banal passage juxtaposing the two figures (Fatima and Jesus Christ) seems to me central for the characterization of vengeance in this novel as a cornerstone of its meaning.

In effect, isn't Marouane suggesting and even indicating that "le pardon, la compassion, la merci constituent des comportements très valorisés auxquels l'Église et la société en général offrent de puissants renforcements positifs, la vengeance étant perçue comme un sentiment primitif, une attitude blâmable, un acte morbide, grossier et simpliste" "pardon, compassion, mercy constitute highly valued behaviors that the Church and society in general offer as powerful positive reinforcements, with vengeance being perceived as a primitive sentiment, a blameworthy attitude, a morbid, crude, and simplistic act," in the words of Suzanne Robert (1999, 22)?

The answer to this question appears to be in the affirmative, as it is quite clear that Fatima, the avenging woman, seems to bring together in their fullness the criteria, characteristics, and conditions of possibility and effectivity of vengeance as enumerated by Robert, namely, "de l'imagination, de la lucidité, de la subtilité, de la finesse, de la logique, de la méditation, de la ténacité et de la solitude, surtout. Elle exige du courage, celui d'aller à l'encontre de tous et de forger dans cet univers de bien-pensants un couloir parallèle, isole, secret, éclatant de sa noirceur où, enfin, l'indignation guérira par la fureur" "imagination, lucidity, subtlety, finesse, logic, meditation, tenacity, and solitude, above all. It demands courage, that of going forth to meet all and to forge in this universe of self-righteous a parallel hallway, isolated, secret, exploding from its darkness where, finally, indignation will cure through fury" (1999, 22).

We thus find, thanks to the detour of vengeance, a loophole in madness and an access that is finally made possible for a new identity to take form at the point of juncture, in the interstitial space that opens up when, at the end of the novel, in a prophetic vein, Mlle Kosra and Mme Amor encounter each other through the memory of the other, a true condition for the emergence of a "self" that, having transcended trauma, can finally begin to be rebuilt. *Le châtiment des hypocrites* by Leïla Marouane is probably, from that viewpoint, the most vibrant testimony of what Shoshana Felman has said about madness, namely:

> Raison et folie sont liées; la folie est essentiellement un phénomène de la pensée: d'une pensée qui dénonce, en la pensée de l'autre, l'Autre de la pensée. La folie n'est possible que dans un monde en conflit de pensées. La question de la folie n'est donc autre que la question de la pensée. La question de la folie, c'est précisément ce qui fait de l'essence de la pensée, une *question*. (1978, 37)

> Reason and madness are thereby inextricably linked: madness is essentially a phenomenon of thought: of thought that claims to denounce, in another's thought, the Other of thought: that which thought is not. Madness can only occur

within a world in conflict, within a conflict of thoughts. The question of madness is nothing less than the question of thought itself: the question of madness, in other words, is that which turns the essence of thought, precisely, *into a question*. (Felman 51–52)

In linking Felman's thought to Marouane's novel, it becomes clear that madness alone allows Fatima to collapse, to expose the madness that characterizes and haunts the thinking of men, who are holders of patriarchal power. Furthermore, by denouncing the patriarchal thought that enslaves women in postcolonial Algeria, the militant Algerian writer skillfully employs madness to open up a debate on the question of rape, to lift the veil from a judiciary system that, under the pretext of maintaining social—and often religious, order—blames victims and reduces to nothingness the vindictive function of the judiciary, by offering the rapist an excuse that legitimizes, indeed even encourages rape: a way out of the penal consequences if the criminal agrees to marry his victim.

In such a world marked by "conflict of thoughts," through her main character the writer thus poses the question about the status of the woman, doubly exiled from the interior and exterior of her native land, reduced to a simple sounding board for the will of men, who are moreover the depositaries of state and religious power. We can also note, furthermore, that this work is made possible, in Marouane's writing, by the tension between the need for a woman who has been victimized by rape to mourn, her inability to obtain justice, and the imperative for vengeance without which the crime cannot be forgotten. This tension can be read through a subversion of Paul Ricoeur's thesis on forgetting and forgiving. In *La mémoire, l'histoire, l'oubli* (2000), the philosopher sketches a phenomenology of memory that seeks to go beyond memory of the past. This approach is important for its attempt to understand the ways in which Fatima, the profaned and humiliated woman, positions herself according to her condition as a female object. How to mourn a symbolic death? Answering this question requires us to leave the literary world to engage with a more ethical and moral perspective that can be rooted in a conversation between literature and human rights. In examining novels as historical and sociological contexts, we must build on what the novel offers to reflect on the ethical dimension of the world projected by the author. Resolving the tension between victimization, the inability to obtain justice and vengeance necessarily calls for achieving an appeased memory for the female character. To achieve an appeased memory, then, Ricœur arrives at a solution by distinguishing, on the one hand, the need to forgive and, on the other hand, the impossible need to forget. He tells us: "L'oubli et le pardon désignent, séparément et conjointement, l'horizon de toute notre recherche. Séparément, dans la mesure où ils relèvent chacun d'une problématique distincte: pour l'oubli, celle de la mémoire et de la fidélité au passé; pour le pardon, celle de la culpabilité et de la réconciliation avec le passé" (2000, 536) / "Forgetting and forgiveness, separately and together, designate the horizon of our entire investigation. Separately, inasmuch as they each belong to a distinct problematic: for forgetting, the problematic of memory and faithfulness to the past; for forgiveness, guilt and reconciliation with the past" (2004, 412). I find this theoretical stance particularly pertinent and useful for highlighting the uniqueness of *Le châtiment des hypocrites*. If indeed, in Cathy Caruth's words, "trauma describes an overwhelming experience of sudden or catastrophic events in which the response to the event occurs in the often delayed, uncontrolled repetitive appearance of hallucinations and other intrusive phenomena" (1996, 11), then the resort to a work on memory might constitute a way of healing the wound.

In fact, Ricœur's thought on this matter reveals the complex relationship between memory and forgetting. In this sense, remembering would be forgetting. Nevertheless, and this nuance is necessary, Ricœur emphasizes that it is not a matter of forgetting by erasing but a forgetting that makes memory possible. Nothingness would thus account for the existence of a forgetting that is legitimate in that it does not silence evil but speaks of it in a pacified tone. In the context of Marouane's novel, we easily see that Fatima's trajectory is radically removed from memory and reconciliation with the past following the model put forth by Ricœur. By choosing the means of reparation of crime by crime, she places herself outside the "cercle de l'accusation et de la punition" (Ricœur 2000, 619) / "the connection between forgiveness and punishment" (2004, 470), by indicating that, for her, pardon is only possible if she repairs through violence the offense that she experienced. In other words, if Ricœur makes a plea for an amnesia and an amnesty thought of as the "travail de mémoire, complété par celui du deuil, et guidé par l'esprit de pardon" (2000, 589) / "work of memory, which work is completed by the work of mourning and guided by the spirit of forgiveness" (2004, 456), Fatima communicates the quest for her identity that was distorted by the murders through the punishment of the hypocrites, putting to death her tormentors. Through a significant prolepsis on the very first page of the novel, one that functions to frame what is to follow in detail throughout the rest of the narration, Marouane evokes the moment of encounter between two personalities that are in effect but the doubling of the same person: "Ce jour de canicule exceptionnelle sous le ciel parisien, barbotant dans une marre de sang, Mme Amor se remémora enfin Mlle Kosra" "On that exceptionally hot summer day under the Parisian skies, splashed in a pool of blood, Mme Amor was finally able to remember Mlle Kosra" (prologue). It transpires from this anamnesis that the efforts to plunge into oblivion that had been rendered impossible by the trauma of rape and mutilations can only be accomplished through the surfacing of a memory brought on by the murder of her husband.

Finally, *Le châtiment des hypocrites* assures a double sociohistorical and philosophical function. As for a social-historical function, Marouane's novel offers a way back for Algerian women whose rapes and other forms of torture have very often been passed over in silence in the official discourse of the Algerian War and even independent Algeria, with respect to the Penal Code that does not automatically sanction rape. From that perspective, in response to a society in which rape is not considered a crime of blood, the Algerian writer, through her imaginary, liberates the female character who takes it upon herself to rectify the failure of the State and protect the dominated sex. If Marouane's writing is considered cathartic, it is also because the catharsis of the writer mimics that of her female characters, who emerge from the darkness of night thanks to vengeance. And that vengeance is not be subjected by the novel's reader to an axiological evaluation, to a value judgment. Vengeance in the work of Leïla Marouane is not an outgrowth of madness but is located beyond good and evil, such that, as Michel Erman writes, "la vengeance ne méconnaît ni la capacité de juger ni le projet concret, et dans bien des situations il n y a pas lieu de douter que celui qui se venge est bel et bien un sujet qui veut défendre sa dignité" "vegeance is neither unaware of the ability to judge nor the concrete project, and in many situations, there is no room to doubt that the one seeking to avenge himself or herself is first and foremost a subject that wants to defend his or her dignity" (2012, 20). The concept of dignity spoken about by the French philosopher in that quotation leads me to the philosophical function of *Le châtiment des hypocrites*: the characterization of the Algerian woman as "slave" that I spoke about earlier and the concept by which, as a marginal figure, the woman can emerge from her slavery through vengeance. Consider another gloss of the philosopher Erman on vengeance:

Car ne pas répliquer à une offense, refuser la logique de la riposte, c'est reconnaître la supériorité de qui vous a agressé et accepter de lui être soumis en abdiquant sa fierté et son honneur. L'honneur, qui recoupe l'estime ou l'amour de soi, ne dépend pas d'un quelconque calcul mais du regard d'autrui et de la dignité qu'il nous reconnaît ou nous accorde, voire de la renommée qu'il confère. L'honneur est donc une donnée de la vie en société, son contraire étant la honte. En termes hégéliens, ne pas laver un affront, c'est vouloir oublier son état d'humilié alors que l'opprobre vous frappe publiquement: c'est être un esclave. (2012, 14)

For by not responding to an offense, refusing the logic of counterattack, is to recognize the superiority of the one who has been the aggressor against you and accepting to be subject to him by abdicating one's pride and honor. Honor, which overlaps with esteem or self-love, does not depend on just any calculus, but on the regard of another and the dignity that he recognizes in us or gives us, indeed, on the reknown he confers. Honor is thus a give in life in society, its opposite being shame. In Hegelian terms, not to wipe off an affront, is to want to forget one's state of humiliation when hatred strikes you publicly: it is to be a slave.

In opting therefore for murder, Fatima renounces her condition of slave and reclaims her honor, all while deciding to renounce shame, to make use again of Erman's oppositional pair. Murder as reparation stands out, in the novel, as filling the legal that Moussaoui commented on with regards to the criminalization of the victim of rape. It also brings light to the absence of reflexion and recognition of war crimes in the history of colonialism and postcolonial violence. I would go even further in saying that in freely choosing prostitution rather than suicide, Fatima marks her choice and determination to re-possess her body that has been abused by abduction and rapes, and to transform the site of her killing (her body) into a perfect weapon of combat. The moral choice is a choice of freedom to repair and to survive when the state is not taking care of the victims.

In a rigorously philosophical logic inspired by Giorgio Agamben, we could say that she remedies the "profanation" of her body by a purely profanatory act itself, but in reverse. In effect, if we consider the kidnapping and the service to which her body was placed as a profanation, I would suggest rather that it corresponds to a sacralization, with her body having been removed from outside the sphere of its common usage by the terrorists, and enclosed in a realm that is outside of human rights.

To understand this seeming confusion, we must again follow the thought of Agamben and return to Ancient Rome to find the meaning of "profanation." Agamben tells us that in its proper sense, profane means what, from once being sacred or religious, is now restored to use and ownership by humans. By thus distinguishing between secularization and profanation, we find that profanation "neutralizes what it profanes. Once profaned, that which was unavailable and separate loses its aura and is returned to use" (2007, 77). Agamben further argues that this neutralization of the profaned object and its return to use are both political operations that guarantee the exercise of power by returning it to a secret model, deactivate the apparatus of power, and return to common use the spaces that power had seized. From the preceding, we can then postulate that Fatima's body had been isolated in a religious sphere of fundamental Islamism by her rapists, then experienced a profanation that deactivated the means of power that had formerly been confiscated by her abductors and rapists, and subsequently returned her body to her own use, unlike the unproductive use of the body of a slave. By achieving this coup de force, Marouane confers upon a female character a double quality that is eminently philosophical, "destituent potential" and "inoperativity," which have in common, according to Agamben, "the capacity to deactivate something and render it inoperative—a power, a function, a human operation—without simply destroying it but by liberating the potentials that have remained inactive in it in order to allow a different use of them" (2015, 273). Through the character of Fatima Amor, or Fatima Kosra, whose choices and actions, but above all vengeance render inoperative the power of life and death of man over woman, empty the sexual and reproductive function of its contents, and deactivate male domination that reduces woman to a marginal being, *Le châtiment des hypocrites* ultimately suggests the possible path to a future for woman as subject and not simply as an object. Marouane's choice to name her protagonist Fatima, the preferred daughter and political advisor of the prophet, a woman who was given a lot of agency, therefore acquires all its significance: the novel signals the path to the recognition by the state of trauma and violence against women. There is a clear testimonial dimension to the novel that again fills the gap of human rights resolutions, and points to the woman as a *homo expendibilis* who, from being disaffiliated and kept out of the weft of the nation's system of protections, resist precarity and gain visibility.

NOTES

1. For further reading, see Vince (2015).
2. Stora's comments are in relation with the 1984 Code de la famille.

Chapter 4

Precarious Lives
Slum Dwellers and Social Outcasts

SLUMDOG TERRORISTS: CHILDREN, MARGINALIZATION, AND RADICALIZATION IN *LES ETOILES DE SIDI MOUMEN*

The title "Slumdog Terrorists" is an allusion to Danny Boyle's *Slumdog Millionaire* (2008), which was a true hit film, as seen in the many awards garnered by the British filmmaker the year it came out. In this drama, which interweaves a personal story with political or more accurately social questions, slum life in Mumbai, India, is presented in the most straightforward of ways. It is the story of two orphans, Jamal and Salim, who live a life of extreme poverty in the streets of Mumbai. Where Salim joins the world of crime to survive, his brother Jamal lives off small jobs and puts his imagination to use in fighting poverty, until the day he wins the grand prize on a television game show, without previously having been the victim of abuses assuredly linked to his social origins. The police have a hard time believing that this child of the notorious slums, without any education at all, could accomplish such an achievement without the benefit of fraud. The plot of Boyle's film is of interest to me specifically for two reasons: first, the film pushes us to reflect on the condition of a childhood of abandonment and poverty; second, by inscribing the detention of the hero, whose only crime is his origin, in an exceptionally disadvantaged setting, then by paralleling it with the trajectory of his brother, who finds refuge in criminality, Boyle gives his film a distinctly social dimension, and thus one that is eminently political. The slums are also the setting for *Les étoiles de Sidi Moumen* by Mahi Binebine (2010). Mohammed Choukri's *For Bread Alone* (1972) had already introduced us to the life of street children in Morocco. Only, in the Moroccan slums that are represented in Binebine's novel, the children follow a trajectory closer to the criminal Salim in *Slumdog Millionaire,* but even more of a criminality that is pushed to the extreme. We know that Morocco was shaken by terrorist attacks in the city of Casablanca in May 2003. And whether by chance or coincidence, the perpetrators of these attacks were, based on the reports that followed, inhabitants of Sidi Moumen, the same slum that is featured in Binebine's novel. By following the trajectory of the young children in the novel, I propose to show, first, the ways in which the slum is a space of segregation. Then, and because of the segregation and exclusion that afflict this slum's inhabitants, I will suggest that the vulnerability of its inhabitants becomes the road to radicalization, which itself leads to the terrorist attacks. Clearly distinguishing between the terroristic violence perpetrated by the children in the novel and the violence that results from a religious ideology in the strict sense of the word, I will show that, despite everything, irrational violence preserves a rational dimension, in that it becomes the sole means of existence for an entire population of the socially excluded and the marginal. I maintain that, from this perspective, by fostering insensitivity or even remaining insensitive to the social disaffiliation of certain segments of the population, slum inhabitants whose bodies are reduced to pure biological life and deprived of social and civil protections, the State indirectly and unconsciously creates conditions that are favorable to a rise in security threats that weaken both the precarious classes and the socially integrated, dominant classes. While it might be argued that work on marginal bodies is not the place to explore the reasons of terrorism, I will submit that by imagining the circumstances and motives behind the attacks, Mahi Binebine uses fiction as a site of reflexion on the link between precarity and insecurity. In doing so, the Moroccan writer also mediates and invites his reader to rethink the slum child as a *homo expendibilis,* caught between social disaffiliation and various options for becoming-subject.

The Slum: A Biopoliticized Space

Les étoiles de Sidi Moumen tells the story of the inhabitants of a slum of Casablanca, excluded in its poverty and misery, exposed to all sort of maladies and perversions. In this novel, it is the children/youth who occupy a central place and who constitute the turning point in the story. The account is narrated by Yachine, a young boy who will lead the reader's gaze not only across the atrocious living conditions of his peers but also across the ways in which a group of his friends and he himself, under the influence of "the men with beards," turn to terrorist violence. From the very start, Binebine's novel is a canvas that strips away the veneer of the two-tiered Moroccan society, where city dwellers enjoy relative social and civil protection, whereas those on the periphery are reduced to captivity. In her article "Zones of

Perceptual Enclosure: The Aesthetics of Immobility in Casablanca's Literary *Bidonvilles*" (2016), Katarzyna Pieprzak bases her study on the work of Frantz Fanon in *Les damnés de la terre* (1961) with respect to the division of space in the colonial context, to show the lack of mobility and the captivity as significant elements in two Moroccan novels, one of which is this one by Binebine. While the emphasis on the oppositional construction related to city and slum is absolutely pertinent in Pieprzak's analysis, I would like to shift the reflection on the slum from the question of mobility toward the political status of its inhabitants. While emphasizing the description of space as a field of failure, enclosure, and absence of any horizon, I will go further and reflect on segregation by attempting to inscribe the marginalization of the children and inhabitants of the novel's slum within a biopolitical perspective. A concept borrowed from Michel Foucault, *biopolitics* refers to a form of power that is no longer applied to the control of territories, but to the control of individuals. By biopolitics, Foucault meant "the attempt starting from the eighteenth century, to rationalize the problems posed to governmental practice by phenomena characteristic of a set of living beings forming a population: health, hygiene, birthrate, life expectancy, race" (2008, 317). As we see, the question of government is at the heart of the problem of biopower, inasmuch as the rationalization of the problems Foucault discusses presupposes that the State has deployed techniques of power that belong to itself alone in its mission to manage and control human lives. To view how this management/ administration of slum populations in Binebine's novel is organized, we must first stop and consider the aesthetic and ethical parameters of the representation and carving-up of the space.

The novel opens with a description of Sidi Moumen, summing up the relationship between the occupation of space and the lives of those who inhabit it, as opposed to those who live in the world outside it, through the narrator's own statement that "un promeneur pourrait longer notre quartier sans se douter de son existence. Orné de crénelures, un imposant mur en pisé le sépare du boulevard où un flot interrompu de voitures fait un bruit de tous les diables. Dans ce mur, on avait creusé des fentes semblables à des meurtrières d'où l'on pouvait contempler à loisir l'autre monde" "a pedestrian could walk along our quarter and never doubt its existence. Decked out with crenelations, an imposing mud wall separates it from the boulevard where a ceaseless flow of cars makes a hellish sound. In this wall, there are cracks like arrow slits where you could leisurely contemplate the other world" (2010, 9). This description of the slum, recalling the unawareness of the lives of its inhabitants and the contrast between two worlds, is highly revealing of a space that is doubly beyond space and time. The wall alluded to by the narrator marks the very edge between the slum and the other world, a division that is all the more paradoxical because the slum appears to be excluded in its inclusion. Likewise, the description of the house where the narrator and his family live, sleeping "à six dans une pièce grande comme un caveau . . . cocktail de relents à peine identifiables: odeur de chaussures, transpiration, de fond de culotte" "sleeping up to six in a room that is large like a cave [with] a mix of stenches that could scarcely be identified: smells of shoes, sweat, panties" (22) reinforces the reading according to which, beyond the simple framework of the house, Sidi Moumen is a space of rot and putrefaction. We must note, as already observed by Fredj Stambouli (1972), that the appearances of slums in the Maghreb are a direct consequence of the massive urbanization that took place after the dispossession of land during the colonial period. In fact, for Stambouli, "c'est dans ce contexte d'une urbanisation massive qu'émerge pour la première fois, au Maghreb le phénomène de bidonville qui s'impose comme une réalité massive" "it is in this context of a massive urbanization that for the first time, we see the emergence in the Maghreb of the phenomenon of the slum, which establishes itself as a massive reality" (1972, 31). These slums, which Stambouli rightly calls "ceintures de misère" "poverty belts," are endlessly proliferating because of a demographic explosion, to the point that, as the narrator states, "s'il avait existé un livre de records à Casablanca, Yemma y aurait figuré en bonne place: quatorze grossesses en quatorze ans! Qui dit mieux?" "if there had been a book of records in Casablance, Yemma would have held a special position in it: fourteen pregnancies in fourteen years! What more can be said?" (14). The mention of demographic gift is important here because it speaks to the particular context of Morocco, as has been shown by Brahim Elmorchid, a Moroccan economist. Without attemoting a synthesis of Elmorchid's argument, I will underline that he states that in Morocco, while demographic growth was an opportunity for economic development, it has produced the contrary, with its social consequences. Elmochid writes:

> Recent theoretical studies and the experiences of some emerging countries demonstrate that this exceptional phenomenon is a favorable opportunity for economic take-off. It represents an ambitious development project that, if utilized properly, can lead to massive savings, thereby increasing the pace of investment and accelerating growth with the potential to create new jobs, decrease the unemployment rate, and reduce negative migration. In the case of Morocco, it is clear that this opportunity for development did not come with any real gains. Rather, it transformed into a curse. In addition to the lack of improvement among macroeconomic indices, some sensitive social indices recorded negative results. In particular, the unemployment rate among educated youth experienced a worrisome rise and negative migration, both domestically and abroad, reached alarming numbers. (2018, 89)

From what precedes, it is clear that youths stand out as the most vulnerable category, in that their integration into working life did not follow demographic growth, a gift that, according to Elmorchid, has turned into a curse.

The above examples, along with the fact that the division of urban space dating back to the colonial period is still a reality in today's Maghreb, bear strong witness to the marginality that, in Africa, is not a phenomenon tied to a specific period, and is not only permanent but undoubtedly derives from a polemical division of the resources in these countries. Clearly, with regard to Sidi Moumen, we can state that if colonization favored the pauperization of the peasants, the local political authorities who followed after colonization added into the mix the marginalization of the urban proletariat. Consequently, Binebine's Sidi Moumen, doubtless like other slums in the Maghreb and in Africa in general, is a segregated space where the life of the human being has no value. In that space, which can be summed up as a public dump site, with its trash cans spilling over with waste, according to the narrator, "on s'habitue à tout par nos contrées, comme à cette odeur de pourriture et de mort devenue si familière et qui collait à la peau de chacun de nous" "people get used to everything in our parts, like the smell of rot and death that is so familiar and that stick to the skin of every one of us" (2010, 24).

Sidi Moumen, this space of chaos and degradation, is the result of a politics of the exclusion of undesirables and its sources are to be found in a technique of the government of men that requires discussion. This slum is an illustration of urban apartheid—to use the expression from Chantal Tetrault and Paul Silverstein on the subject of French *banlieues*—that follows the oscillations of a politics of exclusion, erasure, and concealment of a reality that consecrates the relegation of the marginal, the poor, and the minorities to a space that is literally cut off from the rest of the city. The geographical location of the slum (on the city's periphery) and its collective perception (zones without rights) basically follow the same logic, and effectively lead to segregation, since it is understood that the populations of Sidi Moumen "non seulement connaissent une forte concentration spatiale, mais qui de surcroit se trouvent plus ou moins assignées à cette concentration, sous l'effet des pratiques et de logiques d'exclusion ou de relégation dont elles sont en quelque sorte 'l'objet'" "not only experience a strong spatial concentration, but additionally find themselves more or less assigned to that concentration, because of practices and logics of exclusion or relegation of which they are in some way the 'object,'" to use the second condition for identifying segregation according to Yves Grafmeyer (1994, 95). It then becomes a question for the authorities in Morocco to monitor the "invisibilization" of this social category and this section of the population relegated to the slums.

The notion of segregation I am referring to here can be polemical—given that in a general manner, segregation commonly refers to a racial context.

However, in my analysis here, and unlike in French or American ghettoes, slum dwellers in Morocco cannot be said to be of different races than those occupying visible spaces. Nevertheless, and beyond the aspect of relegation that marks the slum, we can even postulate that this segregation is built upon a "différence de races" "difference in races," if we consider the doctrine of races developed by Arthur de Gobineau in his *Essai sur l'inégalité des races humaines* (1853) in which he made a distinction between the aristocracy and the bourgeoisie as two distinct races. Bringing class distinction as the origins of race, it must be noted that the political regime of Morocco is a monarchy, and as such, it informs all social interactions and discourses. Thus, by admitting that the separation is marked on the basis of social class, the segregation that I am speaking about here corresponds, moreover, to a "pratique délibérée de relégation d'une fraction de la population à l'écart des zones d'habitat occupées par les catégories plus favorisées" "deliberate practice of the relegation of one fraction of the population to the outside of the living areas occupied by the more advantaged categories" (Brun 1994, 24). As we have seen, segregation necessarily implies a social inequality, and in the Moroccan context of Binebine's novel, the unequal division of social privileges impels us to consider the reasons for and process of violence and domination that force the excluded of the slum off to the side. One of the most interesting aspects of segregation found in the novel is indeed space. Again, the spatial organization is unique there because of the creation and maintenance of a margin, the banlieues, a periphery that is truly not found inside or outside the privileged space, and neither in public nor in private.

My thesis is that the banishment of the slums is inscribed in a vast governmental measure of governmental control over marginalized bodies, one that corresponds to what Foucault saw as "a triangle-sovereignty-discipline-government, which has as its primary target the population and its essential mechanism the apparatus of security" (1991, 102). We should note that even though the figure of the sovereign is rarely if ever evoked in the novel, the governmentality I am speaking of here does seem to reinforce sovereign power, one that in today's Morocco tends to blame the poor, especially in the slums where they are part of what can be called the criminalization of poverty. With respect to the forsaking of the slums, we see a movement from compassion to the culpabilization of the poor, according to the gradation described by Serge Paugam: "Dans cette optique, les pauvres sont en quelque sorte accusés de ne pas suffisamment se prendre en charge eux-mêmes et les pouvoirs publics n'ont pas à les aider davantage. Chaque individu est responsable de lui-même et seul son courage peut lui éviter de connaître la pauvreté" "In this light, the poor are in some way accused of not sufficiently taking care of themselves and so the public authorities do not need to help them anymore. Each individual is responsible for himself or herself, and only his or her courage can help avoid the experience of poverty" (1991, preface). While Paugam's observation can be applied as an observation of French society, it seems appropriate for understanding the decline seen in Binebine's novel. Furthermore, and therein probably lies the nuance that must be emphasized between the poor and the marginal, the inhabitants of Sidi Moumen are not part of the work chain and capitalist production. They are marginal beings with precarious jobs—when they have them—reduced to an enclave at the city limits, and condemned to survive through their own resourcefulness and petty crime, or in the case of women, prostitution. That is why I use the concept of biopolitics to explain segregation for the slums of Sidi Moumen. If the difference between the notion of biopolitics in Foucault and in Agamben lies at the level of life as an object of power (Foucault) and of the relationship between sovereignty and naked life (Agamben 1997), nevertheless the approaches of these two philosophers seem valuable for characterizing biopower in *Les étoiles de Sidi Moumen*.

In Agamben, I find the notion of camp particularly pertinent for characterizing the slums' geographic isolation. If the slum is not properly speaking the consequence of a disciplinary isolation or a detention, it is still a place of banishment; but even more, it is what Agamben perceives as "a piece of territory that is placed outside the normal juridical order; for all that however, it is not simply an external space . . . what is being included in the camp is captured outside, that is, it is included by virtue of its very exclusion," to use his words (1997, 40). As can be seen in the novel by Binebine, the presence of the police station that the youths of Sidi Moumen will set on fire, evoked on page 31, is the palpable sign of what happens when the State is disengaged, though not completely absent, from this space of reclusion. The slum is thus included by its exclusion, and even though its inhabitants are not in a penitentiary, the slum is controlled by police, who abuse the marginal people who are in a space that is simultaneously open and closed, where every attempt at mobility comes down to a never-ending starting over. Regarding the biopoliticization of the space of the slum, I would add that in effect everything transpires as if this urban body, due to its gangrene, is symbolically cut off from the rest of the city, as illustrated by the wall in which the youths have to make holes to be able to look out onto the other world, the real world, since they exist in a world outside. The body and space thus show a strong relationship that allows us to look at the value of bodies in terms of the spaces they occupy or that they do not occupy. Seen in this light, we can then understand that this isolation is eminently biopolitical, and can be summed up as fear of the Other, and more precisely, fear of contagion.

Foucault referred to the plague and leprosy as two pathologies that allow us to understand human actions. The idea of "impurities" in the preceding thought echoes the two paradigms used by Foucault to describe the management by humans of leprosy and the plague, which correspond to the "great confinement" on the one hand, and "the correct training" on the other. He writes:

> The following, according to an order published at the end of the seventeenth century, were the measures to be taken when the plague appeared in town. First, a strict spatial partitioning: the closing of the town and its outlying districts, a prohibition to leave the town on pain of death, the killing of all stray animals; the division of the town into distinct quarters, each governed by an intendant. (1995, 195)

In the same way, Foucault adds, "The leper was caught up in a practice of rejection, of exile-enclosure; he was left to his doom in mass among which it was useless to differentiate; those sick of the plague were caught up in a meticulous tactical partitioning in which individual differentiations were the constructing effects of a power that multiplied, articulated, and subdivided itself" (1995, 198). Thus, the Sidi Moumen slum, due to its contagious impurities, was cut off from Casablanca so that the two spatial realities, even though coalescent, function only on a parallel, but never complementary parallel. Due to their social status, which also becomes pathological, the inhabitants of the slum are held at the periphery, in short, made invisible and symbolically quarantined in a quasi-medical isolation for the sick with contagious illnesses, in the apparent desire to preserve the good health of the advantaged classes. If we admit that the inhabitants of Sidi Moumen are the natural confluence of every kind of decline, according to the narrator, and that the lepers and plague-bearers that Foucault speaks of are significant in characterizing the treatment of the marginal, then we must allow that because of the fear that they inspire, Moroccan society by arranging their sidelining seeks to shelter itself from danger.

Michela Marzano's observation on the fear of the Other and his or her exclusion is then pertinent for interpreting the exclusion, rejection, and societal indifference that isolates the "Other," the "abnormal," all the better to remove him from sight. Regarding lepers and the plague-inflicted, she writes: "Leur enfermement et leur mise à l'écart sont censés effacer les peurs collectives et sauvegarder le lien social. Comme dans le cas des épidémies de peste et de lèpre, la société cherche à éviter le danger de la contagion, du désordre, de l'éclatement" "Their imprisonment and sidelining are thought to erase the collective fears and safeguard their social ties. As in the case of plague epidemics and leprosy, society seeks to avoid the danger of contagion, disorder, and eruptions" (2009, 28). Still, if the goal of setting aside the "abnormal" is aimed at reassurance, there is still the matter, Marzano, emphasizes, of knowing whether we can really be reassured by covering up what we don't want to see or hear about with a veil of silence. That is the question that Binebine sets out to answer by underscoring in his novel not merely a justification of terrorist violence, but the processes of social disqualification that can push the marginal into fighting their own Others, sometimes through extreme methods like terrorism. Finally, I will analyze the emergence of terrorism by highlighting the close, but often ignored, relationship between terrorism and sociopolitical conditions.

Up against Marginalization: Terrorism as an Outlet?

In an essay entitled *Confronting Poverty* (2010) Corinne Graff, a senior adviser at the United States Institute of Peace, authors a chapter where she links poverty, underdevelopment, and violent extremism in weak States, citing among others, the terrorist attacks of 2003 in Casablanca. Graff concludes her analysis by noting that terrorist Attacks are growing more numerous and deadlier in the developing world, where security control tend to me more lax. She goes on to note that preventing terrorist attacks would save lives first and foremost in developing countries. And more interesting to my analysis of the link between social disqualification and insecurity, she notes that "in addition to protecting US national security, incorporating development assistance into an international counterterrorism strategy is a long-overdue global solution to a global problem" (2010, 80) In the same volume, Peter Warren Singer, a political scientist, entitles his chapter "The New Children of Terror." In this chapter, he reflects on the reasons why children are increasingly present in conflicts, both as targets and participants. Singer makes it clear that "focusing solely on the leadership of terrorist organizations also misses the larger socioeconomic context of radicalism and terrorism, as well as how and where terrorists thrive. Successful terrorist groups are based in (and thrive in) zones of chaos, poor governance, and lawlessness" (2010, 118). While it can be argued that both Corinne Graff and Peter Singer are writing from an American perspective, I insist that, as social scientists and security experts, they clearly see marginalization and poverty as potential sources for terrorist violence. Building on their works, I argue that it is particularly difficult, even illogical, to want to understand the emergence of terrorist violence and terrorism in *Les étoiles de Sidi Moumen* by separating them from their geopolitical and sociopolitical contexts. I am not maintaining here that terrorism is a path of response to injustices, and far be it from me to seek to justify terrorist violence. But on the other hand, I find it important to underscore that in a global context marked by the rise in fear and insecurity, there can be a strong temptation to privilege emotions and blindly condemn violence without seeking to understand its deep causes, without in fact trying to explain this violence. In a remarkable article on the creation of terrorism in Binebine's novel,

Mustapha Hamil provides a lengthy analysis of the human condition that led to the terrorist attacks. I will not repeat Hamil's long, pertinent analyses, but for the purposes of my discussion, I will select a passage that is significant to me: "Two weeks after the 'May 16 attacks,' King Mohamed VI visited Sidi Moumen and promised to improve its housing conditions but nothing concrete on the ground was accomplished, except perhaps that Sidi Moumen got the reputation as a hotbed of fanatic kamikazes" (2011, 566). Then, Hamil continues by stating: "As Chifaa Nassir puts in the weekly Maroc Hebdo International: Certaines mosquées des environs ont été fermées, et celles qui restent sont surveillées pour qu'elles ne puissent servir que de lieux de prières. This raises the common issue of literature's role and ability to influence the course of politics, especially in the country where illiteracy is alarming high" (2011, 566). [Certain area mosques were closed, and the rest were monitored so that they couldn't serve as places of worship]. The author of the cited article indeed has reason to see in the unkept promises of the King of Morocco to ameliorate the living conditions of the inhabitants of the slum an illustration of literature's inability to provoke social change. For my part, and as a complement to that reading, I maintain that the hidden matrix of the tenacity of terrorism in the Moroccan context can be found precisely in the never-kept promises of the king, and furthermore in the stigmatization of Sidi Moumen as a cradle of terrorism. At the end of the novel, from the realm of the dead, the narrator observes that if that points to the futility of terrorist attacks, it nevertheless appears as the element that authorizes the understanding of the motivations of violence by the *sans-parts* of the slum: "Le bidonville n'a pas changé. Il s'est même étendu et les baraquements autrefois séparés forment désormais une ville" "The slum hasn't changed. It's even spread and the barracks that used to separate is now form a city" (2010, 153). What I hope to achieve in my analysis of the relationship between terrorism and marginalization with respect to Binebine's novel is the understanding that, as Ann Norton puts it, "no one should have to argue any longer that terrorism can be a rational and reasonable strategy" (2013, 89).

With respect to keeping Sidi Moumen at the periphery in the days following the attacks and despite the heavy media coverage that followed it, and literary contributions such as Binebine's novel, to understand the security situation in Morocco, we should make a detour over into neighboring Algeria. Algeria achieved independence in 1962 after eight long years of war that led to deep separations within Algerian society. In this country adjacent to Morocco, the military and psychological damages of war continued to weigh on the nation's moving forward. An entire generation of sincere young patriots dedicated to the revolutionary cause, acquired in spite of themselves, the status of "traitors." Such were the conditions whereby, thirty years after independence, Algeria succumbed to total chaos when "dans les années quatre-vingt/quatre-vingt-dix, plusieurs processus majeurs se développent au Maghreb et entrent en résonance avec un courant politique qui, les années précédentes, avait fait 'profil bas,' du moins sur la scène publique: l'islamisme" (Stora 2001, 77) / "in the 1980s and 1990s several major processes developed in the Magrheb and began to resonate with Islamism, a political current that in previous years had had a 'low profile,' at least on the public stage" (trans. 2001, 179). What we must understand is that the Islamist violence or even the Islamist era is a logical consequence of the long history of decolonization in Algeria, and this explains the detour we must make through the long-ago past to better identify the question of insecurity linked to Islamic terrorism. This necessary passage, is joyfully inscribed by Algerian writer Rachid Boudjedra in his novel *Les figuiers de Barbarie*, as, through oscillations between poignant episodes of the war of liberation and the present, the time of enunciation by the narrator who is sitting in an airplane, he inserts an important reflection that strongly suggests the direct link between the failure of the elite in post-independence Algeria and the rise of Islamist networks. After recalling the assassination of Abbane Ramdane by his own brothers in arms and struggle, the novelist hammers out the role of the elite in the days following the independences in an extract that deserves attention, despite its length:

> Nous parlions souvent du ratage de l'Indépendance, de la corruption généralisée, et de la lutte des clans. Nous nous posions, alors, cette question inévitable: Comment l'Organisation qui, pendant les sept années de la guerre, avait été quasi parfaite s'est-elle transformée en un pouvoir véreux, enrichi, arrogant et finalement, idiot? Dès les premiers jours de l'indépendance les factions de l'Organisation se sont mises à se combattre avec une violence, une sauvagerie et un acharnement qui nous avaient bouleversés, Omar et moi. Après quelques jours de liesse populaire, la Kasba, bastion à Alger de l'Organisation pendant les sept longues années de la guerre, devint le centre d'affrontements sanglants entre groupes rivaux. La foule refusait cette folie fratricide et ne criait qu'un seul slogan: "Sept ans, ça suffit" Nous nous mêlâmes tous les jours à cette foule en colère et désarmée qui dénonçait cette guerre civile. Comme si, après sept ans de guerre, une année de mise à sac et de tueries organisées par l'OAS dans les grandes villes du pays n'avait pas suffi. Il nous fallait encore cette guerre de la Kasba qui allait inaugurer, en fait, un cycle de violences qui n'est pas terminé, à ce jour. (2010, 158–59)

> We often spoke of how Independence had turned sour, of widespread corruption and tribal bickering. We therefore posed ourselves this inevitable question: How had the Organization, which had comported itself so impeccably throughout the seven-year war, turned into such a dishonest, money-grubbing, arrogant and

finally idiotic government? From the first days of Independence, the factions in the Organization had started fighting amongst themselves with a violence, savagery and furious determination that had distressed Omar and I [sic]. After a few days of public jubilation, the Kasbah in Algiers—the Organisation's stronghold during the seven long years of the war—became the focal point of bloody clashes between rival groups. The crowd refused to accept such fratricidal madness and kept shouting a single, simple slogan: 'Seven years is enough!' Every day we took part in the angry, unarmed crowds that denounced this civil war. As if seven years of war, a year of looting, and organised carnage by the OAS in the country's main cities hadn't sufficed. We still had to go through this Kasbah war, which in fact ushered in a cycle of violence that has yet to end. (2012, 96–97)

In my reading of this passage, two things stand out. First, the citation sheds light on what Frantz Fanon called the "trials and tribulations of national consciousness" in *The Wretched of the Earth*, in that it enlightens us on the ways that, by inheriting a power that was formerly in the hands of the colonial administration, the political elite (and not always the intellectual elite, since the intellectual elite of the FLN had been liquidated around the time of independence) turns away from its initial responsibility, that of guaranteeing the prosperity of its people, and slowly but surely becomes a simple substitute for the colonial elite that was formerly in control. The observations and the question contained in the preceding citation are testimonials to what in Algeria, and in postcolonial Africa in general, became the bankruptcy of what Fanon saw as the bourgeois dictatorship that simply replaced the metropolitan bourgeoisie. Thus, the leaders of the Organization, who after heroic struggles were transformed into holders of a wormy, now-rich and arrogant authority, truly correspond to the elite about whom Fanon writes:

> Before independence, the leader, as a rule, personified the aspirations of the people—independence, political freedom, and national dignity. But in the aftermath of independence, far from actually embodying the needs of the people, far from establishing himself as the promoter of the actual dignity of the people, which is founded on bread, land, and putting the country back in their sacred hands, the leader will unmask his inner purpose: to be the CEO of the company of profiteers composed of a national bourgeoisie intent only on getting the most out of the situation. (2004, 112)

Second, the war of the Kasbah recalled by Boudjedra's narrator is unique in that in his opinion, and I agree completely, it inaugurates a new cycle of violence. That cycle of violence then leads to an unfortunate war that is unleashed after the great war of national liberation, that is, the civil war that will favor the emergence of radical Islamism in its most brutal and bloody form. This failed transition from colonization to independence will facilitate Islamic terrorism in a context of the single party that must face the enduring challenges of the exercise of individual rights and the press's vague notions of independence. The result, Benjamin Stora explains, is that "incontestablement, une mutation se produit, avec la volonté de passer d'un sujet constamment soumis à des impératifs familiaux, religieux, traditionnels, à un sujet faisant la loi, la loi humaine. En Algérie, l'islamisme se présentera comme une réponse à ce trouble très profond. D'autant que le système politique du parti unique bloque le développement de la société" (2001, 78) / "Unquestionably, a shift came about, a desire to move from a subject constantly subjugated to the imperatives of family, religion, and tradition, to a subject who was master of his own human destiny. In Algeria, Islamism presented itself as a response to this very profound unrest, especially since the single-party political system was blocking the development of society" (2001, 180). In reality, the date of October 1988, which is explicitly mentioned in Boudjedra's novel on page 178, is a fundamental date for situating and better understanding the rise of Islamists in Algeria. A bit more than two decades after achieving independence, Algeria is faced with extreme poverty, unemployment, in short, a widespread absence of both civil protections that guarantee basic freedoms and assure the safety of property and persons by the rule of law, and social protections that themselves guard against the risks for a degradation of the situation of individuals, to use the terms offered by Robert Castel (2003).

This long digression on Algeria allows me to adopt the following thesis: By comparing Algerian and Moroccan contexts, if the attacks in Morocco on May 16, 2003, was not necessarily the consequence of a war of decolonization as was the case in Algeria, it still remains that in both cases we can speak of political power having taken part, despite itself, in spreading the call to jihad. In both cases, we could say, the population that was betrayed by the national bourgeoisie, which, as Fanon describes, was simply transformed into a substitute for the colonial bourgeoisie set in place by the metropole, and resorted to extreme measures to emerge from invisibility. That is implicitly what the narrator of *Les étoiles de Sidi Moumen* is saying when he reflects on the conditions that led them—himself, his brother, and his friends—to commit acts of terror: "Au commencement, il y eut la décharge et la colonie de garnements qui germait au dessus. La religion du foot, les bagarres incessantes, les vols à l'étalage et les courses effrénées, les avatars de la débrouille, le haschich, la colle blanche, les errances qu'ils entraînent, la contrebande et les petits métiers, les coups à répétition qui pleuvent, les fugues et leurs rançons de viols et de maltraitance" "At the beginning, there was the landfill and the gang of hoodlums that were sprouting up. The religion of soccer, endless brawls, theft from displays and frantic escapes, typical forms of ingenuity, hashish, glue sniffing and the endless roaming around that is involved, contraband and small jobs, the beatings that rain down endlessly, the running away and its price in rape and abuse" (2010, 72). Abou Zoubeïr exploits the young people lack of education, anxieties and extreme vulnerability, as well as their limitations, to build in them a sense of belonging. In fact, this character was especially important to the slum's abandoned children because he incarnated victory over the mediocrity of their lives:

> Il était parvenu à nous rendre notre fierté avec de mots simples, des mots ailés qui nous transportaient aussi loin que le pouvait notre imagination. Nous n'étions plus des parasites, des rebuts d'humanité, des moins que riens. Nous étions propres et dignes et nos aspirations trouvaient résonance dans des esprits saints. Nous étions écoutés, nous étions guidés. La logique avait remplacé les coups. Nous avions ouvert la porte à Dieu et Il était entré en nous.

> It happened that we go tour pride through simple words, words with wings that took us as far as our imaginations would take us. We were no longer parasites, dregs of humanity, nobodies. We were clean and worthy, and our dreams resonated in godly minds. We were heard, we were guided. Logic replaced the beatings. We had opened our door to God and He had entered into us. (110)

We then can easily understand the context in which the terrorist recruiter Abou Zoubeïr, himself a former prisoner, readily exploits the vulnerability of the children of Sidi Moumen to transform them and push them over to the side of the holy war.

Clearly, for these youths the corrupter of consciences legitimately fulfills the functions normally assigned to the State and society, namely, promoting a self-esteem that involves being seen, being heard, having property, and dare we mention, escaping the pathological bodily conditions that I recalled earlier with respect to biopoliticization of the space of the slums. Given the privileged classes' fear of contagion that fills the public authorities with dread, and which results in the quarantining the slum's inhabitants, the State creates favorable conditions for brainwashing by religious extremists.

In substituting the terrorist preacher for the figure of the State and by entrusting in him its sovereign function, namely, guaranteeing civil and social protections, as transpires from my above interpretation of the novel, Binebine directs the reader onto the path of the thesis that, whether unconsciously or even sometimes simply by negligence or by political ruse, the State creates insecurity. And that creates conditions that are more favorable for religious fanatics to transform fear into an instrument to endlessly discomfit the urban pariahs. From that viewpoint, the suicide candidates, the youth of Sidi Moumen, are trapped in a logic that is a priori irrational but nevertheless troubling: terrorizing those who terrorize. The notion of "human trash" that confers an extremely important power to indoctrination by religious extremists is very well summarized by Hamil as he shows the impact of Abou Zoubeïr on the slum youths:

> His "regime of truth," to use Foucault's phrase, and turns the topographical opposition between their slums and the rest of the city into an overarching opposition between the haves and have-nots, the righteous and the corrupt, Good and Evil, Islam and the West. To restore social justice and equality as ordained by God involves the removal of that opposition; that frontier which indicated the line of demarcation between the powerless, the privileged and the neglected, the virtuous and the corrupt . . . Consciousness of their humiliation makes the prospect of self-sacrifice more logical and less horrible. (2011, 553)

In the same vein, Yachine and the other children of the "tribu de va-nu-pieds" "tribe of the barefoot" who wear "les ceintures du paradis" "heaven's belts," as the bombs are called, consider themselves the "elect" in the death that in their minds becomes the only condition for rebirth away from Sidi Moumen (2010, 137), and they feel particularly distinguished for having been chosen as those who will bear "le titre de martyr avec la clé du paradis" "the title of martyr holding the keys of Paradise" (135). Therefore, it is as administrators of justice for slum children that the youths of Sidi Moumen will sacrifice their lives so that they no longer have to "voir ces machines monstrueuses déverser sur l'enfance leurs détritus et leurs vomis" "see these monstrous machines pouring their detritus and vomit upon children" (138). By admitting that this violence is all the more unproductive since it changes nothing in the situation of the marginal and those who are cut off from society, could we not, moreover, see in the choice for terrorism a kind of rationality?

Is there not, despite the horror of violence and the irreversible consequences of the choice to sow the seeds of death, a certain rational grounding based on the very condition of those who resort to violence as a unique means of expression? That is perhaps what Norton wants us to understand when she says that we should no longer have to explain that there is something rational in terrorism and that it is a quite reasonable strategy. In any case, in glossing terror, she writes, "'If I'd been born Palestinian,' Ehud Barak declared in the course of an Israeli election campaign, 'I would have been a terrorist.' For Barak, terrorism is not alien, but familiar; not irrational, but rational; not a nihilistic choice, but a political one" (2013, 89). Drawing on the issues caused by demographic growth discussed by Brahim Elmorchid, as well as the works of Corrine Graff and Peter Singer, all referred to above. It could well be, in the final analysis, that confronted with spatial relegation, marginalization, and simple reduction to diseased bodies that constitute a danger for the rest of the population, the children of Sidi Moumen who are fictionalized by Binebine, rather than having chosen the road of jihad, were simply trying to emerge from invisibility by hoping, rightly or wrongly, that their actions would place their slum at the center of the concerns of Morocco's political elite. Furthermore, in coldly approaching the plot of Mahi Binebine's novel, that is, without emotion and without value judgments, and by placing ourselves in the perspective of the living conditions that have led these characters to take on death through perpetrating these attacks, it seems to me that it would then be appropriate to attribute an ethical dimension to jihad, in the sense offered by Faisal Devji. In *Landscapes of the Jihad* (2005), the historian maintains that "as ethical practices, the acts of jihad bear a family resemblance to other global movements like environmentalism or the anti-globalization protests, with which they share many other things besides, including forms of history and individuality" (160–61). Thus, it is possible that the terrorist might be someone who opposes the world as it is today, that is, a world where injustices thrive in general. I therefore want to propose, to conclude, that if we reflect upon the conditions that lead to violence before responding emotionally to their irreversible consequences, as for example, those laid out by Binebine in *Les étoiles de Sidi Moumen*, we might be able to see that the terrorist is the marginal figure who comes as a reminder of the vulnerability of the power-holders in the advantaged classes. That is why I will conclude with Norton's comment on terror:

> The terrorist preys on our fears, but not only on the simple fear of death. The suicide bomber reminds us that we are always a mystery to one another. The suicide bomber holds the terror and the promise that the world could be blown asunder in any moment, and that this could be the work of one alone. The terrorist is the dark side of individualism. We fear terror because we know that power always lies within our reach. (2013, 93)

Mahi Binebine's novel, like many novels dealing with terrorist violence in North Africa in particular and Africa in general, invites us to reflect upon the link between insecurity and the State's abdication of responsibility for an unvarnished investigation of the responsibility of power-holders themselves in the rise of radical violence as an alternative to a democratic expression for the voiceless and the people without a place in society. Binebine's work as an author can be said to unveil marginality in Morocco. In Assia Belhabib's words, *Les étoiles de Sidi Moumen* does not excuse or justify terrorism, raises a poignant observation about the wretched of the earth: "Ce roman, sans excuser ou justifier l'acte terroriste, dresse un constat poignant des damnés de la terre" (2014, 204). Pursuing the analysis of social outcasts and pariahs, it is to the study of another category of marginal bodies in Binebine's fiction that I will now turn to as the last example of expendable person: black woman slave in Morocco.

RACIALIZED AND SEXUALIZED BODIES IN MOROCCO: BLACK WOMEN SLAVERY IN *LE SOMMEIL DE L'ESCLAVE*

In her work *La prostitution coloniale*, Christelle Taraud strives to analyze the relationship of the double domination that affected the women of North Africa between 1830 and 1962, a period corresponding to the French presence first in Algeria, then in the rest of the Maghreb. Beyond emphasizing that the relationship of domination over the indigene by the colonist was multiplied by or prolonged by the domination of men over women, the historian equally sets out to "exposer en pleine lumière, la réalité d'un esclavage sexuel et racialisé" "bringing out into the open the reality of a sexual, racialized slavery" (2003, 16). What is particularly interesting about Taraud's study is that she sheds light on the ways that, contrary to an idea that is quite often widespread among historians of colonization, prostitution in North Africa was well and truly anterior to colonization, for at heart, the historian maintains, such a postulation would come down to a definition of prostitution in the Maghreb as a function of colonization. That approach would then have the disadvantage of maintaining silence about or ignoring "les relations sexuelles illicites monnayées et le statut des femmes dans un monde dominé par les hommes et par l'Islam; le rapport à la centralité et à la marge" "paid illicit sexual relations and the status of women in a world dominated by men and by Islam" (2003, 11). This exploration of the double—masculine and colonial—marginality to which women in North Africa are subjected, and which highlights the contours of a sexual, racialized slavery, then becomes significant in two ways. First, as we know, social ties are defined by the relationships between the sexes, in any case those sexualized relationships that respect the line that is drawn between men on one side and women on the other. Secondly, the racial dimension of this slavery introduces, in the context of the Maghreb, a separation in society that is based on the color of skin and ethnicity, such that if the European woman is also included in the catalogue of prostitutes and sources of sexual pleasure, the colonized woman is doubly so, because in not being European, her female alterity is increased by her racial alterity as an indigenous woman. The third level of female subalternity in the Maghreb, and one on which the imaginary as well as literary criticism has not often insisted, is a particularly rare figure in literature, the black female slave in North Africa, who is both black and a slave in a North Africa that itself is prey to the demons of colonization, and ends up being added to an anterior, permanent context of male domination, such as the main character in Mahi Binebine's first novel, *Le sommeil de l'esclave*, published by Editions Stock in 1992. In this section, I will attempt to analyze the double marginality of the black female slave, marginal firstly because of her race and then because of her sex, a double disqualification manifested by the place she occupies in Moroccan society in general and in Binebine's novel in particular. In other words, the focus will be on the highly paradoxical, significant status of the black slave woman who is an object of both attraction and repulsion, desired but at the same time banished, and whose body becomes the object of her master's sexual fantasies even as she continues to be kept in a situation of, if not nonexistence, then at least invisibility.

The question of freedom is central in Binebine's novel, inasmuch as the plot sheds light for the reader on the atrocious living conditions of those who are generally denied the right to exist. Nevertheless, the freedom that I deem decisive in the novel goes beyond the realm of simple enclosure and associates precarity, confinement, deprivation of freedom, and reduction of human beings to the status of an object. Clearly, a schematization of the social links in the plot allows us to see a superposition of both social classes and gender (men versus women), but also and above all, races. While *Le sommeil de l'esclave* is a novel whose plots unfolds in all likelihood in an independent Morocco, after the abolition of slavery, the figure of the slave is still central in the text, as witnessed in the title. This is the story of Dada, the novel's slave, a black woman who fluctuates between speaking and silence, visibility and invisibility in the midst of a Moroccan family of very high social status. The major paradox characterizing the female slave in this work is found at the core of the tension between the need for her and her expendability. If this characteristic is generalizable in the context and in the history of slavery in general, in Morocco it deserves special attention inasmuch as we are not dealing with the transatlantic slave trade, but a trade of human beings taking place inside Africa itself. Moreover, as Chouki El Hamel points out in the introduction of his remarkable study *Black Morocco*, the official and even the academic discourse on Morocco in particular and the Maghreb in general unfortunately tends to wrap a cloak of silence around if not refute the racial oppositions and slavery that built these societies, and whose effects can be felt in our time. El Hamel writes:

> Although slavery has practically ceased to exist in Morocco since the 1950s, its legacy persists in a form of prejudice and inherited marginalization. Morocco has traditionally been described in local historiography as racially and ethnically homogeneous nation, defined religiously by Islamic doctrine and linguistically and politically by Arabic nationalism. Written history is generally silent regarding slavery and racial attitudes, discrimination, and marginalization, and paints a

picture of Morocco as free from such social problems, problems usually associated more with slavery and its historical aftermath in the United States. (2013, 2)

El Hamel's study allows us to understand how a slavist exploitation of certain individuals, sometimes but not always on the basis of race, could be implemented on the African continent and among the peoples of Africa. The historian informs us that it is undeniable that Muslims accepted enslaving non-Muslims as normal, regardless of their race or ethnicity, whereas Islamic beliefs and thinking explicitly prohibit the practice of slavery. As we can see in El Hamel's citation above, the abolition of slavery in Morocco was not accompanied by a disappearance of the slave practice, and even more interesting, the descendants of slaves were said to have inherited through genetics their marginalization and the injustices that were the lot of their ancestors' lives. Spatial segregation was then based upon corporal markers, and notably upon skin color, even though in Morocco there were also European slaves. The fundamental difference between European slaves and black slaves is that in the case of Europeans, the practice ended once abolition was proclaimed or the prisoners who had been made slaves were freed, whereas in the case of blacks, the heavy heritage of the black condition was reified and race mutated into a social class, if the two criteria were not simply united and consolidated. As for women, distinction between prostitutes of all origins was articulated around the practice of slavery. As Taraud emphasizes, "pour comprendre pourquoi le phénomène apparaît globalement, jusqu'à la colonisation qui procède comme un révélateur, si invisibilisé et minoré au sein des sociétés maghrébines, il faut mettre la prostitution en lien avec un autre mode de régulation de la sexualité masculine, alors plus massif et plus évident: l'esclavage" "to understand why the phenomenon appeared worldwide, until colonization acted as a indicator, that invisible and of lesser value in the heart of Maghrebian societies, prostitution must be tied with another mode of regulation of masculine sexuality, one that is much larger and more obvious: slavery" (2003, 26). Despite ethnic mixing, black blood remained a permanent marker of marginality.

Moreover, it could be that the prostitution of black slaves was often hidden because their condition as slaves placed them outside the circle of paid prostitution, for example, and their sexual practices did not therefore point to any social deviancy. The consequences for generations of descendants of these slaves remains permanent, for as we can read in the report made for Huffpost Morocco by Adeline Bailleul, more than a skin color, black mutated in Morocco into a social class. "Plus qu'une couleur de peau, Bailleul writes, le 'Noir' s'est mué ici en classe sociale."[1] The journalist goes on to quote a black Moroccan inhabitant of Zagora who affirms that in the past, blacks could not share the same space with whites, and were expected to act as their servants. That means that blacks in Morocco by themselves constitute a distinct category of marginality inasmuch as their lives were, so to speak, made precarious throughout the centuries, even though racial or tribal discrimination is strongly condemned by the Quran (El Hamel 2013, 62), the holy book of Islam, which has often been presented as the basis for the justification of slavery. Why then is the figure of the black female slave unique in understanding the processes of reification of the human being in the Maghreb? Why does slavery occupy a central position in the interpretation of sexuality as a practice of social disqualification and a crucible for the domination of women's lives that are precarized in this way? The answers to these questions are found in Taraud's work, as she indicates that domestic slaves and concubine slaves were inserted into the sexual organization of Maghrebian societies and their function was to fulfill the sexual needs of their buyers, all the more so because "au Maroc d'ailleurs, les concubines-esclaves noires sont très prisées, non seulement pour leurs qualités sexuelles, mais aussi pour leurs vertus prophylactiques" "in Morocco, moreover, black concubine-slaves were highly prized, not only for their sexual qualities, but also for their prophylactic properties" (2003, 29).

Binebine's *Le sommeil de l'esclave* explores the subaltern condition of Moroccan blacks, with a special emphasis on the female black slave. The trajectory of Dada, the novel's black slave, is instructive of the special place occupied by black women in a Moroccan society that is fully practicing slavery. The tone is set from the very first pages when we read that the slave Dada had been offered to the grandfather of the child who is recalling his past and to whom the story of his family is told, which naturally includes the tragic story of the black female slave. The description of Dada, as having "un visage d'esclave [qui] ne vieillit jamais" "a face of a slave that never grows old," "une bossue à l'envers, courbée par l'usure. Et par la honte" "a hunchback in reverse, hunched over by wear and tear. And by shame" (1992, 11), who was given a freedom she never understood, is highly revealing. And we see quite early on in the narration that there is an absence of values characterizing the life of the slave when the narrator learns that the feast given in honor of Dada on the day of her freedom was meant less to mark her release from captivity than to add to the luster of the image of the master's family, a family that was highly respected in the neighborhood.

In the course of retrospective narration, the novel tells of the raid on blacks in Morocco to explain Dada's arrival in the family where she is to be, like an object, offered as a gift to a former army officer. The story then goes back to a time when the female black slave was still an adolescent at best, and paints a picture of a quasi-impossible existence for blacks, one compared to animals, through a significant metaphor; according to the narrator, Dada had the expression of being "en laisse comme un chien, un chien de race, bien sûr" "on a leash like a dog, a race dog, really" (13). The animal metaphor bears witness to a Moroccan society that was a place where slaves were not only likened to and reduced to the state of animals but equally considered like merchandise. More precisely, the slave in general and the black slave in particular is thus inscribed in the core of the process of depersonalization and reduction to the status of object in the sense understood by Claude Meillassoux:

> De-personalization was completed through the *reification* of the slave. This was more frequent in regions where trade was intense, like Sahelo-Sudanese regions, where captives were sold on the market. They were, successively, *commodities* in the hands of the merchants (the so-called "slave trade captives"), then *use-goods* and *patrimony* in the hands of the buyers. In all these cases, they were *objects*. Since they were seen as livestocks, and thus de-personalized, their re-socialization, in juridical terms, was improbable and in fact unknown, since it presupposed not only the rebuilding of links with other, similarly de-personalized captives, but also permission to build links with gentles of the sort which constitute the social person. (1991, 109)

The caravan of slaves crossing the Moroccan desert, as described in the novel, recalls in fact those slave ships in which slaves destined for labor were transported to the plantations of Europe and America. The long procession of slave children, including Dada, is likened in the novel to a "collier de perles noires" "necklace of black pearls," which speaks volumes on the commercial value of these slaves. By way of illustration, the leader of the men on the camels, the slave seller, despite his desire for sexual relations with Dada, never dared penetrate her, not because he was impotent, but because "il y avait des règles et l'une d'entre elles se dressait comme une barrière, aussi raide que son sexe raide, entre lui et son désir de prendre l'enfant les yeux fermés, de la posséder éperdument" "there were rules and one of them stood out as a barrier, as strongly as his stiff member, between him and his desire to take the child with eyes closed, to possess her wildly" (1992, 21). The rule, as we learn in the novel, was that women slaves had to submit to a test of virginity, and if they failed, the price at which they could be sold was considerably reduced. On this point, we already observe a merging between control over the body and commercial value. From that viewpoint, and even before considering the theorizations of Foucault and Agamben on biopower, it is useful to note that the body of the black slave was inserted into an economic practice that specifically involved control, management, and bodily preservation. In this particular case, biopower is not directly linked to the sovereign State, as seen by Foucault, but is linked to the financial and symbolic capital that determined the position of the slave seller on the social ladder. The gender of the black slave thus not only becomes an object of investment for sexual fantasies but also acquires a certain monetary value.

The relationship that is generally admitted between capitalism and slavery assumes another dimension here, in the sense that the commercial value is determined not only by the productive capacity of the slave but also in the case of women, by sexual attributes. Thus, the black slave is attributed a status even more inferior to that of male slaves of the same race, because of gender. If we apply the theory of subalternity developed in the case of India by Gayatri Chakravorty Spivak (1995), we can say that if the slave was reduced to invisibility, the black female slave was simply nonexistent, precisely because her color of skin was added to the gender to which she belonged. In this Moroccan society where we are dealing with a type of relationship that was based on the regulation of prostitution, the black slave woman, if we look to the character in this novel, can also be seen in terms of force. From subjection to forced labor to sexual exploitation, the slavery of blacks in Morocco thus assumed the shape of a negation of universal rights and basic freedoms, the liberty of peoples, but above all the liberty of women. It would not then be wrong to attempt a graphic representation or an outline of the stratification of the victims of Moroccan society that led to a pyramidal separation, with the sultan at the very top, his subjects of all genders beneath him, then below them the male slaves, and finally, at the very bottom, the female slaves. Slavery in Islam had other norms than European slavery: women slaves were white too, as Fatima Mernissi powerfully reminds us: "One of the traumatic events studied by historians, which they always view from the point of view of the palace, is the revolt of the zanj, black slaves, which took place under the Abbasids in 255/869. However, it could be argued that the first revolt was that of women slaves, the jawari, who well before that date lanched an assault on the caliphs" (2006, 37). Clearly, if we consider that the horrors of slavery in the Maghreb affected blacks in their totality, it is important to remain attentive to the fact that the nature of the damage was uniform, with difference in degree being a function of its victim, and thus the black female slave being made a figure of suffering and sorrow.

Sexuality thus introduced into slavery likely crystallizes the basic difference that was constructed around gender in the slave practice in Morocco. In this regard, El Hamel appropriately recalls that under the reign of Mawlai Isma'il, there was an army in Morocco made up of black soldiers who established the basis of his kingdom and guaranteed the stability of the country: "The black army provided the means to realize the dream and the vision of the sultan to bring security and unity to the country" (2013, 191). On the other hand, concubines were women slaves who were forced to satisfy the sexual desires of their masters. One of the wives of Sultan Mawlai Isma'il, a former concubine, as we are told by Chouki, was an extremely powerful black woman, a former slave whose power over the sultan was generally explained by magic, thereby reducing the quality of the intelligence of women to a kind of superstition (193). We see that at this period, the status of the slave allowed for a certain degree of social mobility, whether for slave-concubines, legitimate slave wives, or even members of the army who had pledged total allegiance to the sultan. Nevertheless, the plot in Binebine's novel, set during the reign of the sultan, suggests that the black female slave throughout time and space seems never to have escaped her first function as servant and satisfier of sexual desire.

But how do we then explain that during the reign of Sultan Mawlai Isma'il there were slaves fulfilling enviable social functions, and even female slaves with positions of political influence, long after blacks had been degraded to their primary position of subjects reduced to the labor and production force, but also to sex, and deprived of rights by the practice of slavery, as we see in Binebine's novel? It could in fact be that the relegation of blacks, both men and women, to the bottom ranks of the social ladder in Morocco long after Mawlai Isma'il finds its justification in the fact that once they became envious of the roles, choice positions, and possibilities offered by the sultan to the slaves who were faithful to him, the Moroccan people gradually mentally devised the construction of an enemy within, one that was black and powerful. In fact, if we consider along with El Hamel that "whenever concubines succeeded in forging emotional bonds with their master or patrons they were able to survive, thrive and negotiate better conditions" (2013, 193) and if we add that "the black army's strong loyalty to the sultan and the prerogatives they enjoyed threatened the interests of Moroccan tribes and caused resentment and jealousy [which] also focused on the army and revived and reinforced the negative perception of black people" (2013, 203), then we can easily understand the persistence of discrimination based on skin color in Morocco years after the reign of the sultan. First, slaves in general recall a past that is not in the past, during which the sultan's reliance on an army of blacks directly created a feeling of resentment in the Moroccan population that worsened due to the negative perception of the black. Yet, and despite the fact that members of the sultan's army, the blacks, made progress toward their autonomy on the basis of legal structures in effect in Morocco, the domestic and often sexual slavery of black women carried over into the twentieth century, that is, well after official abolition of slavery by the French Protectorate in 1923. Also, the skin color discrimination in Morocco might also be an effect of colonization.

Thus, was progressively implemented an economy of labor and sex, with the female black slave being reduced to the very lowliest domestic work and sexual duties. These women constitute an important female grouping and become a kind of outlet for men who, hypocritically respectful of the laws of Islam, are in search of a body whose use will keep them from the defilement that they would incur by having sexual contact with prostitutes. Because deep down, the female black slave, precisely because she is a slave, is simply fulfilling her social, sexual function of fulfilling the desires of men, without that situation ever being considered a moral problem. It is furthermore interesting to read Taraud on the subject of prostitution in North Africa, suggesting that this practice varied according to race and social class:

> La question de l'esclavage, et par extension celle de son rôle dans la régulation de la sexualité masculine, est donc déterminante en Afrique du Nord. Son existence permet en effet à de très nombreux hommes (donc à de nombreuses familles, les esclaves libérant les épouses d'une part importante des travaux domestiques et sexuels) de disposer d'une ou de plusieurs esclaves sexuelles à demeure. Dans les couches les moins aisées de la population, ce sont les "Négresses" qui cumulent souvent les fonctions de servantes et de concubines, permettant ainsi de joindre l'utile à l'agréable. Quant aux élites, elles préfèrent généralement les Blanches pour le lit et les Noires pour le service domestique.
>
> The question of slavery, and by extension that of its role in the regulation of male sexuality is thus determinant in North Africa. Its existence in effect allows numerous men (thus, numerous families, with the female slaves freeing the spouses from an important part of domestic and sexual duties) to have one or several sexual slaves permanently in the household. In the less wealthy layers of the population, it was "Negresses" who combined the functions of servants and concubines, thereby joining the useful with the agreeable. As for the élites, they generally prefer Whites in bed and Blacks for domestic work. (2003, 29)

Two observations should be made. First, recourse to the sexuality of the female black slave was then also a function of the social class to which the men belonged, if it is true that the wealthy elites preferred whites in matters of sexual activities rather than for blacks, who were reduced to domestic work. Next, it is also noteworthy that in a context of male domination, there is no female solidarity if female black slaves were considered to be human beings of the same sex as Moroccan wives, who, we should point out, also benefited from the sexual slavery inasmuch as the female black slaves relieved the wives from domestic and sexual tasks, as Taraud noted. This leads us, then, to observe that at heart, the female black slave was reduced to her biological life, with the devaluation of her body being understood in every sense of the expression. Not only the need for her as a slave, that is, as a "body-machine" that ensures production but even more as a "sexual body" that ensures and fulfills libidinous desires.

The body of the black female slave racialized and sexualized in this way is to become the locus of inscription for the paradox between necessity and expendability that I referred to in the introduction to this chapter. In *Le sommeil de l'esclave*, this body takes on specific forms and invests the field with a practice that is strange at least and extremely worthy of our interest: it is a particular form of the use of the body of the female black slave that is both included and excluded from humanity. Throughout Binebine's novel, we see Dada reduced to silence and total submission, permanently subjected to surveillance: "Dans son habit de joie, l'esclave avait l'impression qu'on épiait le moindre de ses mouvements. Elle ne savait pas où poser ses bras. Ni d'ailleurs son regard. Dure épreuve que celle de devoir lever les yeux en public" "Dressed in her unusual new clothes, the slave woman had the impression that they were spying on her least movements. She didn't know where to place her arms. Nor, moreover, her gaze. A tough ordeal if she raised her eyes in public" (1992, 81). But at the same time, she fulfills a basic role in regulating male sexuality, not only by fulfilling the master's desire but also in introducing young men to sex. In fact, as we read in the novel, "il est bien connu que la chaleur des corps noirs atténue la douleur des circoncis" "it is well known that the heat of black bodies relieves the pains of the circumcised" (77). During the circumcision ceremony of a young boy, the black slave Dada is the object of an exposition and her body is subjected to the gazes of the men who are present at the ceremony while she is simultaneously subjected to her household role as servant. Yet it was always difficult for her to raise her eyes in public.

This contradiction between being made a spectacle of, or rather exposing the black slave woman's body, and her invisibilization is perhaps best explained in an article by Cilas Kemedjio on the subject of the black body, as he sums up the situation in the following way: "faire taire les silences du corps noir" "keep the silences of the black body silent." Kemedjio's project in that article is to explore "la réduction du mutisme qui est au principe de la mise en spectacle du corps noir, de l'esclavage aux cirques humanitaires en passant par les mailles du Code de l'indigénat" "explore the mutism at play in making a spectacle of the black body, from slavery to humanitarian circuses as well as the chains of the Code of Indigeny" (2006, 13). In effect, the slave Dada's black body is essentially alienated, reduced to its most profound alterity, and surrounded by silence, and from this perspective it in every way resembles that "corps-esclave pris dans les chaines du collier de la servitude, [qui] ne peut supposer ou supporter une parole de manière libre" "slave-body taken in the neck chains of servitude, [which] cannot suppose or supporter any speech that is free" (12), to use Kemedjio's words.

Even when the ritual scene following the circumcision of the child whose sorrow she must assuage because of his burning member, Dada is mute when threatened by Milouda, her master's white spouse who promises that there will be hell to pay if she doesn't calm the child: "Espèce de bourrique, l'enfant est circoncis et il souffre. Prends garde si tu ne parviens pas à calmer ses pleurs, Dieu te maudira, si toutefois il existe un état plus maudit que le tien" "You ass, the child is circumcised and is suffering. Take care if you don't calm his cries, God will curse you, if ever there was a more cursed state than yours" (1992, 84). Later, on the same page, we read that after the women have prepared the black slave before she is to offer sex to the circumcised child, "Dada resta immobile, les yeux mi-clos. Le sang de l'enfant se répandit sur son caftan. Un sang de maitre. Un caftan d'esclave" "Dada remained immobile, her eyes half-closed. The child's blood spilled onto her caftan. The master's blood. The slave's caftan." The association between the master's blood and the slave's caftan is in the end telling and suggestive of the inaugural scene of slave practice, rape. It indicates too the fusional proximity between the body of the slave and the body of the master, if we agree with Agamben whose reflection on slavery tells us that "the slave's body in its relationship of organic exchange with nature is thus used as a medium of the relationship of the master's body with nature" (2015, 14). Nevertheless, slave rape was not considered criminally reprehensible, since, in a way, for the masters and other males of the dominant class, it was more a right than anything else, because in reality, El Hamel tells us, "in Islamic law, the man had a license to enjoy a female slave's sexuality, but he also had the obligation to assume the legal consequences when his slave bore him a child" (2013, 193). El Hamel's affirmation, set against the practice of silencing the black body, according to Kemedjio, leads us to the point of rupture for this silence in Binebine's novel.

The black female slave in the novel slept very little during the night. And for good reason, and in that can be found the symbolism of the title chosen by the Moroccan author: her sleep was constantly interrupted by the nocturnal visits made by her master and for which, even though she was the victim, she often paid a heavy price: "elle se souvint du jour où la maîtresse avait appris les visites que lui faisait le Fqih, à l'aube, après la prière. Comment oublier l'échelle sur laquelle on l'avait étendue une journée entière, mains et pieds attachés ? Elle ressentait encore les brulures de piment de Cayenne avec lequel Milouda avait frotté son sexe encore pubère" "she remembered the day when the mistress learned of the visits made to her by the Fqih, at dawn, before prayer. How could she forget the ladder on which she had been stretched out for the entire day, hands and feet bound? She still felt the burnings of cayenne pepper with which Mioud had rubbed her still pubescent genitals" (1992, 69–70). As can be seen in Binebine's novel, not only does the master's wife humiliate and assault the female black slave who is the victim of rape but that slave is condemned to endure her sorry condition. Considering that fiction is inspired by a true story, its status as sociological text allows us to displace the interpretation from the literary to the sociological and philosophical. We therefore can easily understand why and how in such a situation, with the manual and sexual work that is both valorized and repressed, the black slave succumbs to a certain and true depression, as we see is true in reading Guillaume le Blanc: "L'ennui et l'humiliation qui sont le pendant de la détresse et de l'insatisfaction révèlent un 'je' littéralement épuisé et pour lequel la souffrance psychique ne peut plus être contenue" "Ennui and humiliation which are the two sides of distress and insatisfaction reveal an 'I' that is literally exhausted and for which psychic suffering can no longer be contained" (2007, 191). But in this condition of invisibility and permanent silence, is it possible for the female black slave to formulate an "I," that is, to speak out and affirm herself as a subject that can speak and is capable of emotions and decision? If yes, how?

In *Le sommeil de l'esclave*, the figure of the child will be the triggering element of self-affirmation and the breaking of the chains of silence by the black female slave. Analyzing desexualization as a process following desocialization, itself the logical result of depersonalization, Meillassoux observes that in societies where slavery is practiced, "since the slave class was reproduced through the plundering of alien societies and through purchase on the market, the 'procreative' function was in the hands of men, whether warriors or merchants: it was they who, by force of arms or by payment, 'procreated' the individuals who were to reconstitute the exploited class" (1991, 112). He then adds that the producing role of the woman is weakened at the expense of functions linked to work, for example, relieving the function of *mother*. On the other hand, he emphasizes, and this is what interests me in particular in attempting to interpret the role of the child in the taboo performed by the black female slave in Binebine's novel: "Il n'y a, par contre, aucune sacralisation de la femme dans l'esclavage . . . Elle n'est pas recrutée pour procréer mais pour travailler aux tâches féminines; si elle s'accouple, elle n'est pas mariée; si elle engendre, elle est réduite au rôle de génitrice, sa progéniture appartient au maître, elle peut lui être arrachée à tout moment" "There is, however, no sacralization of the woman in slavery. . . . She is not recuited to procreate but to do female chores; if she mates, she is not married; if she gives birth, she is reduced to the role of birth-giver, and her progeny belongs to the master and can be taken from her at any time" (1992, 113). That description certainly corresponds to the forms of the presence of Dada the black female slave in the novel.

When she discovers that she is pregnant, she is even more traumatized and terrorized because, in any event, as the narrator asks: "Comment imaginer l'honneur du maître souillé par une histoire de fornication avec l'esclave? Qu'allaient-elles dire, les langues du quartier?" "Can you image the honor of the master sullied by a matter of fornication with a slave? What would people say, all those wagging tongues in the neighborhood?" (69). Even more, when

Dada confides the heavy secret of her pregnancy due to rape by her master to M'bark, another character in the novel, he replies that not only have they not taken away her property but that Dada is a slave who was bought at a high price and she is lucky that she knows it, unlike so many others who are slaves but are unaware of their condition. At the same time, during the slave's pregnancy, an unusual calm settles within the house, the kind of calm that precedes a storm, that is, the scandal that the slave's pregnancy will cause. This form of profoundly eloquent silence serves to help instill doubt in the black female slave and thus force her to "re-personalize" herself in a way. She asked herself the following questions, in response to the mutism that met her pregnancy: "Sont-ils devenus aveugles ou bien ont-ils choisi de ne rien voir? Quelle sorte de châtiment allait-on lui infliger? La torturer par leur indifférence? Et jusqu'à quand? . . . Comment [son ventre] avait-il pu échapper à la maîtresse?" "Have they become blind or have they chosen not to see anything? What kind of punishment would they inflict upon her? Torture her with their indifference? And how long? How could [her belly] have escaped the mistress's eye?" (85).

The decisive point for Dada's return to visibility, even if only at a symbolic level, will be effected at the height of her pregnancy, between a master who has stopped his nocturnal visits because of her pregnancy, and his wife who ostensibly looks away, even though Dada "sentait son ventre se rétrécir, comme si le bébé s'accommodait déjà de l'espace réduit que la vie lui réservait" "felt her stomach shrinking, as if the baby was already dealing with the reduced space that life had reserved for it" (87). I maintain that it is the awareness of the fate that will be transmitted from slave mother to son, despite his father being the master and, as El Hamel observed, supposed to guarantee a better social status for him, that will force the black slave woman to confront her mistress for the very first time, thus breaking the chains of silence, exiting the status of owned objects confined to a living-dead status and lifting herself up to the same level of speech as her *owners*. In an almost epic scene of confrontation between the black slave and her mistress, Dada reappropriates her language and, according to the narrator, "pour la première fois de sa vie, elle refusait de se soumettre, de s'aplatir" "for the first time in her life, she refused to submit, to bow down" (91). In so doing, in announcing to the mistress that she carried within her womb the child of the master, Dada confirms her determination to cross over from being the body-machine destined for sexual pleasure that she was, to becoming a body-witness to rape by her master, with the testimony made manifest by the child whose origin is no longer a secret. Then, when she is ordered to "mettre bas son bâtard" "put down her bastard" (note the animal metaphor) without any noise, without help, and in maximum solitude, the black slave will some time later experience yet another trauma that is even more decisive.

Not only is the fathering of her progeny by her master denied by his wife, but Dada is forced to hand over the child to religious women; then, faced with her mistress's indifference to her supplications, the black slave commits the worst: infanticide. Before burying her dead child with her own hands, the black slave confers upon him a mission that rather effectively sums up her position for emerging from marginality, breaking the circle of desocialization and depersonalization, re-civilizing herself, and becoming the sole owner of her body: "Mon image est morte, mais des milliers d'autres sont vivantes. Les milliers à venir sont encore plus vivantes! Tu leur diras qu'ils devront eux-mêmes incendier le silence qui leur brûle les ailes, lapider sa fumée qui les étouffe" "My image is dead, but thousands of others are alive. The thousands to come are even more alive. You'll tell them that they must themselves burn the silence that burns their wings, stone the smoke that suffocates them" (1992, 128). This testament to struggle and revolt pronounced by the black slave woman shows that because of this child she delivers unto death, she has finally become aware of her status and now resolves to overturn the scales, in showing that her ability to free her child from a fate similar to hers is the affirmation of her move from the periphery to the center. Even though she remains a slave, Dada shows that she is henceforth mistress of her fate, and therefore she has decided to kill her child to make him free, while waiting to reunite with him in a certainly unreal world, but one where the child of the slave, a slave himself, will no longer be the property of anyone whosoever, but where he will wait for her "libre pour l'éternité" "free for eternity" (128).

The scorn, indifference, and relegation that victimizes the black female slave is in fact but the ensemble of acts that bear witness to the fact that as a slave, the black woman did not exist, and her work, if we can talk about work in the sense of a productive activity, is simply reduced to nothing. It could even be, then, that in the final analysis the specific kind of paradoxical relationship of need and expendability that characterizes the life of the black female slave can be explained by its reduction to what Agamben, following Aristotle, has named the function of the body. In fact, Agamben writes: "Unlike the cobbler, the carpenter, the flute player, or the sculptor, even if he carries out these activities—and Aristotle knows perfectly that this can happen in the *oikonomia* of the household—is and remains essentially without work, in the sense that, in contrast to what happens with an artisan, his praxis is not defined by the work that he produces but only by the use of the body" (2015, 15). If it is true that the praxis of the slave is not defined by the result of his or her work and that he or she really exists for nothing other than the use of his or her body, would it not be possible to interpret Binebine's novel through the prism not only of the denunciation of injustices set upon the marginal whose body is subject to disposal after being used but rather of the subtraction of this slave body from the vicious circle of its reduction to its use.

Doesn't the decision made by Dada to confront her mistress and reveal the source of her pregnancy signal that Dada has understood that the black slave knew that the use of her body abundantly implied the use of her sexual parts by her master, and that finally, she has become aware that, as Agamben notes in one of his commentaries, "in the indetermination of the two bodies, the 'serviceable' hand of the master is equivalent to the service of the slave" (1992, 18). In accepting this hypothesis, then, we can affirm that the slave's speaking out signals the beginning of her emergence from subalternity, and in a certain way, by affirming her awareness that the master who used her as a slave sex has dishonored himself, the black slave intends to restore her voice that was rendered mute, and finally, she will now give voice to the silences of her black body, to use the inverse of Kemedjio's (2006) expression given above.

Mahi Binebine thus succeeds, through his novel, not only in giving voice and visibility to the visible minorities forced into invisibility and silence but also in restoring speech, in a way, to the body of the black slave. Binebine's *Le sommeil de l'esclave* thus postulates the possibility of a new black slave, different from one who is reduced to the use of the body, and who is "the human being without work who renders possible the realization of the work of the human being, that living being who, though being human, is excluded—and through this exclusion, included—in humanity, so that human beings can have a human life, which is to say, a political life" (Agamben 2015, 23). The black female slave reappropriates her body for herself even as she remains in the service of the master, for by affirming her awareness of the part she plays in realizing the humanity in the life of her master, she literally breaks the link between *bien d'usage* (goods for consumption), *patrimoine* (property), and *objet (*object) that tied her to her master, and she becomes a subject. Thus, we can understand her decision to kill her child to allow him to live, in a word, to remove her child from the fate of the slave and the oppressed, thereby signaling the need to rethink the notions of subject and object, and also of center and periphery. In short, the black female slave invents for herself an art of finding an alternative that, though not placing her in power, allows her at least to emerge symbolically from her absolute precarity and define by herself conditions necessary for her happiness.

NOTE

1. https://www.afriqueconnection.com/article/02-02-2016/%C3%A0-zagora-les-fant%C3%B4mes-de-la-s%C3%A9gr%C3%A9gation-raciale-reportage-vid%C3%A9o-texte

Conclusion

Decentering the Center, Recentering the Periphery

The exploration of marginal bodies and lives at risk, which has been the subject of analyses that have provided the framework for this study, allows us to emphasize the ways in which in North Africa, colonial and postcolonial powers have been organized in what can rightly be called human bankruptcy. Whether through social disqualification, social disassociation, or general exclusion, it is clear that certain human lives are valuable only insofar as, being ostracized, they confirm the primacy of the powerful over the vulnerable. Summing up and extending the thought of Fabien Eboussi Boulaga in *La crise du Muntu* (1977), we can say that if socialization is what transforms primitive man into a human, we thereby observe that socialization, which goes hand in hand with personalization and ends in civilization (collectivities who see each other as groups of humans), can only be understood when it is seen as that which allows humankind to become human. Now, inscription in the world of at-risk lives in North Africa is not as human beings who take part in the future of humanity, but as beggars, colonized, prostitutes, slaves—in short, as subalterns.

Whether we are speaking of the indigenes of colonial Algeria, North African immigrants and exiles who have been racialized and then reduced to the condition of foreigner, black slaves, or children of the slums of Morocco, their contribution to the future of humanity is denied or rendered impossible precisely because they are not "protected," so that "la sécurité et l'insécurité sont des rapports aux types de protection qu'une société assure, ou n'assure pas, d'une manière adéquate" "security and insecurity are linked to types of protection that a society guarantees, in an inadequate way," to cite Robert Castel, who concludes masterfully that "être protégé, c'est aussi être menacé" "to be protected is also to be threatened" (2003, 7). First during the colonial era, then even more so in the days after the independences, these marginal bodies existing at the border of the *polis* (in the sense of the city) are either deprived of integration by not being able to take advantage of stable employment and therefore not able to take part in stable social relations or they are reduced to insecure jobs, indeed reduced literally to joblessness, which leads to their social isolation. Marginalization and exclusion, which victimize the excluded subjects from North Africa, comes down to poverty, insecurity, failure of social adaptation, and other forms of exclusion that may be summed up by what Serge Paugam calls social disqualification and what Robert Castel calls social disaffiliation. We should note, however, that in the case of space, the relationship of interdependence between the category of the poor and the social services that could bring them various forms of aid is literally nonexistent. The originality of the marginal bodies in my analysis resides in the fact that marginality or exclusion transcends economic borders (unemployment, underemployment, insecure employment, etc.) and leads to a philosophical conception of insecurity. Thus, we read in the thoughts of the anonymous authors of *Gouverner par le chaos*:

> La culture de l'inégalité ne concerne pas que le domaine économique. Elle touche aussi à la configuration du champ perceptif. En effet, le fondement des théories de la surveillance, tel que résumé par le principe panoptique de Jeremy Bentham, est la dissociation du couple "voir et être vu." La politique comme ingénierie sociale consiste alors à bâtir et entretenir un système inégalitaire où les uns voient sans être vus, et où les autres sont vus sans voir. Le but de la manœuvre est de prendre le contrôle du système de perception d'autrui sans être soi-même perçu, puis d'y produire des effets en réécrivant les relations de cause à effet de sorte qu'autrui se trompe quand il essaie de les remonter pour comprendre sa situation présente.

> The culture of inequality does not concern the economic sphere. It also touches upon the configuration of the field of perception. In fact, the bases for theories of surveillance, such as summarized by the panopticon scheme of Jeremy Bentham, is the dissociation of the pair "see and be seen." Politics as social engineering therefore consists in building and maintaining an inegalitarian system where some see without being seen, and others are seen without seeing. The goal of that maneuver is for the one to take control of the other's system of perception without being seen, then to produce effects upon it by rewriting cause and effect relationships so that the other is mistaken when trying to apply them to the present situation. (2014, 32)

The philosophical dimension of insecurity in the way that I understand it is articulated around what might be summed up as follows: What is the value of the North African citizen when he or she is inscribed in a relationship of political power that makes him or her into a living dead? This question is all the more pertinent because on the whole, from the colonial period to the days following the independences, everything has occurred in fact as if the ordinary citizen, this *homo sacer* whose killing does not qualify as a homicide, is seen as the endless victim of a crisis whose foundations derive from the city's method of administration.

By considering Algeria as a synecdoche, indeed a metaphor of North Africa, yet without denying the singular colonial and postcolonial trajectories of each of the three former French colonies in North Africa, a novel by Rachid Boudjedra allows us to put the political power in the systemization of the gift of death into perspective. *Les figuiers de Barbarie* (2010; translated by André Naffis-Sahely as *The Barbary Figs*, 2012) by Boudjedra is likely the best rendering of the political turbulences that shook Algeria from its colonial occupation until the fratricidal wars of the 1990s. During a flight from Algiers to Constantine, two men find themselves together and through a kind of cathartic anamnesis, review the history of their country. In doing so, they question the truths, lies, and manipulations that shook the destiny of an entire people that was subject to colonial occupation, freed at the cost of an appalling war, but left visibly trapped in violence, underdevelopment, and insecurity. The first trait of Boudjedra's novel deals with the fact that events are not recounted in a linear manner, but are articulated around a dialogical coming and going, and sometimes one that is simply mental, between Rachid and Omar, two young men who had rejoined the underground Front de Libération Nationale (FLN) during the struggles for decolonization. The novel shifts back and forth between two precise historical periods, the years of the struggle against the French military occupation and those of the unleashing of Islamist violence, with the trajectory of the characters crystallizing around the notion of fear. In one passage, the narrator summarizes the entire history of violence that has shaken his country: "Adulte, j'étais écœuré par les horreurs coloniales d'hier et par celles commises par le pouvoir de mon pays, aujourd'hui. Comme si ce pays était voué au malheur d'une façon définitive" (2010, 241)/ "Now as an adult, I was sickened by the horrors perpetrated by the colonial power in the past, as well as by the present-day atrocities committed by my own country's potentates. As if this country were irremediably doomed to a tragic fate" (2012, 145). The encounter between the novel's two cousins, Rachid the doctor and Omar the architect, serves as a pretext for the evocation of the present and past history of Algeria, and everything happens in fact as if the long exposition of colonial violence, were, for Rachid Boudjedra, an invitation to inscribe the rise of Islamists and fratricidal wars into the age-old history of this country.

Why do I find Boudjedra's novel central in sketching out a better understanding of the pernicious role of political power in the manufacture of at-risk lives that are subject to death and yet not worthy to be mourned? In the case of Algeria—and the same could be said of Morocco, shaken by attacks in 2003, and of Tunisia, which experienced a revolution less than a decade later—civil war and the rise to power of the Islamist at the beginning of the 1990s are the direct consequence of the failure of the FLN to guarantee justice and social equity to the millions of people who had hoped that the independence they gained in 1962 would mark a new beginning, or in any case different living conditions from those under which the people had lived during the period of French domination. Rather than giving back to this people their dignity and freedom, the Algerian government decided at that time to implement a strategy at the intersection of the political and the religious, by making rebels into martyrs and thus constructing a national mythology. From that point of view, the appropriation of religion with an intent of radicalizing minds and justifying violence can be seen as related to security in the State in Algeria. In fact, that contributed to the creation of a form of generalized insecurity, by displacing the goal of its combat in the struggle for the conquest of the State, into the struggle against its citizens. In the Algerian context, the legacy of the struggle for independence does not consist in conquering the autonomy of the nation, but in struggling against the humanity that rose up to confront the prevailing of injustice and poverty.

The heirs of the war who make up the State have thus slid from resistance against the colonial yoke toward repression of the victims of colonization. A refusal to take into account the popular masses in the "partage du sensible"[1] "distribution of the sensible" thus created the bed of religious, namely, Islamic radicalism. For in encouraging or tolerating Islamist violence, the government created conditions that were favorable to the development of insecurity. The latter is doubly problematic, first because it can escape all control, and then because the initiatives that were set in place for control only exacerbated the situation, as seen in the passage of the FIS into the Groupe Islamique Armé, Armed Islamic Group (GIA). Thus, the State's creation of internment camps in the Algerian Sahara for imprisonment of members of the Islamist party could only exacerbate the tensions, and in fact create fertile ground for the promotion of ideologies that support the Holy War, as stated by Algerian journalist and writer Abed Charef (1994) and further explored by Saphia Arezki (2019).[2] Therefore, in a general way, it appears that the multiplication of marginalized bodies that are abandoned to their own destiny and in some way punished for their social conditions—which, moreover, they have not chosen—expose a North African social context in which "les pouvoirs oppresseurs se sont toujours abrités derrière la nécessité de lutter contre la violence pour fonder eux-mêmes leur propre violence" "powers of oppression are always sheltered behind the need to struggle against violence to establish their own violence" and where "créer du désordre justifie même la revendication des mesures d'ordre" "creating disorder itself justifies the demands for measures of order" (Braud 2004, 221).

Thus, when the individual is not left in permanent fear by reason of the State's abandonment of its sovereign function, that individual must confront insecurity and very often the possibility of death at the hands of the same States that were supposed to guarantee protection. That, at least, is what seems to me to be the deep reason for the questions of security that have now become the central preoccupations in Africa. In fact, whether it is a question of political violence arising at the time of the colonial encounter, the management of the lives of the repugnant (women reduced to their bodies, inhabitants of slum condemned to living in disastrous conditions, immigrants and exiles deprived of life in a city, etc.) who are excluded from the political sphere by a quasi-biological—and therefore biopolitical—enterprise, or even the young people who are living lives that are generally condemned to what François Dubet (1987) has called hell in his reflections on the specific situation of youths in France's ghettoes, it is implicitly clear: understanding the process of the banishment of entire populations has a great deal to do with the State's abdication of responsibility or its propensity to create, and make everlasting, social fractures.

My approach therefore aimed at understanding the relationship between *homo expendibilis* and the colonial or postcolonial State, which has allowed me to identify the deep matrix of the past and recent situation of North African society, namely, that insecurity is not so much the consequence of a society considered uncivilized, as it is the result or the means of production of an indecent society. Basically, by appropriating the distinction established by Avishaï Margalit between the two types of societies, we understand that in outlawing those whom I call precarious lives and marginal bodies, society manages to produce and maintain an indecency that goes apace with humiliation, so that, for Margalit, "une société civilisée est celle dont les membres ne s'humilient pas les uns les autres, alors qu'une société décente est celle où les institutions n'humilient pas les gens" "a civilized society is one whose members are not humiliated by each other, whereas a decent society is one where the institutions do not humiliate the people" (2007, 13). If humiliation effectively ends in the desocialization and disaffiliation of the groups that are involved, in a word in their social decline, then the obvious relationship between socialization and security emerges in a clear manner. Barry Buzan's reflections in *People, States and Fear* (1991) show this quite well: security is linked to socialization: (in)security cannot be felt except through respect to the Other. And the security of each is the sole condition for possibility of security for all.[3] More interesting and pertinent in the framework of this work, Buzan establishes the link between individual security and national security, because the better the organization of the societies it deals with, the State can both assure and threaten individual security.

The forms of threat to individual security that can easily become national threats are many: famine, epidemics, criminal violence, economic exploitation, ecological and nuclear disasters, incurable illnesses, and the like. According to Buzan:

> Most threats to individuals arise from the fact that people find themselves embedded in a human environment which generates unavoidable social, economic and political pressures. Societal threats come in a variety of forms, but there are four obvious types: physical threats (pain, injury, death), economic threats (seizure and destruction of property, denial of access to work or resources), threats to rights (imprisonment, denial of normal civil liberties) and threats to position or status (demotion, public humiliation). (1991, 37)

According to Buzan's thoughts, we can affirm that generally and particularly in North Africa with respect to the body analyzed here, precarization becomes an important instrument of governmentality, and this corresponds to the third dimension of precarity identified by Isabell Lorey:

> Governmental precarization thus means not only destabilization through employment, but also destabilization of the conduct of life and thus bodies and modes of subjectivation. Understanding precarization as governmental makes it possible to problematize the complex interactions between an instrument of governing and the conditions of economic exploitation and modes if subjectivation, in their ambivalence between subjugation and self-empowerment. (2015, 13)

With regard to the preceding, we need to state that the precarious human is the one who is deprived of socialization and weakened to the point where it is nearly impossible to have a narrative stance. The paradox is that these precarious lives are inscribed in the process of qualification that is in itself disqualification.

In *Precarious Life: The Powers of Mourning and Violence* (2004), Judith Butler reconsiders that very question of the value of human life by taking as her point of departure the attacks of September 11, 2001, which revealed their state of vulnerability to Americans, to which the United States reacted by affirming its power over life and death of those who were deemed guilty. The philosopher therefore questions the status of the human being by means of a remarkable use of the concept of face that she borrows from Emmanuel Levinas. In the second chapter of her study, Butler asks questions that I find central to the reflection and that I have tried to explore in the preceding pages. She asks: "Who counts as human? Whose lives count as lives? And finally, What *makes for a grievable life?*" (2004, 20). I in my turn take up these questions raised by Judith Butler and I position them within the context of wars between nations to resituate it within the framework of relationships between sovereign power or State power (and all the figures that incarnate it or monitor its expansion) and the individual, whom Guillaume le Blanc identifies as "the Being without," that is, the one who has been weakened and whose power of action (in the sense of *agency*) has been reduced to the point that he becomes an "être pour qui la perte est sans réponse évidente, un être dont le seul espoir est suspendu à la perte de la perte" "being for whom los sis without an evident response, a being whose sole hope is suspended upon the loss of loss" (2007, 84). From this perspective, it is remarkable that the North African "being without," from the colonial period up to our days, is not simply a being deprived of something that would make his or her socialization possible, but a being whose capacity to undertake the search for that thing has been rendered inoperative by the apparatus of power. For after all, if these invisible and unheard voices are relegated to the city's periphery, it must be because they belong to those lives that Butler characterizes as "lives that are not considered lives at all, they cannot be humanized . . . they fit no dominant frame for the human, and their dehumanization occurs first, at this level, and . . . this levels gives rise to a physical violence that in some sense delivers the message of dehumanization that is at work in the culture" (2004, 34).

Once again, despite the difference in the frame of interaction and the nature of the entities in conflict, as observed by Butler and other scholars who are of interest to me, it seems to me that the precarious lives fictionalized in the North African novel, through their bodily contact with colonial authorities and the national bourgeoise who replace the former, perfectly unite the characteristics of these lives that are more than just disposable and do not even deserve to be lamented, precisely because they have already been dehumanized. These precious lives, dehumanized and unworthy of being mourned in the case of death, are an example of what I call *homo expendibilis*, a triple *homo sacer* (Agamben), "living dead" (Mbembe), and the faceless (Butler). But what is common to the novels under analysis in this study is that the fictionalization of marginal bodies shows that these bodies indeed have a critical awareness of their situations through time and space. In other words, the North Africans who are excluded and at risk, at least those who emerge in the fiction that is analyzed, conjure up, so to speak, their vulnerability and propose a new configuration of relationships between the individual and the political authorities, who rely on the biopolitical, necropolitical, and thanato-political. Regarding the resistance to stigmatization that results from the humiliating situation of accepting social exclusion and living in a world of disadvantage, Serge Paugam has pointed out that "ces individus, diminués physiquement et psychologiquement, résistent malgré tout à cette déchéance morale en mobilisant des défenses pour résister à la stigmatisation" "these individuals, physically and psychologically diminished, resist this moral decline in spite of everything by mobilizing defenses to resist stigmatization" (1991, 29). As the articulations of resistance to their real, lived, discredited lives as shame, the sociologist therefore proposes two types of real experiences, namely, *conjured marginality* and *organized marginality*.

The first experience concerns the will to have a recognized social status, in short, to try to make a social move upwards, while the second experience does not aim to ameliorate social condition, and especially salary, but rather to reconstruct in a symbolic way an acceptable framework for the marginal. It therefore seems to me, with respect to the body under analysis, that North African marginal bodies very often opt for organized marginality, for

> par l'espace vécu qui contient potentiellement leur histoire faite de conflits, d'échecs mais aussi de fêtes et de moments heureux, ils accèdent à une forme d'identité positive. Il ne s'agit pas pour autant d'une volonté de changement de statut mais plutôt d'une adaptation individuelle à une condition dont on peut dire qu'elle est à la limite de l'exclusion sociale.

> through the lived space that potentially contains their history composed of conflicts and failures, but also of celebrations and happy moments, they give way to a form of positive identity. It is not a matter, however, of a will to change status but rather an individual adaptation to a condition that one could say is at the limit of social exclusion. (Paugam, 129–30)

Nevertheless, conjured marginality (the exiles and immigrés of Albert Bensoussan and Mehdi Charef who in living the experience of marginality try to give a meaning to their lives despite the inherent difficulties in their condition as foreigner) and organized marginality also cross paths, sometimes to the point of encountering what is crystallized in violence. The same pertains to the peasants of colonial Algeria in the works of Mohammed Dib and Azzédine Bounemeur, as do the women victims of male domination who are sometimes obliged to resort to violence or murder in the works of Leïla Marouane, or even suicide in the works of Fawzia Zouari and Mahi Binebine.

In the particular case of the kamikaze bombers in *Les étoiles de Sidi Moumen* by Mahi Binebine, certainly in the black slave in that same author's other novel, it is important to note that in a certain measure, resistance and self-destruction become synonymous, but also, they are sometimes the ultimate condition for escaping, as Achille Mbembe has emphasized in his reflection on the terrorists in Palestine. Focusing upon the martyr's body, he writes:

> The body in itself has neither power or value. The power and value of the body result from a process of abstraction based on the desire for eternity. In that sense, the martyr, having established a moment of supremacy in which the subject overcomes his own mortality, can be seen as laboring under the sign of the future. In other words, in death the future is collapsed into the present. . . . The body duplicates itself and, in death, literally and metaphorically escapes the state of siege and occupation. (2003, 37)

Even though Mbembe's analysis concerns the specific case of the Palestinian martyr, it is still a matter of real pertinence in understanding the trajectory of the bodies of the marginal and nefarious lives who through resistance, combat, civil disobedience, or suicide choose to give a meaning to their lives.

If the Palestinian martyr escapes the state of siege through suicide, the North African citizen, for his or her part, escapes a kind of state of permanent exception to become more than a *homo sacer*, or a living dead, but a *homo expendibilis*. It is therefore remarkable that in North African society as fictionalized in the texts that are being studied, death paradoxically becomes a condition of survival. I therefore am proposing the concept of profanation that was theorized by Giorgio Agamben as the central key to understanding how those who are socially disaffiliated take charge of their destiny, which means not only emerging from invisibility but finding a voice. To understand this idea of profanation and the reasons, it is pertinent to this interpretation of the relationships between marginal bodies and power (political, male, religious), it is absolutely imperative to return to the Italian philosopher Giorgio Agamben's theorization.

According to Agamben, to profane means "to open the possibility of a special form of negligence, which ignores separation, or rather, puts it to a particular use" (2007, 75). So, it appears that in Agamben's thinking, the profane is what has passed from the religious, or the sacred, to the human. In that sense, the philosopher continues his analysis by positing that the term "religious" basically does not derive from the link between the human and the divine, but from the word *relegere*, which indicates the attitude of scruples and attention in the management of the relationship between men and gods. There is thus a double play at work in the terms "religion" and "religious." Agamben writes:

> Religion can be defined as that which removes things, places, animals or people from common use and transfers them to a separate sphere. Not only there is

no religion without separation, but every separation also contains or preserves within itself a genuine religious core. The apparatus that effects and regulates the separation is sacrifice: through a series of meticulous rituals, which differ in various cultures and which Henri Hubert and Marcel Mauss have patiently inventoried, sacrifice always sanctions the passage of something from the profane to the sacred, from the human sphere to the divine. What is essential is the caesura that divides the two spheres, the threshold that the victim must cross, no matter in which direction. That which has been ritually separated can be returned from the rite to the profane sphere. (2007, 74)

If we attempt to discover the pertinence of this theorization, we will observe that profanation takes shape in a specific "usage" of the sacred, which in the postcolonial context can certainly be applied to what pertains to sovereign power or at least the figure that incarnates power, whether civil, military, or political. Thus, I find it pertinent to interpret the marginal person's decision to take action or to resist as a gesture that assures the passage of his or her body in this inverse sense, from the sacred to profane. The marginalized, having already been killed by the social rite that placed them at the margins of society, opt for violence and risk death to be able to live free, including in eternity. If the first death of the marginal subject is symbolic in the sense that he or she is sacrificed by social and practical conventions, can we then see in the second death the very sign of total redemption of his or her body?

I maintain in fact that by risking death, the precarious North Africans are implementing the rite that allows them to pass from the level of the sacred to that of the profane, to the extent that by affirming their becoming-subject, they have successfully returned their marginal bodies that had been moved to the sacred sphere to the profane sphere. Whether it is peasants organizing a revolt against the oppressive colonial order, exiles going on a hunger strike and ending up dead, even women who break the chains of silence and defy male domination, or even the black slave who makes the double choice of suicide and infanticide, it seems to me that there is an affirmation of their freedom in those acts, which ranges from the restitution of their bodies to a use that is no longer decided by the authorities, but by themselves. From the philosophical viewpoint, these precarious lives, through an act of reversal, take charge of their lives that have been made repugnant by the authorities to give a new meaning: what Katia Genel (2004) articulates through the remarkable formula of "la vie comme résistance au pouvoir" "life as resistance to authority." Genel reflects on Foucault's *La volonté de savoir* (1976) along with Agamben's *Homo sacer: Le pouvoir souverain et la vie nue* (1997) and suggests that if it is true that political struggles are rooted in life, then that life can be turned against the system that exercised its control over it. To Foucault's conception of the link between life and power, she proposes localizing "the subtraction of power" in the theory of "whatever singularity" put forth by Agamben in his work entitled *La communauté qui vient*—in effect, by considering that the coming community is one of "whatever singularities" that will no longer be a state authority, but a "struggle between the State and the non-State (humanity), an insurmountable disjunction between whatever singularity and the State organization" (1993, 85).

I therefore am proposing my final thesis based on the moment that marginal bodies give themselves a voice, speak for themselves, and thus succeed in removing themselves from the circle of those lives without faces and effectively escape the symbolic loop of the inaudible and the invisible—what Guillaume le Blanc refers to as the loop of precarity (2007,165), the precarious lives and marginal bodies from North Africa decenter the center and recenter the periphery through a spectacular displacement of the locus of power, which reminds us of the common vulnerability of every single human being, both the included and the excluded. From this perspective, adopting article 35 of the Declaration of the Rights of Man and the Citizen of 1793, which stipulates that "quand le gouvernement viole les droits du peuple, l'insurrection est, pour le peuple et pour chaque portion du peuple, le plus sacré des droits et le plus indispensable des devoirs" "When government violates the people's rights, insurrection is, for the people and for each segment of the people, the most sacred of rights and the most indispensable of duties," the marginalized, in fact abnormal, come face to face with the society composed of visible and audible people, in short, "normal" people, to exercise their most indispensable duties and their most sacred right. The subtraction of marginal bodies that allows them to free themselves from the State and the erection of "whatever singularities" as modalities of life, such as resisting authority, ultimately lead me to suggest a way of furthering this reflection on the link between marginal bodies and political power in North Africa. In the epilogue of *The Use of Bodies*, Agamben sets out the theory of a violence that will never put forth a new right, taking inspiration from Walter Benjamin's critique of violence, which calls for a pure violence, one that deposes the law but without establishing a new law. Agamben then emphasizes that "what is in question is the capacity to deactivate something and render it inoperative—a power, a function, a human operation—without simply destroying it, but by liberating the potentials that have remained inactive in it in order to allow a different use of them" (2015, 273).

From this perspective, conjured marginality and organized marginality are prolonged through profanation in the instance of marginalized bodies in North African, and end up with another use in that, again according to Agamben, "what has been divided from itself and captured in the exception—life, anomie, anarchic potential—now appears in its free and intact form" (ibid.). We could support the thesis that within the question of the representation of these fragilized bodies of North African precarious lives is the issue that they destroy not only the social or political order that keeps them at the periphery but renders them inoperable by establishing a different use for their lives. These marginal bodies are precarious lives, appearing not to be, through an attempt at undoing where finally they are not limited to conjuring their marginality but making use of their conditions as social disaffiliates. There is, in my opinion, a whole study to be undertaken on the marginal bodies' dismissal of maneuvers by authorities, which itself would be the subject of an entirely different work on forms of life, with the content needing to be identified and the philosophical dimensions articulated.

What I have concluded with certainty in my study is that the novels analyzed here signal that the multiplication and maintenance of lives that do not merit being grieved, these marginal bodies and precarious lives from North Africa, will make the bed of a permanent insecurity not only in the Maghreb but in all of Africa. There is thus an urgency for African countries to take seriously the words of the Invisible Committee that reports on proliferation in the global context (and this is also valid for the African continent) with an insurrectional logic that is revealed as follows:

> It's useless to wait—for a breakthrough, for the revolution, the nuclear apocalypse or a social movement. To go on waiting is madness. The catastrophe is not coming, it is here. We are already situated within the collapse of a civilization. It is within this reality that we must choose sides. To no longer wait is, in one way or another, to enter the logic of insurrection. It is once again to hear the slight but always present trembling of terror in the voice of our leaders. Because governing has never been anything other than postponing by thousand subterfuges the moment when the crowd will string you up, and every act of government is nothing but a way of not losing control of the population. We're setting from a point of extreme isolation, of extreme weakness. An insurrectional process must be built from the ground up. Nothing appears less likely than an insurrection, but nothing is more necessary. (*The Invisible Committee* 2009, 96)

The political lesson contained in the thought of the Invisible Committee seems to me central for understanding the ways in which the North African *homo expendibilis* undoubtedly represents the very site for redefinition of the relations between life and sovereign power. As I have attempted to show, from the figures of the colonized to the youth of the slums as well as the female figure and the migrant, these lives are controlled and reproduced by the authorities. Now if the powers that manufacture and maintain precarious lives and marginal bodies are not careful, as in the colonial era which experienced Algeria's long fratricidal war, they risk being totally surprised by the coming insurrection, of which the October 1988 riots in Algeria, the attacks in Casablanca in 2003, and even the 2011 revolution in Tunisia, to mention only those examples, are annunciatory signs. As suggested by the analysis of the trajectories of marginal bodies and precarious lives in the novels of Albert Bensoussan, Mahi Binebine, Azzédine Bounemeur, Mehdi Charef, Fawzia Zouari, and Leïla Marouane, the periphery will multiply the strategies to contest the center, unless they can participate in the advent of a just and equitable management of the city, a city where entire segments of humanity do not see themselves being refused citizenship, the right to the city, or more simply, the right to exist. We have seen that for the North African *homo expendibilis*, suicide, armed struggle, civil disobedience, and even murder become not only alternative projects for doing but alternative arts for being and acting.

Thus, the ultimate epistemological lesson to draw from the study of North Africa's precarious lives and marginal bodies lies in the central place that the excluded subjects must occupy in the heart of the city, to summarize the thought of Guillaume le Blanc in his work entitled *Que faire de notre vulnerabilité?* (2011) where he shows that being fragilized does not exclude the excluded person's ability to hold citizenship. And this work, I hope, has tried to put into perspective the conceptions that the vulnerable subjects create of the city that has vulnerabilized them, and the ways they react to the social and political mechanisms that have excluded them, by emphasizing the ways in which the periphery returns to the center and obliges us to reconsider the hypothesis of democracy.

NOTES

1. Expression borrowed from Jacques Rancière and referencing the distribution of political power and its advantages. See Jacques Rancière, *Le Partage du sensible. Esthétique et politique*, Paris, La Fabrique, 2000, 14.

2. This idea is also mentioned and explored in the documentary by Malik Ait-Oudia and Séverin Labat, *Algérie 1988–2000. Autopsie d'une tragédie*, Compagnie des Phares et Balises, 2003, 150 minutes.

3. On this, see the work of Ronnie D. Lipschutz (dir.), *On Security,* New York: Columbia University Press, 1995.

Bibliography

Agamben, Giorgio. 1997. *Homo Sacer: Sovereign Power and Bare Life*. Trans. Daniel Heller-Roazen. Stanford, CA: Stanford University Press.
Agamben, Giorgio. 2000. *Means Without End*. Trans. Cesare Casarino and Vincenzo Binetti. Minneapolis: University of Minnesota Press.
Agamben, Giorgio. 2007. *Profanations*. Trans. Jeff Fort. New York: Zone Books.
Agamben, Giorgio. 2015. *The Use of Bodies*. Trans. Adam Kotsko. Stanford, CA: Stanford University Press.
Alcaraz, Emmanuel. 2013. "La mise en scène de la mémoire nationale: De la guerre d'indépendance algérienne au *maqam al-chahid* d'Alger." In *Autour des morts de guerre: Maghreb-Moyen-Orient*, ed. Raphaëlle Branche, Nadine Picaudou, and Pierre Vermeren, 21–45. Paris: Publications de la Sorbonne.
Amrane-Minne, Danièle Djamila. 1999. "Women and Politics in Algeria from the War of Independence to Our Day." *Research in African Literatures* 30(3): 62–77.
André, Marc. 2016. « Algériennes: quelle citoyenneté? (Années 1930–années 1960) », *Clio. Femmes, Genre, Histoire* 43: 94–116.
Arezki, Saphia. 2019. "Les camps d'internement du sud en Algérie (1991–1995). Contextualisation et enjeux." *L'Année du Maghreb* 20: 225–39.
Ayadi, Hanna. 2014. "D'une rive à l'autre, littératures et pratiques culturelles: la virginité dans les romans de Leïla Marouane." *Babel* 30: 293–302.
Bachelard, Gaston. 1969. *The Poetics of Space*. Boston: Beacon Press.
Bailleul, Adeline. 2016. "À Zagora, les fantômes de la ségrégation." Huffpost Maroc Jan 2, 2016. Last consulted March 25, 2019. URL: https://www.huffpostmaghreb.com/2016/02/01/zagora-maroc-segregation-_n_9132500.html.
Balandier, Georges. 1985. *Le Détour. Pouvoir et modernité*. Paris: Fayard.
Bancel, Nicolas, and Pascal Blanchard. 1998. *De l'indigène à l'immigré*. Paris: Gallimard.
Bancel, Nicolas, et al. 2002. *Zoos Humains*. Paris: La Découverte.
Bancel, Nicolas, Pascal Blanchard, and Sandrine, eds. 2005. *La fracture coloniale*, Paris: La Découverte.

Barkat, Sidi Mohammed. 2005. *Le corps d'exception. Les artifices du pouvoir colonial et la destruction de la vie*. Paris: Éditions Amsterdam.
Bassalah, Iman.2012. *Hôtel Miranda*. Paris: Éditions Calmann-Lévy.
Belhabib, Assia. 2014. "Lever le voile sur la littérature de la marge au Maroc.» *Présence Africaine* 190: 199–211.
Ben Jelloun, Tahar. 1976. *La réclusion solitaire*. Paris: Denoël.
Bencheikh, Jamel Eddine. 2000. *Dictionnaire des littératures de langue arabe et maghrébine francophone*. Paris: Presses Universitaires de France.
Benguigui, Yamina, dir. 1997. *Mémoire d'immigrés. L'héritage maghrébin*. Canal+/-Bandits, 1997. Film. DVD
Bensoussan, Albert. 1989. *Mirage à 3*. Paris: L'Harmattan.
Bernault, Florence. 2009. "Colonial Syndrome: French Modern and the Deceptions of History." In *Frenchness and the African Diaspora*, ed. Charles Tshimanga, Didier Gondola, and Peter J. Bloom, 120–45. Bloomington: Indiana University Press.
Binebine, Mahi. 1992. *Le sommeil de l'esclave*. Paris: Éditions Stock.
Binebine, Mahi. 2010. *Les étoiles de Sidi Moumen*. Paris: Flammarion.
Blanc, Guillaume le. 2011. *Que faire de notre vulnérabilité?* Paris: Bayard Éditions
Blanchot, Maurice. 1978. *L'espace littéraire*. Paris: Gallimard.
Boëtsch, Gilles, Christian Hervé, and Jacques Rozenberg, eds. 2007. *Corps normalisé, corps stigmatisé, corps racialisé*. Bruxelles: De Boeck.
Bonn, Charles. 1988. *Lecture présente de Mohammed Dib*. Alger: ENAL.
Bonn, Charles. 2016. *Lectures nouvelles du roman algérien. Essai d'autobiographie intellectuelle*. Paris: Classiques Garnier.
Bonn, Charles. 2016. *Lectures nouvelles du roman algérien*. Paris: Classiques Garnier.
Bouchareb, Rachid. 2010. *Hors la loi*. Tessalit Production/Studio Canal.
Bouchareb, Rachid., dir. 2006. *Indigenes*. Mars Distribution. Film. DVD.
Boudjedra, Rachid. 1975. *Topographie idéale pour une agression caractérisée*. Paris: Denoël.
Boudjedra, Rachid. 2010. *Les figuiers de Barbarie*. Paris: Grasset. Trans. André Naffis-Sahely as *The Barbary Figs*. London: Arabia Books, 2012.
Boudjedra, Rachid. 2012. *The Barbary Figs*. Trans. André Naffis-Sahely. London: Arabia Books.
Bounemeur, Azzédine. 1983. *Les bandits de l'Atlas*. Paris: Gallimard.
Bourdieu, Pierre. 1998. *Masculine Domination*. Stanford, CA: Stanford University Press.
Bozon, Michel. 2008. *Sociologie de la sexualité*. Paris: Nathan/VUEF.
Branche, Raphaëlle. 2013. "Au temps de la France: identités collectives et situation coloniale en Algérie." *Vingtième Siècle. Revue d'Histoire* 117: 199–213.
Braud, Philippe. 2004. *Violences politiques*, Paris: Éditions du Seuil.
Brugère, Fabienne, and Guillaume le Blanc. 2018. "Le courage de l'hospitalité." *Esprit* 7: 49–53.
Brun, Jacques. 1994. "Essai critique sur la notion de ségrégation et sur son usage en géographie urbaine." In *La ségrégation dans la ville*, ed. Jacques Brun and Catherine Rhein, 21–57. Paris: L'Harmattan.

Butler, Judith. 2004. *Precarious Life: The Powers of Mourning and Violence*. New York: Verso.
Buzan, Barry. 1991. *People, State and Fear*. Boulder: Lynne Rienner Publishers.
Caruth, Cathy. 1996. *Unclaimed Experience: Trauma, Narrative, and History*. Baltimore: Johns Hopkins University Press.
Castel, Robert. 1995. "Les pièges de l'exclusion." *Lien social et politique* 34: 13–21.
Castel, Robert. 2003. *L'insécurité sociale*. Paris: Éditions du Seuil et La République des Idées.
Cazenave, Odile. 1996. *Femmes Rebelles: naissance d'un nouveau roman africain au féminin*. Paris: L'Harmattan.
Césaire, Aimé. 2000. *Discourse on Colonialism*. New York: Monthly Review Press.
Chamoiseau, Patrick. 1997. *L'esclave vieil homme et le molosse*. Paris, Gallimard.
Charef, Abed. 1994. *Algérie, le grand dérapage*. La tour d'Aigues: Éditions de l'Aube.
Charef, Mehdi. 1983. *Le thé au harem d'Archi Ahmed*. Paris: Mercure de France "Folio."
Chikhi, Beïda. 1996. *Maghreb en textes*. Paris: L'Harmattan.
Chraïbi, Driss. 1955. *Les Boucs*. Paris: Denoël.
Colonna, Fanny and Zakya Daoud (dirs.) 1993. *Être marginal au Maghreb*. Paris: CNRS Éditions.
Debordeaux, Danièle. 1994. "Désaffiliation, disqualification, désinsertion." *Recherches et Prévisions* 38: 93–100.
Déjeux, Jean. 1984. *Dictionnaire des auteurs maghrébins de langue française*, Paris: Karthala.
Devji, Faisal. 2005. *Landscapes of the Jihad*. Ithaca: Cornell University Press.
Dib, Mohammed. 1954. *L'incendie*. Paris: Editions du Seuil.
Djellali, Abderrazak. 1992. "Le caïdat en Algérie au XIXe siècle." *Cahiers de la Méditerranée* 45(1): 37–49.
Donadey, Anne. 2016. "Gender, genre and intertextuality in Rachid Bouchareb's *Hors la loi*." *Studies in French Cinema* 16(1): 48–60.
Donadey, Anne. 2001. *Recasting Postcolonialism: Women Writing Between Worlds*. Portsmouth: Heinemann.
Dubet, François. 1987. *La galère*. Paris: Fayard.
Dubet, Francois. 1987. *La galère: jeunes en survie*. Paris: Fayard.
Dugas, Guy. 1983. "Le thème du regard dans *L'incendie* de Mohammed Dib." *Revue CELFAN* 2(2): 2–7.
Dugas, Guy. 1991. *La littérature judéo-maghrébine d'expression française: entre Djéha et Cagayous*. Paris: L'Harmattan.
Dugas, Guy. 1994. *Études littéraires maghrébines. Bibliographie critique de la littérature judéo-maghrébine d'expression française*. Paris: L'Harmattan.
Eboussi Boulaga, Fabien.1977. *La crise du Muntu*. Paris: Présence Africaine.
El Hamel, Chouki. 2013. *Black Morocco: A History of Slavery, Race and Islam*. Cambridge: Cambridge University Press.
Elmorchid, Brahim. 2018. "The Demographic Gift in the Arab World: a Blessing or a Time Bomb for Morocco?" *AlMuntaqa* 1(3): 74–91

Esposito, Roberto. 2012. *Terms of the Political: Community, Immunity, Biopolitics*. Trans. Rhiannon Noel Welch. New York: Fordham University Press.
Evans, Jane. 2009. "Re-Inscribing the body: A Study of Leïla Marouane's *Le châtiment des hypocrites*." In *Aimer et Mourir: Love, Death and Women's Lives in Texts of French Expression*, ed. Eileen Hoft-March, and Judith Holland Sarnecki, 190–211. Cambridge: Cambridge Scholars.
Evans, Martin, and John Phillips. 2007. *Algeria: Anger of the Dispossessed*, New Haven and London: Yale University Press.
Fanon, Frantz. 1965. *A Dying Colonialism*. New York: Grove Press.
Fanon, Frantz. 2004. *The Wretched of the Earth*. Trans. Richard Philcox. New York: Grove Press.
Farès, Nabile. 1971. *Un passager de l'Occident*. Paris: Le Seuil.
Felman, Shoshana. 1978. *La folie et la chose littéraire*. Paris: Éditions du Seuil. In English: *Writing and Madness*. Trans. Martha Evans. Redwood City: Stanford University Press, 2003.
Fontaine, Jean. 2004. *Le roman tunisien de langue française*. Tunis: Sud Éditions.
Foucault, Michel. 2003. *"Society Must Be Defended": Lectures at the Collège de France, 1975–1976*, ed. Mauro Bertani, and Alessandro Fontana. New York: Picador.
Foucault, Michel. 2008. *The Birth of Biopolitics: Lectures at the Collège de France, 1978–1979*. Trans. Graham Burchell. New York: Picador.
Foucault, Michel. 2009. *Security, Territory, Population: Lectures at the Collège de France 1977–1978*. Trans. Graham Burchell. New York: Picador.
Foucault, Michel. 1995. *Discipline and Punish: The Birth of the Prison*. New York: Vintage Books.
Genel, Katia. 2019. "Le biopouvoir chez Foucault et Agamben." *Methodos* 4, accessed 29 April 2019. URL: http://methodos.revues.org/131. DOI: 10.4000/methodos.131.
Girard, René. 1990. [1972]. *La violence et le sacré*. Paris: Éditions Albin Michel.
Goldhammer, Jesse. 2005. The *Headless Republic*. Ithaca: NY Cornell University Press.
Gontard, Marc. 1992. "Francophone North African Literature and Critical Theory." *Research in African Literatures* 23(2): 33–38.
Grafmeyer, Yves. 1994. "Regards sociologiques sur la ségrégation." In *La ségrégation dans la ville*, ed. Jacques Brun et Catherine Rhein, 85–117. Paris: L'Harmattan.
Greimas, Algirdas Julien. 1966. *Sémantique structurale*. Paris: Larousse.
Guénif-Souilamas, Nacira. 2005. "La réduction à son corps de l'indigène de la République." In *La fracture coloniale. La société française au prisme de l'héritage colonial*, ed. Pascal Blanchard, Nicolas Bancel, and Sandrine Lemaire, 203–12. Paris: La Découverte.
Hamil, Mustapha. 2011. "Plotting Terrorism: Mahi Binebine's *Les étoiles de Sidi Moumen*." *International Journal of Francophone Studies* 14(4): 549–69.
Hamon, Philippe. 1984. *Texte et idéologie*. Paris: Presses Universitaires de France.
Harbi, Mohammed. 2008. "Frantz Fanon et le messianisme paysan." *Tumultes* 31: 11–15.

Hargreaves, Alec, and Moura, Jean-Marc. 2007. "Editorial introduction. Extending the boundaries of francophone postcolonial studies." *International Journal of Francophone Studies* 10(3): 307–11.

Heggoy, Alf Andrew. 1974. "On the Evolution of Algerian Women." *African Studies Review* 17(2): 449–56.

Hiddleston, Jane. 2016. "État Présent: Francophone North African Literature." *French Studies* 70(1): 82–92.

Hollis, Isabel. 2009. "Metamorphoses in Migration: Fawzia Zouari's *Ce pays dont je meurs*." In *Expressions of the Body: Representations in African Text and Image*, ed. Charlotte Baker, 213–30. Bern: Peter Lang.

Hron, Madelaine. 2005. "Pathological Victims: The Discourse of Disease/Dis-Ease in Beur Texts." *French Literary Studies* 16: 159–74.

Ireland, Susan. 2006. "Deviant Bodies. Corporeal Otherness in Contemporary Women's Writing." *Nottingham French Studies* 45(3): 39–52.

Jay, Salim. 2001. *Tu ne traverseras pas le détroit*. Paris: Mille et une nuits.

Jouve, V. 1992. *L'effet-personnage dans le roman*. Paris: Presses Universitaires de France.

Katia Genel. 2004. "Le biopouvoir chez Foucault et Agamben," *Methodos* 4, accessed June 2019. URL: http://methodos.revues.org/131; DOI: 10.4000/methodos.131.

Kemedjio, Cilas. 2003. "L'arrière-pays contre la violence coloniale." *Etudes Littéraires* 35(1): 41–54.

Kemedjio, Cilas. 2006. "Faire taire les silences du corps noir." *Présence Francophone* 66(1): 12–36.

Kemp, Anna. 2016. "'Le passeport de la douleur ou rien': Fawzia Zouari's *Ce Pays dont je meurs* and the Politics of Pain." *Contemporary French Civilization* 41: 49–67.

Komlan Gbanou, Selom. 2003. "Azzédine Bounemeur ou la guerre d'Algérie en questions." *Etudes Littéraires* 35(1): 73–86.

Kristeva, Julia. 1980. *Pouvoirs de l'horreur*. Paris: Éditions du Seuil.

Lacan, Jacques. 1988. *Les complexes familiaux*. Paris: Navarin Éditeur.

Laronde, Michel. 1993. *Autour du roman beur. Immigration et identité*. Paris: L'Harmattan.

Le Blanc, Guillaume. 2010. *Dedans, dehors. La condition d'étranger*. Paris: Editions du Seuil.

Le Blanc, Guillaume. 2011. *Que faire de notre vulnérabilité?* Paris: Bayard Éditions.

Le Blanc, Guillaume. 2007. *Vies ordinaires, vies précaires*. Paris: Le Seuil.

Le Cour Grandmaison, Olivier. 2010. *De l'indigénat. Anatomie d'un "monstre juridique: Le Droit colonial en Algérie et dans l'empire francais*. Paris: Editions la Découverte.

Le Cour Grandmaison, Olivier. 2005. *Coloniser. Exterminer. Sur la guerre et l'Etat colonial*. Paris: Librairie Arthène Fayard.

Lorey, Isabell. 2015. *State of Insecurity: Government of the Precarious*. London: Verso.

Maingueneau, Dominique. 1981. *Approche de l'énonciation en linguistique française*. Paris: Hachette.

Margalit, Avishaï. 2007. *La Société décente*. Paris: Flammarion.
Margalit, Avishai. 1998. *The Decent Society*. Trans. Naomi Goldblum. Cambridge: Harvard University Press.
Marouane, Leïla. 2005. *La jeune fille et la mère*. Paris: Editions du Seuil.
Marouane, Leïla. 2001. *Le châtiment des hypocrites*. Paris: Éditions du Seuil.
Marouane, Leïla. 2007. *La vie sexuelle d'un islamiste à Paris*. Paris: Albin Michel.
Martin, Claude. "Désaffiliation," in Paugam Serge (dir.), *Les 100 mots de la sociologie*, Paris, Presses universitaires de France, coll. "Que Sais-Je?", 61–62.
Marzano, Michela. 2009. *Visages de la peur*. Paris: Presses Universitaires de France.
Mbembe, Achille. 2004. "Essai sur le politique en tant que forme de la dépense." *Cahiers d'Études Africaines* 44(173/174): 151–92.
Mbembe, Achille. "Necropolitics." *Public Culture* 15(1): 11–40.
Mbembe, Achille. 2019. *Out of the Dark Night: Essays on Decolonization*. Trans. Daniela Ginsburg. New York: Columbia University Press.
Mbembe, Achille. 2009. "The Republic and Its Beast: On Riots in the French Banlieues." In *Frenchness and the African Diaspora,* ed. Charles Tshimanga, Didier Gondola, and Peter J. Bloom, 47–54. Bloomington: Indiana University Press.
Mbembe, Achille. 2010. *Sortir de la grande nuit*. Paris: La Découverte.
Mdarhri Alaoui, Abdallah. 2006. *Aspects du roman marocain*, (1950–2003): approche historique, thématique et esthétique. Rabat: Éd. Zaouia.
Meddeb, Abdelwahab. 1986. *Phantasia*. Paris: Sindbad.
Meillassoux, Claude. 1991. *The Anthropology of Slavery*. Trans. Alide Dasnois. Chicago: Chicago University Press.
Memmi, Albert. 1968. *Dominated Man: Notes Towards a Portrait*. Boston: Beacon.
Memmi, Albert. 1968. *L'homme dominé*. Paris: Éditions Gallimard.
Mernissi, Fatima. 1987. *Beyond the Veil: Male-Female Dynamics in Modern Muslim Society*. Bloomington and Indianapolis: Indiana University Press.
Mernissi, Fatima. 2006. *The Forgotten Queens of Islam*. Minneapolis: University of Minnesota Press.
Mernissi, Fatima.1991. *The Veil and the Male Elite: A Feminist Interpretation of Women's Rights in Islam*. Cambridge: Perseus Books.
Meynier, Gilbert. 2014. "L'Algérie et les Algériens sous le système colonial. Approche historico historiographique."*Insaniyat* 65–66: 13–70.
Meynier, Gilbert. 2003. "Les femmes dans l'ALN/FLN." In *Des hommes et des femmes en guerre d'Algérie*, ed. Jean-Charles Jauffret, 307–19. Paris: Autrement.
Michel, Andrée. 1965. "Les classes sociales en Algérie." *Cahiers Internationaux de Sociologie* 38: 207–20.
Mildonian, Paola. 2002. "Identité multiculturelle et développement d'un 'je' anthropologique chez Elias Canetti et José Maria Arguedas." In *Multiculturalisme et identité en littérature et en art*, ed. Jean Bessière and SylvieAndré, 331–48. Paris: L'Harmattan.
Mitterand, Henri. 1980. *Le discours du roman*. Paris: PUF.
Mohanram, Radhika. 1999. *Black Body: Women, Colonialism and Space*. Minneapolis: University of Minnesota Press.

Moles, Abraham, and Elisabeth Rohmer. 1978. *Psychologie de l'espace*. Paris: Casterman.
Mortimer, Mildred. 2018. *Women Fight, Women Write: Texts on the Algerian War*. Charlottesville & London: University of Virginia Press.
Moudileno, Lydie. 2002. "Le droit d'exister. Trafic et nausée postcoloniale." *Cahiers d'Études Africaines* 165: 83–98.
Moura, Jean –Marc. 1999. *Littératures francophones et théorie postcoloniale*. Paris: Presses Universitaires de France.
Moussaoui, Abderrahmane. 2016. "Violence, viols et symbolique sexuelle. L'Algérie d'une guerre à l'autre." In *Guerre d'Algérie: le sexe outragé*, ed. Catherine Brun, and Todd Shepard, 399–410. Paris: CNRS.
Nancy, Jean-Luc. 2003. *Noli Me Tangere: Essai sur la levée du corps*. Paris: Bayard.
Nassir, Muhammad Ali. 2017. "Biopolitics, Thanatopolitics and the Right to Life." *Theory, Culture and Society* 34(1): 75–95.
Ngal, Georges. 1979. *L'errance*. Yaoundé: Editions Clé.
Norris, Andrew. "Giorgio Agamben and the Politics of the Living Dead." *Diacritics* 30(4): 38–58.
Norton, Ann. 2013. *On the Muslim Question*. Princeton: Princeton University Press.
Nossery, Nevine El. 2012. *Témoignages fictionnels au féminin: une réécriture des blancs de la guerre civile algérienne*. Amsterdam: Rodopi.
Olosegun-Joseph, Yomi. 2012. "African Literary Criticism, North African and the Politics of Exclusion." *The Journal of Pan African Studies* 5(12): 218–31.
Orlando, Valérie. 1999. *Nomadic Voices of Exile. Feminine Identity in Francophone Literature of the Maghreb*. Athens, OH: Ohio University Press.
Orlando, Valerie. 2017. *The Algerian New Novel: The Poetics of a Modern Nation*, 1950–1979. Charlottesville and London: University of Virginia Press.
Pageaux, Daniel Henri. 1994. *La littérature générale et comparée*. Paris: Colin.
Paugam, Serge. 2011[1991]. *La disqualification sociale*. Paris: Presses Universitaires de France.
Philippe. 2004. *Violences politiques*. Paris: Éditions du Seuil.
Pieprzak, Katarzyna. 2016. "Zones of Perceptual Enclosure: The Aesthetics of Immobility in Casablanca's Literary *Bidonvilles*." *Research in African Literatures* 47(3): 32–49.
Press, Robert. 2017. "Dangerous Crossings: Voices from the African Migration to Italy/Europe." *Africa Today* 64(1): 3–27.
Rahal, Malika. 2012. "Fuse Together, Torn Apart. Stories and Violence in Contemporary Algeria." *History & Memory* 24(1): 118–51.
Ramonet, Ignacio. 1997. *Géopolitique du chaos*. Paris: Galilée.
Rancière, Jacques. 2004. *The Politics of Aesthetics*. New York: Continuum.
Repo, Jemina. 2016. "Thanatopolitics or Biopolitics? Diagnosing the Racial and Sexual Politics of the European Fra-Right." *Contemporary Political Theory* 15(1): 110–18.
Revel, Judith. 2007. "De la vie en milieu précaire (ou comment en finir avec la vie nue)." *Multitudes* 27. http://multitudes.samizdat.net/De-la-vie-en-milieu-prec aire-ou

Rice, Allison. 2012. *Polygaphies: Francophone Women Writing Algeria.* Charlottesville and London: University of Virginia Press.

Rice, Susan, Corinne Graff, and Carlos Pascual (eds.). 2010. *Confronting Poverty: Weak States and National US Security.* Washington DC: Brookings Institution Press.

Ricœur, Paul. 2000. *La mémoire, l'histoire, l'oubli.* Paris: Seuil. Trans. Kathleen Blamey, and David Pellauer as *Memory, History, Forgetting.* Chicago: University of Chicago Press, 2004.

Rigouste, Mathieu. 2009. *L'ennemi intérieur: la généalogie coloniale et militaire de l'ordre sécuritaire dans la France contemporaine.* Paris: La Découverte.

Saada, Emmanuelle. 2002. "The Empire of Law: Dignity, Prestige and Domination in the Colonial Situation" *French Politics, Culture & Society* 20(2): 98–120.

Saada, Emmanuelle. 2007. *Les enfants de la colonie. Les métis de l'Empire français entre sujétion et citoyenneté.* Paris: La Découverte.

Said, Edward. 2000. *Reflections on Exile and Other Essays.* Cambridge: Harvard University Press.

Sembene, Ousmane. 1960. *Les bouts de bois de Dieu.* Paris: Pocket.

Shepard, Todd. 2006. *The Invention of Decolonization.* Ithaca, NY: Cornell University Press.

Sibony, Daniel. 1997. *Le "racisme." Une haine identitaire.* Paris: Christian Bourgeois.

Silverstein, Paul A., and Chantal Tetreault. 2006. "Postcolonial Urban Apartheid." *Social Science Research Council*, accessed 15 September 2018. http://riotsfrance.ssrc.org/Silverstein_Tetreault.

Smail Salhi, Zahia. 2003. "Algerian Women, Citizenship, and the Family Code." *Gender and Development* 11(3): 27–35.

Smith, Stephen. 2018. *La ruée vers l'Europe.* Paris: Grasset.

Spensky, Martine, ed. 2015. *Le contrôle du corps des femmes dans les empires coloniaux: Empires, genre et biopolitiques.* Paris: Karthala.

Spivak, Gayatri Chakravorty. 1995. "Can the Subaltern Speak?" In *The Post-Colonial Studies Reader*, ed. Bill Ashcroft et al., 28–37. London: Routledge.

Stambouli, Fred. 1972. "Sous-emploi et espace urbain: les bidonvilles au Maghreb." *Manpower and Unemployment Research in Africa* 5(2): 28–48.

Stora, Benjamin. 1986. "Faiblesse paysanne du mouvement nationaliste Algérien avant 1954." *Vingtième Siècle. Revue d'Histoire* 12: 59–72. Passages included in *Algeria 1830–2000: A Short History*, Trans. Jane Marie Todd, 2001. Ithaca, NY: Cornell University Press.

Stora, Benjamin. 2001. *Histoire de l'Algérie depuis l'indépendance. 1962–1988.* Paris: La Découverte.

Stora, Benjamin. 2007. "Un besoin d'histoire." In *La situation postcoloniale: les postcolonial studies dans le débat français*, ed. Marie-Claude Smouts, 293–98. Paris: Presses de la Fondation Nationale des Sciences Politiques.

Tar, Adejir. 1992. "Breaking Out of the 'Cryptostasme': The Fellah Strike in Dib's *L'Incendie* as a Precursor to the Algerian Revolution." *Revue CELFAN* 8(3): 1–12.

Taraud, Christelle. 2003. *La prostitution coloniale.* Paris: Payot.

Taraud, Christelle. 2012. *"Amour interdit": Marginalité, prostitution et colonialisme (Maghreb, 1830-1962)*. Paris: Petite bibliothèque Payot.
Tchumkam, Hervé. 2018. "Remapping Islamic Terrorism in Algeria." *Peace Review* 30(4): 463–69.
Tchumkam, Hervé. 2015. *State Power, Stigmatization and Youth Resistance Cultures in the French Banlieues: Uncany Citizenship*. Lanham: Lexington Books.
Toso Rodinis, Giuliana. 1994. *Fêtes et défaites d'Éros dans l'œuvre de Rachid Boudjedra*. Paris: L'Harmattan.
Vendetti, Maria. 2016. "Quel étranger ici ne se sent pas chez lui?'': Leïla Marouane and the Pathology of Failed Integration." *The Journal of the Midwest Modern Language Association* 49(2): 111–36.
Vince, Natalya. 2015. *Our Fighting Sisters: Nation, Memory and Gender in Algeria, 1954–2012*. Manchester: Manchester University Press.
Vingtième Siècle. Revue d'Histoire 12 (1986): 59–72. Passages included in *Algeria 1830-2000: A Short History*. Trans. Jane Marie Todd. Ithaca: Cornell University Press, 2001.
Woodhull, Winifred. 2000. "Mohamed Dib and the French Question." *Yale French Studies* 98: 66–78.
Woodhull, Winnifred. 1993. *Transfigurations of the Maghreb: Feminism, Decolonization, and Literatures*. Minneapolis: University of Minnesota Press.
Zaid, Afaf. 2016. "L'espace littéraire de Mahi Binebine: pour une esthétique du désenchantement social." *Contemporary French and Francophone Studies* 20(1): 122–30.
Zouari, Fawzia. 1999. *Ce pays dont je meurs*. Paris: Ramsay.

Index

abjection, Kristeva on, 96–97
Africa, migration to Europe, xxii
African diaspora, 2005, 1, 54, 55, 64, 69n3
Agamben, Giorgio: biopolitics and, 111; on biopower, 125–26; on camp, 111; on French suburbs, 79; on homo sacer, xiii, xx, 12, 13, 15, 141, 144; on necropolitics and thanatopolitics, xiii–xiv; on profanation of bodies, 103, 133, 143–44; on religion, 143–44; on slavery, 90, 130; on sovereignty, xiii; on violence, 145
Alcaraz, Emmanuel, 87
Algeria: assimilationist system and, 6; French citizenship and, 6, 14; Grandmaison on dictatorship in, 24; internment camps in, 138; Islam nationalization attempts, 87–90; laws imposed upon women in, 88; living dead of colonial, 1–32; migration to France, 95; rape Penal Code in, 102; Stora on history of, 87, 117; terrorist attacks in, 138; war of national liberation in, 14, 72, 82, 85, 116–17; women as metaphor for, 79–80, 84; women liberation contribution, 72, 82, 85; youth riots in, vii, 118

Algerian nationalist movement: Gbanou on, 29–30; Stora on, 28
Algerian riots, 1988, vii, 117, 146–47
Les alouettes naïves (Djebar), 73
alterity, exile and, 39–40
Amrane-Minne, Danièle Djamila, 82
Ancien Régime of historicity, Hartog on, 42–43
apartheid, slum as illustration of, 109
Armed Islamic Group (GIA), 138
assimilationist system, in Algeria, 6
audibility, 2, 11, 74

Bailleul, Adeline, 123–24
Les bandits de l'Atlas (Bounemeur), 17–32
Barak, Ehud, 119
Barkat, Sidi Mohammed: on bodies of exception, 56, 67; on immigration, xxii
being without, le Blanc on, 141, 147
Bencheikh, Jamel Eddine, 36
Benguigui, Yamina, 57, 59
Benjamin, Walter, 145
Bensoussan, Albert: on cannibalism, 37; on immigration, 35–54, 142
Binebine, Mahi: *Les étoiles de Sidi Moumen* of, 105–13, 120, 142; *Le sommeil de l'esclave* of, 121–34

biopolitics, xi–xii, 139; Agamben and, 111; camp and, 79; Foucault and, 107, 111; governmentality and, xv; slum segregation and, 111; woman body in, xxii; women as victims of, 79

biopower, xiii; Agamben on, 125–26; bodies control and management in, 22–24; Foucault on, xv, 22–23, 107, 125–26; Francophone North Africa and, xvii

Black Body (Mohanram), 72

Black Morocco (El Hamel), 122–23

black women slavery, 125–28, 133–44; invisibility of, 129, 131; prostitution and, 123–24; rape and, 130–32; subaltern condition of, 121–22, 124

Blanc, Guillaume Le: on being without, 141, 147; on exile, 53; on precarity, xxiii, 11, 145; on social disenfranchisement, xxi, 131; on visibility, 11–12, 16

Blanchot, Maurice, 41, 45, 51

bodies: Agamben on profanation of, 103, 133, 143–44; biopolitics and women, xxii; biopower control and management of, 22–24; colonial domination of, 3; colonized, 4; Dib on fellah reduction to, 12; fellahs reduction to, 12; metaphor of, 5; Nancy on assemblage of, 58; racialized and sexualized, 121–34; violated, 87–104; women as slave, xxii. *See also* marginal bodies

bodies of exception, Barkat on, 56, 67

Bonn, Charles, 2

Bouazizi, Mohamed, vii

Bouchareb, Rachid, 1, 56

Les boucs (Chraibi), 73

Boudjedra, Rachid, 35; *Les figuiers de Barbarie* of, 115, 137; *L'escargot entêté* of, 73

Bounemeur, Azzédine, 17–32, 142

Bourdieu, Pierre, 91

Bouteflika, Abdelaziz, viii

Boyle, Danny, 105, 106

Branche, Raphaëlle, 17–19, 30

Butler, Judith, xx; on precarity, 15, 140–41

Buzan, Barry, 139–40

caïd: as colonial order representative, 21–22; Djellali on, 21, 28; housing of, 19; peasantry bodies reduction by, 22–24; power of, 20–21, 23–24

camp: Agamben on, 111; Algeria internment, 138; biopolitics and, 79; women enclosure and control in, 79

cannibalism, Bensoussan on, 37

capitalism, slavery relationship with, 126

capital production, marginal bodies exclusion from, ix

Castel, Robert: on exclusion, ix, 135; on social disaffiliation, x, xiv, 117, 136

Ce pays dont je meurs (Zouari), 54–69

Césaire, Aimé: on colonization, 26; on slavery, 13

Charef, Mehdi, 54–69, 142

Le Chatiment Des Hypocrites (Marouane), 87–104

Chikhi, Beïda: on identity, 39; on inaugural void, 50; on religion, 74

children: marginalization and radicalization of, 105–13; treatment of immigrant, 60

Chraïbi, Driss, 35, 73

citizenship: in Algeria, 6, 14; France urban riots and contested, 55

civil competence, of marginal bodies, xxiii

civilized society, Margalit on, 139

colonial domination: of bodies, 3; of Maghrebian women, 77

colonial order, caïd as representative of, 21–22

colonial Other, in France, 54–69

colonial violence, apologetic discourse on, 64

colonization, xxi–xxii, 2; Branche on, 17–18, 30; Césaire on, 26; divide and conquer tactic, 24–25; Grandmaison on, 33n6; Law of February 23, 2005, 69n3; prostitution and, 121; Saada and Shepard on, 13; stereotypes from, 64; women and subaltern position, 86; women during, 85
colonized, 33n5; dehumanization of, 3, 31; oppression of, 2; Rancière on, 16
colonized bodies, 4
colonized subaltern, 15–16
colonizers: Branche on, 19, 30; housing of, 19
Colonna, Fanny, xx
commodity, human body as, xii
confiscated lands, of peasantry, 1–2
Confronting Poverty (Graff), 113
conjured marginality, 142, 145–46
contested citizenship, France urban riots and, 55
cultural awareness, Moura on, 46

Days of Glory (film), of Bouchareb, 1, 56
death, ix, xviii, 14, 67; before birth, Dib on, 5; of fellah, 15; power of, xiv; power of life and, xii, 20, 33n6, 90; symbolic, xiv, xv, 15, 101
Debordeaux, Danièle, x
Declaration of the Rights of Man and the Citizen of 1793, 145
decolonization, 5; FLN and, 137; peasantry role in, xxii
degradation, xv, xvii, 109, 117
dehumanization, of colonized, 3, 31
depersonalization of slaves, Meillassoux on, 125
Devji, Faisal, 120
Dib, Mohammed: on death before birth, 5; on fellahs, 1–17, 142
Discourse on Colonialism (Césaire), 26
discrimination: of immigrants, 64; imperial heritage and, 64; against peasantry, 12

disenfranchisement, of homo expendibilis, xiv
dispossession, viii–ix, 12, 21, 108
divide and conquer tactic, of colonization, 24–25
Djebar, Assia, 73
Djellali, Abderrazak, 21, 28
domination, 6; bodies colonial, 3; of fellah, 7; Memmi on, 32; slavery and, 12; of women, 77, 89. *See also* male domination
Donadey, Anne, 78, 81, 88
Dugas, Guy, 7–8, 35
A Dying Colonialism (Fanon), 77

Eboussi Boulaga, Fabien, 135
Elmorchid, Brahim, 108–9, 119
Erman, Michel, 102
L'escargot entêté (Boudjedra), 73
Esposito, Roberto, xv
ethnicity, race basis of, 13–14
Les étoiles de Sidi Moumen (Binebine), 105–13, 120, 142
Europe, migration from Africa to, xxii
exception: bodies of, 56, 67; politics of, 62; state of, 56, 62, 67
exclusion, 136, 141–42; Castel on, ix, 135; exploitation and, 38; of marginal bodies, ix; Marzano on, 112–13; slum and, 111; social disaffiliation and, ix
exile: alterity and, 39–40; Le Blanc on, 53; identity and, 39–41; liberation through writing, 44–46; marginal bodies and, 36; as migration form, 36; non-belonging condition of, 52; reality and, 39–40; Said on, 36, 53
exploitation, exclusion and, 38

Fanon, Frantz, xxii, 3, 77, 116; liberating violence of, xv, 28, 31; on national culture, 84–85
Farès, Nabile, 35
fellahs, 1, 4–6, 8–10, 14–17; absence of visibility and voice of, 11; death

of, 15; domination of, 7; peasantry and, 2–3; reduction to bodies of, 12; as sacrificial victims, 7; slavery identification of, 13
Felman, Shoshana, 99–100
Les figuiers de Barbarie (Boudjedra), 115, 137
FLN. *See* Front de Libération Nationale (FLN)
forced marriage, of women, 78, 81, 84
forgiving and forgetting, Ricoeur on, 51–52, 100–101
Foucault, Michel, xiii, 110, 144–45; biopolitics and, 107, 111; on biopower, xv, 22–23, 107, 125–26; governmentality and, xiii; on human management, 79; on impurities, 111–12; on racism, xii
France: African immigrants stigmatization, 56; Algeria migration to, 95; colonial Other in, 54–69; national integrity threat of immigrants in, 59–60; urban riots in, 54, 55; violence in, 54–55; youth riots in, 54–55
Francophone North Africa: biopower and, xvii; literature, xvi–xvii, xix–xx, 47, 71, 73
francophone studies, xvii, 47
freedom of movement, sovereignty relation to, 36
French citizenship, Algeria and, 6, 14
French Protectorate, slavery abolition in 1923, 127–28
French suburbs, Agamben on, 79
Front de Libération Nationale (FLN): decolonization and, 137; peasantry revolt and, 29; women freedom and, 82–83

Gbanou, Selom Komlan, 29–30
ghetto, 110, 139. *See also* slum
GIA. *See* Armed Islamic Group (GIA)
Girard, René: on irrational violence, 92; on sacrificial victim, 92

Goldhammer, Jesse, 91
Gontard, Marc, xvi
governmentality: biopolitical and necropolitical, xv; Foucault and, xiii
Graff, Corinne, 113, 119
Grafmeyer, Yves, 109
Grandmaison, Olivier Le Cour: on Algeria citizenship, 14; on Algeria dictatorship, 24; on colonization, 33n6; on racism of class, 25
Guénif-Souilamas, Nacira, 60–61, 67

El Hamel, Chouki, 122–23, 127; on women slave sexuality, 130, 132
Hamil, Mustapha, 114, 119
Harbi, Mohammed, 32
Hartog, François, 42–43
Hiddleston, Jane, xvi–xvii
Histoire de l'Algérie depuis l'indépendance (Stora), 87
Homer Sacer (Agamben), xiii, xx, 141, 144
homo expendibilis, vii–xxiii, 139; description of, xiv, xv; disenfranchisement of, xiv; dispossessed individuals, viii–ix; North African literature and, xvii; resistance of, xv; sexuality in process of, xii; in slums, xv; symbolic death of, xiv, xv; violence of, xv
homo sacer: Agamben on, xiii, xx, 12, 13, 15, 141, 144; violence exposure, xiii
housing: Benguigui documentary on, 59; of caïd, 19; of peasantry, 19. *See also* camp; slum
human body, as commodity, xii
human management, Foucault on, 79
human rights, 25–26
humiliation, 139

identity: Blanchot on, 31; Chikhi on, 39; exile and, 39–41; present and, 43; religious, 38–39

immigrants: Benguigui documentary on, 57, 59; discrimination of, 64; as France national integrity threat, 59–60; France stigmatization of African, 56; Guénif-Souilamas on, 60–61; indifference to, 57–58; social disqualification of, 68; stigmatization of, 67–68; treatment of children and, 60
immigration: Barkat on, xxii; Bensoussan on, 35–54, 142; Charef and Zouari on, 54–69, 142
imperial heritage, discrimination and, 64
imprisonment, of peasantry, 12
impurities, Foucault on, 111–12
inaugural void, Chikhi on, 50
L'incendie (Dib), fellahs in, 1–17
indecent society, insecurity from, 139
indifference, to immigrants, 56–57
individual security: national security link with, 139–40; threats to, 140
inequality, culture of, 136
infanticide, 133, 144
insecurity, 136–38; from indecent society, 139
insurrection, viii, xix, 26, 145–46
internment camps, in Algeria, 138
The Invention of Decolonization (Shepard), 5
invisibility: of black women slavery, 129, 131; women silence and, 74
Invisible Committee, 146
irrational violence, 92, 106
Islam, 38, 115; Algeria nationalization attempts, 87–90; on sexual intercourse socialization, 75; slavery in, 126; slavery justification by, 124
Islamic terrorism, vii, 137, 138

Jasmine Revolution, vii, 147
La jeune fille et la mère (Marouane), 71–87
Judeo-Maghrebian text, 35–36

Kasbah, war of, 116–17
Kristeva, Julia, 96–97

Landscapes of the Jihad (Devji), 120
Law of February 23, 2005, 69n3
laws, Algeria imposition of women, 88
leprosy, Foucault on, 111–12
liberation: Algeria war of national, 14, 72, 82, 85, 116–17; through writing, of exile, 44–46
literature. *See* North African literature
living dead, xv, 132, 137, 143; of colonial Algeria, 1–32; Mbembe on, xiv, 141
Lorey, Isabell, 140

Mad, Lucio, 66
madness: Erman on vengeance and, 102; Felman on, 99–100; Kristeva on abjection, 96–97
Maghrebian literature, xvi, xix–xx, 35, 71; Orlando on francophone, 73; women literature, 73
Maghrebian women, male and colonial domination of, 77
male domination, 72, 122, 142; of Maghrebian women, 77
Marche des Beurs (March of the Beurs), 1983, 54, 64, 69n1
Marcus Aurelius, 43–44
Margalit, Avishaï, 139
marginal bodies: capital production and social recognition exclusion, ix; civil competence of, xxiii; exile and, 36; homo expendibilis and, xiv; Meynier on women, 82–83; North African literature on, xix; peasantry recognition as, 28
marginality, conjured and organized, 142, 145–46
marginalization, 136; children radicalization and, 105–13; precarious lives and, 113–21; social disaffiliation and, 106; terrorism and, 106, 113–21; of women, following Algeria independence, 88
Marouane, Leïla, 142; *Le Chatiment Des Hypocrites* of, 87–104; *La jeune fille et la mère* of, 71–87

Marzano, Michela, 112–13
Mbembe, Achille: on living dead, xiv, 141; on necropolitics, xii, xviii, 29; out of the dark night phrase of, viii; on Palestinization paradigm, 63–64; on slavery, 62–63; on terrorism, 142–43
Meillassoux, Claude, 125, 131
Memmi, Albert: on domination, 32; on subaltern, 15–16
men: patriarchy and, 72, 76, 79, 81, 84; visibility of, 74. *See also* male domination
Mernissi, Fatima: on Islam slavery, 126; on sexual intercourse socialization, 75
metaphor: of bodies, 5; women as Algeria, 79–80, 84
methodological claims, of North African literature, xvi
Meynier, Gilbert: on peasantry discrimination, 12; on women and liberation role, 85; on women marginal bodies, 82–83
migrant, 69n4; Press on, xii
migration: from Africa to Europe, xxii; from Algeria to France, 95; exile as form of, 36
Mirages (Bensoussan), 35–54
Mohanram, Radhika, 72
Morocco: Elmorchid, 108–9; racialized and sexualized bodies in, 121–34; slavery in, 122–23; terrorist attacks in, vii, 106, 113, 138
Moudileno, Lydie, 66
Moura, Jean-Marc, 46
Moussaoui, Abderrahmane, 93, 103

Nancy, Jean-Luc, 58
national bodies, women bodies parallel with, 80–81
national culture, Fanon on, 84–85
national security: individual security link with, 139–40; threats to, 140
necropolitics: Agamben on, xiii–xiv; Mbembe on, xii, xviii, 29

"New Children of Terror" (Singer), 113
non-belonging condition, of exile, 52
North African literature: Francophone North Africa, xvi–xvii, xix–xx, 47, 71, 73; francophone studies, xvii, 47; Gontard on, xvi; Hiddleston on, xvi–xvii; homo expendibilis and, xvii; Judeo-Maghrebian text, 35–36; Maghrebian text, xvi, xix–xx, 35, 71; on marginal bodies, xix; methodological claims of, xvi; sociological accounts in, xviii
Norton, Ann, 114, 119

oppression, of colonized, 2
organized marginality, 142, 145–46
Orientalism (Said), 81
Orlando, Valérie, 73
out of the dark night phrase, of Mbembe, viii

Palestinian martyr, 143
Palestinization paradigm, 63–64
pathology, women bodies and, 71–104
patriarchy, 72, 76, 79, 81, 84
Paugam, Serge, 142; on social disqualification, xi, xiv, 110–11, 136
pauperization, social disaffiliation compared to, x–xi
peasantry: bodies, caïd reduction of, 22–24; Bonn on emergent speech of, 2; confiscated lands of, 1–2; decolonization role of, xxii; discrimination against, 12; fellahs and, 2–3; FLN and revolt of, 29; housing of, 19; imprisonment, 12; marginal bodies recognition by, 28; resistance of, xxii, 17, 29–30; revolt of, xxii, 17, 20, 31; space of, 19–20; unemployment of, 12; violence, as resistance mode, 18
People, States and Fear (Buzan), 139–40
periphery, xiv, xxi, xxiii, 4, 17, 32, 48; recentering, 135–47; slum and, 106, 109–10, 112, 114

Pieprzak, Katarzyna, 107
plague, Foucault on, 111–12
polemical segregation, 109–10
political violence, 139
politics of exception, Taraud on, 62
(post)colonial order, women transgression and, 79–87
power: of caïd, 20–21, 23–24; of death, xiv;-holders, vulnerability of, 120; of life and death, xii, 20, 33n6, 90
Precarious Life (Butler), xx, 140
precarious lives, 105; marginalization and, 113–21; racialized and sexualized bodies, 121–34; slum, 106–13
precarity, xix; Le Blanc on, xxiii, 11, 145; Butler on, 15, 140–41; Lorey on, 140
present: Aurelius on, 43–44; identity and, 43
Press, Robert, xii
profanation of bodies, 103, 133, 143–44
prostitution: of black women slaves, 123–24; colonization and, 121; Taraud on, 121, 128
La prostitution coloniale (Taraud), 121

race: ethnicity based on, 13–14; slum and segregation by, 110; social class and, 123
racism, 32; of class, 25, 26; Foucault on, xii; March of the Beurs on, 54
radicalization: children marginalization and, 105–13; religion and, 138
Rancière, Jacques, 74; on colonized, 16
rape, 75–76, 80, 86, 89; Algeria Penal Code on, 102; black women slavery and, 130–32; Moussaoui on, 93, 103; stigma of, 92
reality, exile and, 39–40
Recasting Postcolonialism (Donadey), 78
Reflections in Exile (Said), 36
religion: Agamben on, 143–44; Chikhi on, 74; radicalization and, 138

religious identity, 38–39
Repo, Jemina, xv
resistance: Amrane-Minne on women participation in, 82; of homo expendibilis, xv; of peasantry, xxii, 17, 29–30; to stigmatization, 141–42; through terrorism, xxiii; violence as peasantry, 18
revolt: of peasantry, xxii, 17, 20, 31; violated bodies and women in, 87–104; women in, 85
Revolution of 1848, abolition of slavery and, 6
Ricoeur, Paul, 51–52, 100–101
right to exist, 66–67
Robert, Suzanne, 99

Saada, Emmanuelle: on Algeria citizenship, 14; on colonization, 13
sacrificial victim: fellahs as, 7; Girard on, 92
sacrificial violence, Goldhammer on, 91
Said, Edward, 36, 53, 81
Sartre, Jean-Paul, 66
security: individual and national, 139–40; socialization and, 139
segregation: Grafmeyer on, 109; polemical, 109–10; race and, 110; slum and, 106–7, 111; of space, 110
Sembene, Ousmane, 71
sexual intercourse, socialization of, 75
sexuality, 47–49; in homo expendibilis, xii; slavery and, 126–27
sexual relations, Bourdieu on, 91
sexual violence, 62
Shepard, Todd: on assimilationist system, 6; colonization and, 13
Singer, Peter Warren, 113, 119
slavery, 94; Agamben on, 90, 130; black women, 121–34, 144; capitalism relationship with, 126; Césaire on, 13; domination and, 12; El Hamel on, 122–23; fellahs identification with, 13; French Protectorate 1923 abolition of, 127–28; in Islam,

124, 126; Mbembe on, 62–63; in Morocco, 122–23; Revolution of 1848 and abolition of, 6; sexuality and, 128–29. *See also* black women slavery

slaves: Meillassoux on depersonalization of, 125; social disqualification of, xii, 122; women as, xxii, xxiii

slum: as apartheid illustration, 109; description of, 107–8; exclusion and, 111; homo expendibilis in, xv; periphery and, 106, 109–10, 112, 114; precarious lives in, 106–13; resistance through terrorism in, xxiii; segregation, biopolitics and, 111; segregation and, 106–7; space of, 55, 58, 107; Stambouli on, 108

Slumdog Millionaire (film), of Boyle, 105, 106

Slumdog Terrorists, 105

Smith, Stephen, 37

social class: Bailleul on, 123–24; race and, 123

social disaffiliation: Castel on, x, xiv, 117, 136; Debordeaux on, x; exclusion and, ix; marginalization and, 106; pauperization compared to, x–xi

social disenfranchisement, Le Blanc on, xxi, 131

social disqualification, 135; French colonial authorities implementation of, 5; of immigrants, 68; Paugam on, xi, xiv, 110–11, 136; of slaves, xii, 122; of women bodies, 86, 88, 124; of youth, 67–68

social dissociation, 135

socialization: Eboussi Boulaga and, 135; security and, 139; of sexual intercourse, 75

social protections, xi–xii

social recognition, marginal bodies exclusion from, ix

society, women bodies control by, 76

Le sommeil de l'esclave (Binebine), 121–34

sovereignty: Agamben on, xiii; freedom of movement relation to, 36

space, 136; of peasantry, 19–20; segregation of, 110; of slums, 55, 58

Spivak, Gayatri, 16, 126

Stambouli, Fredj, 108

state of exception, 56, 62, 67

stereotypes, 66–67; from colonization, 64

stigmatization: of immigrants, 67–68; of rape, 92; resistance to, 141–42

Stora, Benjamin, 65, 88; on Algeria history, 87, 117; on Algerian nationalist movement, 28

subaltern, 135; of black women slavery, 121–22, 124; colonized, 15–16; Memmi on, 15–16; position, women and colonization, 86; racism of class and, 26; Spivak on, 16, 126; women bodies control and, 72–79

symbolic death, 15, 101; of homo expendibilis, xiv, xv

Taraud, Christelle: on Maghrebian women domination, 77; on politics of exception, 62; on prostitution, 121, 128

terrorism, 105; in Algeria and Tunisia, 138; attacks, in Morocco, vii, 106, 113, 147; Barak on, 119; Hamil on, 114; Islamic, vii, 137, 138; marginalization and, 106, 113–21; Mbembe on, 142–43; Norton on, 114, 119; resistance through, xxiii; Zoubeïr recruiter of, 118–19

thanatopolitics, xi–xii, xv; Agamben on, xiii–xiv

"Thantopolitics or Biopolitics?" (Repo), xv

Le thé au harem d'Archi Ahmed (Charef), 54–69

Transfigurations of the Maghreb (Woodhull), 72

Tunisia: Bouazizi death in, vii; terrorist attacks in, 138

Tunisian Revolution. *See* Jasmine Revolution

unemployment, viii, 136; of peasantry, 12
urban riots, in France, 54, 55
The Use of Bodies (Agamben), 145

veil, women and, 77, 87
Vendetti, Maria, 95
vengeance, 98; Erman on madness and, 102; Robert on, 99
violated bodies, women in revolt and, 87–104
violence, 12, 58–59, 120; Agamben on, 145; apologetic discourse on colonial, 64; Benjamin on, 145; in France, 54–55; Goldhammer on sacrificial, 91; of homo expendibils, xv; homo sacer exposure to, xiii; irrational, 92, 106; Islamic, vii, 137, 138; liberating, of Fanon, xv, 28, 31; as peasantry resistance mode, 18; political, 139; sexual, 62
virginity, 77–78
visibility: Le Blanc on, 11–12, 16; Bounemeur on, 19; fellahs absence of, 11; March of the Beurs demand for, 54; of men, 74
voice, fellahs absence of, 11
vulnerability, of power-holders, 120

war of national liberation, in Algeria, 14, 82, 116–17; women contribution to, 72, 85, 88
women: Algeria laws imposed upon, 88; Algeria liberation contribution, 72, 85, 88; as Algeria metaphor, 79–80, 84; Amrane-Minne on resistance participation by, 82; as biopolitics victims, 79; camp enclosure and control of, 79; (post)colonial order and transgression of, 79–87; during colonization, 85; colonization and subaltern position, 86; domination of, 72, 89, 122, 142; FLN and freedom of, 82–83; forced marriage of, 78, 81, 84; invisibility and silence of, 74; male and colonial domination of Maghrebian, 77; Meynier on marginal bodies of, 82–83; in revolt, violated bodies and, 87–104; veil and, 77, 87; virginity of, 77–78; writing of, 71
Women and Islam (Mernissi), 75
women bodies: in biopolitics, xxii; national bodies parallel with, 80–81; pathology and, 71–104; as slave bodies, xxii; social disqualification of, 86, 88, 124; society control over, 76; subalternity and control of, 72–79
Woodhull, Winnifred, 7–8, 72
Wretched of the Earth (Fanon), xxii, 3, 116
writing: Blanchot on, 45; liberation of exile through, 44–46; of women, 71

youth, social disqualification of, 67–68
youth riots: in Algeria, vii, 118; in France, 54–55

"Zones of Perceptual Enclosure" (Pieprzak), 107
Zouari, Fawzia, 54–69, 142
Zoubeïr, Abou, 118–19

About the Author

Hervé Anderson Tchumkam is an associate professor of French and Francophone Postcolonial Studies and a Fellow of the John G. Tower Center for Public Policy and International Affairs at Southern Methodist University. He is the author of *State Power, Stigmatization and Youth Resistance Cultures in the French Banlieues: Uncanny Citizenship* (Lexington Books, 2015); and, the coauthor with Alexie Tcheuyap of *Avoir peur. Insécurité et roman en Afrique Francophone* (Presses de l'université Laval, 2019).

www.ingramcontent.com/pod-product-compliance
Lightning Source LLC
Chambersburg PA
CBHW020122010526
44115CB00008B/930